EARLY SCHOOLING

EARLY SCHOOLING

The National Debate

EDITED BY SHARON L. KAGAN
AND EDWARD F. ZIGLER

YALE UNIVERSITY PRESS
NEW HAVEN AND LONDON

Designed by Sally Harris
and set in Baskerville type by
Keystone Typesetting Co., Orwigsburg, PA
Printed in the United States of America by
BookCrafters, Inc., Chelsea, MI

Library of Congress Cataloging-in-Publication Data

Early schooling: the national debate / edited by Sharon L. Kagan and Edward F. Zigler.
p. cm.
Includes index.
Contents: Early schooling: on what grounds? / Sharon Lynn Kagan—Formal schooling for four-year-olds?: no / Edward F. Zigler—The case for public school sponsorship of early childhood education revisited / Albert Shanker—From national debate to national responsibility / Bertha D. Campbell—Child care in the public schools: public accountability and the Black child / Evelyn K. Moore—Early childhood education on its own terms / David Elkind—Policy, implementation, and the problem of change / Seymour B. Sarason—Early childhood education: developmental enhancement or developmental acceleration? / Irving E. Sigel—Early education: what should young children be doing? / Lilian G. Katz—Curriculum quality in early education / David P. Weikart—Comparing preschool curricula and practices: the state of research / Douglas R. Powell—Early schooling: a national opportunity? / Sharon Lynn Kagan and Edward F. Zigler.
ISBN 0–300–04124–1 (alk. paper)
1. Education, Preschool—United States. 2. United States—Social conditions. 3. Education, Preschool—United States—Curricula. 4. Education and state—United States. I. Kagan, Sharon Lynn. II. Zigler, Edward, 1930–
LB1140.23.E19 1987 87–21763
372′.21′0973—dc19 CIP

The paper in this book meets the guidelines for permanence and durability of the Committee on Production Guidelines for Book Longevity of the Council on Library Resources.

The editors gratefully acknowledge permission to reprint the following material: Edward F. Zigler, Formal Schooling for Four Year Olds? No., in *American Psychologist,* March 1987, Vol. 42, No. 3, 254–60. Copyright © 1987 by the American Psychological Association. Adapted by permission of the publisher and author.

10 9 8 7 6 5 4 3 2 1

TO JENNI KLEIN

an accomplished professional
who embodies the spirit and wisdom
of early childhood education,
and who has established the
highest standards for the field.

CONTENTS

PART III: *Research and Curriculum: Points of View*

PART IV: *The Policy Challenge*

CONTRIBUTORS

Editors

SHARON L. KAGAN, Director of The Mayor's Office of Early Childhood Education in New York City, is on leave as Associate Director of the Yale Bush Center in Child Development and Social Policy and Coordinator of the Bush Network of programs in Child Development and Social Policy. She is a research associate at the Child Study Center and in the psychology department at Yale University. Dr. Kagan has directed many early schooling programs of national significance, including Project Developmental Continuity and New York City's Giant Step program. Integrating practice and theory, she has lectured and written in areas of child and family policy, early childhood education, child care, educational policy, and parent involvement. She has co-edited *Children, Families and Government: Perspectives on American Social Policy* and *America's Family Support Programs: Perspectives and Prospects*.

EDWARD F. ZIGLER is Sterling Professor of Psychology and Director of the Bush Center in Child Development and Social Policy at Yale University. He served as the first director of the U.S. Office of Child Development and was Chief of the Children's Bureau in the U.S. Department of Health, Education, and Welfare. Serving on many presidential commissions and panels, Professor Zigler was a member of the original Head Start Planning Committee and led the presidentially-appointed committee on the future of Head Start. He has served as a government consultant in the United States and abroad and is the author of numerous books and articles. Professor Zigler received the 1982 Distinguished Contributions to Psychology in the Public Interest Award from the American Psychological Association and the C. Anderson Aldrich Award in Child Development from the American Academy of Pediatrics in 1985. In addition, Professor Zigler received the Award for Distinguished Contributions to Applied Psychology from the American Psychological Association in 1986 and was elected to the Institute of Medicine in 1987.

Contributors

BERTHA D. CAMPBELL has taught the gamut of the educational ladder, from infant and toddler to graduate and adult education programs in public, private, and cooperative schools. Until her recent retirement from the New York State Education Department, she headed the Bureau of Child Development and Parent Education, which carries responsibility for the New York State Experimental Prekindergarten Program. She has been a consultant to Head Start, Parent and Child Centers, Advocacy, Basic Education Skills and other federally funded projects. At present, she serves as a commentator to the Bruner Foundation in its current efforts to contribute to a more discerning evaluation of inner city school programs.

DAVID ELKIND is currently Professor of Child Study and Senior Resident Scholar at the Lincoln Filene Center at Tufts University. He is President of the National Association for the Education of Young Children and a contributing editor to *Parents Magazine*.

LILIAN G. KATZ is Professor of Early Childhood Education at the University of Illinois (Champaign) where she is also Director of the ERIC Clearinghouse on Elementary and Early Childhood Education and Editor-in-Chief of the *Early Childhood Research Quarterly*, a joint publication of the Clearinghouse and the National Association for the Education of Young Children. Professor Katz has extensive experience working with preschool educators in the U.S. and many other countries and has a special interest in the training of preprimary teachers.

EVELYN K. MOORE is the executive director of the National Black Child Development Institute (NBCDI). She co-founded this nonprofit organization in 1970 because the problems facing black children demanded immediate and sustained attention. Drawing on the expertise of affiliates in thirty-three major cities, NBCDI conducts policy research and analysis on emerging trends in child care, education, adoption, foster care, and health. Through her leadership, NBCDI brings new insight to policymakers and new resources to community advocates for black children. An adviser to numerous federal and private agencies, Ms. Moore maintains an active writing and speaking schedule on topics related to the health and welfare of black children. She received her master's degree in education from the University of Michigan.

DOUGLAS R. POWELL is Associate Professor of Child Development and Family Studies at Purdue University. His research on child-care programs, parent involvement, and the professional development of preschool teachers has been published in books and journals. Professor Powell is at present research editor of *Young Children*. Previously, he was a faculty member and Director of Program Development at the Merrill-Palmer Institute, Detroit.

SEYMOUR B. SARASON is Professor in the Department of Psychology and in the Institution for Social and Policy Studies at Yale University. A recipient in 1975 of the Award for Distinguished Contributions to Community Psychology and Mental Health, Division of Community Psychology, from the American Psychological Association, he served as President of the APA's Division of Clinical Psychology in 1978–79. He is a recent recipient of the APA's Distinguished Contributions in the Public Interest Award.

ALBERT SHANKER has been president of the 650,000 member American Federation of Teachers since 1974. A noted statesman in the fields of American public education and labor, Mr. Shanker serves on the Carnegie Forum on Education and the Economy's Task Force on Teaching as a Profession and was recently named to the National Academy of Education. Mr. Shanker has been a guest lecturer at Hunter College and Harvard University. He writes a weekly column, "Where We Stand," which appears in the Sunday *New York Times*.

IRVING E. SIGEL, Distinguished Research Scientist at Educational Testing Service, is a developmental psychologist. His research and extensive publications deal with children's cognitive development as influenced by the family and the school.

DAVID P. WEIKART is President of the High/Scope Educational Research Foundation, a nonprofit research, development, and training organization in education. He is the project director for the longitudinal studies of the Perry Preschool Project and the Curriculum Comparison Project. He is also Coordinator of the International Association for the Evaluation of Educational Achievement (IEA), Preprimary Study, a twenty-one-nation study of four-year-old children in and out of home care and the relationship of these experiences to achievement in formal schooling.

PREFACE

A national debate regarding early schooling is being waged throughout America. Concern is not limited to a single ethnic or economic group, nor is it bound by geographic locale. In foundations, state legislatures, and city councils, interest in how America should care for and educate its young children is a contested topic.

Currently, those concerned about young children and their development find themselves at the threshhold of a new era. Rhetoric has been replaced by a new reality. Painful budget cuts have given way to unprecedented commitments to youngsters by states and municipalities. Foundations have taken swift leadership in giving priority to early childhood education and child care and in supporting projects that chronicle legislative efforts and provide technical assistance and analysis. Even the media have provided extensive news and editorial coverage of the events and issues associated with early schooling.

Certainly interest in young children is not new, but the current push is unique in that it is more pervasive and intense and differs in scope and orientation from past efforts. What are the differences and why have they emerged now? What are the issues and why are they debated so? Who are the players and what values do they hold? What, if any, are potential solutions? *Early Schooling: The National Debate* seeks to unravel these dilemmas.

No doubt, America's current interest in children under the age of six derives from more than one source. Certainly changing demographics, the popularization of recent research, and the nation's general concern about children's academic achievement have all precipitated the increased attention. Among the most important of the demographic changes is the rise in the number of single-parent families, many of whose heads, regardless of the ages of their children, must work and therefore require day-care services. In addition, married women with children are joining the work force in unprecedented numbers. The Bureau of Labor reports that the percentage of employed women with children under the age of six has steadily risen from 29 percent in 1970 (Select Committee on Children, Youth, and Families, 1983) to 54.4 percent in 1986 (Bureau of Labor Statistics, 1986) and is expected to continue to rise. Clearly, the need for good quality, affordable care for children while parents work is rapidly escalating.

For many years mothers who worked outside the home have faced the challenge of finding suitable care, and they have come to realize the inadequacies of child-care services: lack of availability, high cost, long distances from home or work, and questionable program quality. But fathers too are now taking a greater interest and role in child rearing, and they have joined working women from all classes (not just low-income mothers) in expressing concern over these shortcomings. With this expanded constituency has come broader exposure of the problem and a more widespread desire for its solution. Precisely because the child-care problem is so acute, desperate parents look to the institution they know for support—the schools. Often propelled by parental pressure, schools attempt to respond, thereby accelerating the debate regarding their role in caring for and educating young children. In short the nearly ubiquitous need for child care has been confounded with the need for early schooling.

Interest in early education is also linked to renewed concern for the scope and effects of poverty on children and families. Currently, one in four youngsters lives in poverty, and only one-third of three- and four-year-old children receive preschool or child-care services (Children's Defense Fund 1986). Recent research, however, indicates that it is precisely low-income and special needs children who benefit most from early intervention.

Beyond dramatically changing demographics, a second force generating interest in early schooling is the media's popularization of research findings regarding the importance of the early years in children's growth and development, and the positive effects of early intervention efforts. For example, research indicates that low-income children who have had quality preschool experiences demonstrate later educational success and greater employability than do their counterparts who have not been enrolled in similar programs (Berrueta-Clement et al., 1984). Other widely publicized data, such as those included in the Consortium for Longitudinal Studies (1983), have also buttressed the belief in the importance of the early years.

Because these findings have received so much public attention, there is grave concern in the academic community about their overgeneralization. Scholars caution against thinking that early schooling will have equally positive results for *all* children, regardless of income level or program quality. They point out that the reported positive results were obtained for economically disadvantaged children and that the intervention programs assessed in the studies may have varied in quality and scope from typical early childhood programs. Yet, in spite of these not so widely publicized cautions, many middle- and upper-class families, hearing of the findings, regard preschool attendance as a necessary step to ensure later college acceptance.

Public concern regarding the general state of education is a third source of pressure for early schooling. Distressed by increases in school drop-out and illiteracy rates and dissatisfied with the performance of public schools, advocates increasingly seek school reform. Although many national reports criticizing our nation's schools have not necessarily advocated early education as a panacea, they have pointed out weaknesses in the educational system that have led to broad education reforms. In some cases—Texas, South Carolina, and Massachusetts—these reforms have included funding for programs for prekindergarten children.

Other current issues—the push for educational excellence and the emphasis on preventive social services—also have precipitated interest in early education. State projects on excellence routinely regard the early years as the time to begin the new push toward educational excellence. The National Governors' Association Task Force on Readiness, for example, considered the possible role of early childhood programs in raising performance levels in the higher grades (National Governors' Association,

1986). Part of the interest in preventive social services in the early years derives from cost-benefit studies demonstrating that investments in services for young children prevent the onset of future difficulties and save tax dollars in the long run. These are persuasive arguments favoring early intervention. In short, the movements for educational excellence and for preventive services in the early years have coalesced, generating renewed interest in early schooling.

Taken together, changing demographics, research findings, and the movement toward excellence and preventive services have created a broader constituency for, and a new approach to, early schooling. The audience of the 1980s is larger and more diverse socially, economically, and politically than in the mid-1960s, so that the call is for expanded services for all children, not merely low-income and special-needs youngsters. Constrained by fiscal realities, however, states and municipalities may not be able to implement universal services immediately; yet the fact that such services are even considered bespeaks a significantly different orientation from that of the 1960s. In addition, the current approach has moved from the remediative or deficit orientation of the 1960s to a focus on excellence and prevention. The movement now may resemble the 1960s call for services, but it is different in scope and orientation.

New concerns about *who* shall be served (targeted or universal populations) and *where* children shall be served (in educational or social service sectors), coupled with some still unanswered questions from the past, have generated a renewed national debate on early schooling. Although decades of research and experience have helped clarify the impact of services on low-income children, the question of the value of more universal services is an open one. And despite the pell-mell rush to create programs, other conceptual, philosophical, and practical issues must be examined: Is early schooling appropriate for young children, or are they better left in the care of parents? What kinds of education and care are appropriate? Do we know what constitutes equality in programs for young children? And if we know, can we afford to provide it? Do all young children benefit equally from out-of-home services? Are schools appropriate vehicles for delivering comprehensive preschool services? Indeed, precisely the issues that surround the sensitive question of early schooling have generated a national debate, but they remain underexplored.

In the spring of 1986, the Yale Bush Center in Child Development and Social Policy, as a part of the Bush Network's activities, sponsored a conference on Four-Year-Olds and the Public Schools. An outgrowth of that conference, this volume continues the examination of key elements in the debate by presenting analyses of the issues by leading authorities. We have not attempted to solve all the questions related to early schooling, but rather to explore the issues and to reveal the complexity of the problem. In so doing, the volume should inform future discussion, enabling the challenges surrounding early schooling to be addressed more thoughtfully.

We have encouraged each author to discuss questions related to early schooling from her or his unique perspective. Thus, there may be some overlap in the issues presented and in the positions taken by the writers. Nevertheless, each essay reflects the best wisdom of a particular scholar, and collectively, the essays reflect the thrust of current thinking on early schooling.

The volume is divided into four parts, with the first providing an overview of the issues. Chapters in the second section address broad programmatic and policy issues, and chapters in the third section focus more specifically on issues related to classroom practice. The contributors to this section have used empirical research to arrive at what they see as appropriate pedagogy for very young children. In the final section of the volume, the editors suggest a possible answer to the serious policy challenge the nation faces as it strives to provide comprehensive, developmentally appropriate services for young children and their families.

Sharon L. Kagan
Edward F. Zigler
August 1, 1987

REFERENCES

Berrueta-Clement, J. R., Schweinhart, L. J., Barnett, W. S., Epstein, A. S., & Weikart, D. P. (1984). Changed lives: The effects of the Perry Preschool Program on youths through age 19. *Monographs of the*

High/Scope Educational Research Foundation No. 8. Ypsilanti, MI: High/Scope.

Bureau of Labor Statistics. (1986, August 20). *News*, U.S. Department of Labor, p. 4.

Children's Defense Fund. (1986). *A children's defense budget*. Washington, DC: Author.

Consortium for Longitudinal Studies. (1983). *As the twig is bent . . . Lasting effects of preschool programs*. Hillsdale, NJ: Lawrence Erlbaum Associates.

National Governors' Association. (1986, August). *Time for results: The governors' 1991 education report*. Washington, DC: Author.

Select Committee on Children, Youth, and Families. (1983, May). *U.S. children and their families: Current conditions and recent trends*. Washington, DC: U.S. Government Printing Office.

ACKNOWLEDGMENTS

We would like to express our gratitude to those who have assisted in making this book a reality. We acknowledge the Bush Foundation, whose financial support made both the conference and the book possible. We thank Leslie Branden, Barbara Emmel, and Gwen Mood for their invaluable assistance in all phases of manuscript preparation. We also acknowledge the assistance and support of our editor, Jeanne Ferris.

PART I

An Overview of the Issues

CHAPTER 1

Early Schooling: On What Grounds?

SHARON L. KAGAN

Very few issues capture the attention of policymakers, academics from diverse disciplines, the media, and the public simultaneously; even fewer precipitate ongoing debate in public and private sectors. What America should be doing to care for and educate its young children is one such issue. Although discussed for decades, early schooling is now a widely contested matter, piquing attention throughout the nation.

Not since the mid-1960s has early schooling commanded such consideration. Within the past several years, we have witnessed a proliferation in the number of commissions and task forces that have recommended the establishment or expansion of programs for young children, and numerous states have increased such services. This expansion builds upon a general increase in the number of children who attend preschool. For example, in 1965, about 11 percent of three- and four-year-old children were enrolled in preschools; recent data indicate that in 1985 this figure had more than tripled to 39 percent. Projections point to an even greater escalation in preschool attendance rates (U.S. Department of Education, 1986). Not only are more youngsters enrolling in preschools, but in some areas more college students are enrolling in preparation programs for early childhood teaching. Further, evidence of increased attention on the early years is manifest in efforts to reinstate or activate special certification in early childhood.

Certainly, this interest in early schooling has not escaped the media. Coverage of the issue has been widespread in the popular press with articles appearing in such newspapers as the *New York Times* ("School at 4," 1985) and the *Christian Science Monitor* ("Should 4- and 5-year-olds be in school?" 1986). *Newsweek* (Salholz, Wingert, Burgower, Michael, & Joseph, 1987) and *Atlantic Monthly* (Bettleheim, 1987), among others, have helped catapult the early schooling issue into national prominence.

Although the field is characterized by vigorous activity and media coverage, there is strong disagreement about whether young children actually need early schooling. What kinds of experiences are appropriate, whether early schooling should take place in the schools, and how cognitively oriented the curriculum should be are all matters of widespread debate. Precisely because of this lack of consensus and because programs are being implemented at unprecedented rates, the intensity of discussion and the need for systematic analysis of the issues are compounded.

The purpose of this chapter is to identify some of the key issues inherent in the debate and to disentangle them so that the reader will have a clearer sense of their complexity and magnitude. These issues will be discussed in three linked categories. Each addresses issues related to the grounds or conditions under which early schooling should be examined: (1) physical grounds (where should early schooling take place?); (2) pedagogical grounds (what should early schooling provide, how, and for how long?); and (3) philosophical grounds (why and with what value assumptions should early schooling be considered?).

More specifically, the first group focuses on the actual *physical* location of where children should be served. Can and should schools serve young children or are there more appropriate settings, such as the home or family day-care or child-care centers? This category addresses questions regarding administrative auspices and capacities of existing settings. Are schools, given their already large responsibilities and their bureaucratic tendencies toward uniformity, the best place to lodge services for young children? What are the implications for private care providers of placing young children in the schools?

Discussion of location and auspices logically leads to issues related to the *pedagogical* grounds of early education. This category focuses on curricular questions regarding how children's needs are best met. How much cognitive emphasis is appropriate and how comprehensive should services to young children be?

Finally, consideration of the first two categories leads to a third group of issues, those that focus on the *philosophical* grounds or conditions under which early schooling should take place. The issues here relate to differences in how we think of services for young children (for example, education or care, or both?); differences in values regarding standardization of services (to what extent should early education be standardized and regulated?); differences in our perceptions of equity (universal versus targeted services for children, and salary and benefit equity for adults); differences in our philosophic orientation to quality (must all services be of very high quality or are there situations under which good-enough care is sufficient?); and finally, differences in who is responsible for the care and education of young children (the family or the state?).

Taken together, these three sets of questions encompass the critical elements of the debate about early schooling. Before we consider these content issues, however, we must detour briefly to address the language of early schooling, a problem that has obscured discussion of the issues. The language problem is twofold: not only are similar words used to mean different things and different words used to convey the same concept, but because of historical precedent, certain words (*day care*, *schooling*) taint the way the issues are conceived. It's not just that our lexicon is imprecise but that interpretations of key words often reflect dramatically different values.

Perhaps the words that warrant attention first are those that label the debate itself—*young children* and *schooling*. For example, when we speak of "young children," who do we actually mean? Titles of recent press articles and commission reports imply that all young children are under discussion. Typically, however, recommended services are for special groups of young children, often designated by age or by special needs. In recently passed legislation for young children, for example, many programs, such as those in South Carolina, are targeted for youngsters who have "significant readiness difficulties." Illinois has approved $12.1 million for school districts that request funds to start up classes for three-to-five-year-olds at risk of academic failure and to establish full-day kindergarten. Maine appropriated $1.7 million to expand its services to Head Start–eligible youngsters (Blank & Wilkens, 1985; Weil, 1986; Schweinhart, 1985). State by state, legislation is being passed that gives the illusion of addressing the early childhood challenge, but actually only targets particular groups of young children.

The second ambiguity associated with the term *young children* concerns what is meant by "young." Gesell (1940) and others have pointed out distinct characteristics of four-year-olds. Although such developmental levels are helpful guideposts, sometimes children's abilities may span several levels, depending upon what characteristics are under consideration. Good teachers know that children vary on nearly every measurable characteristic. Preschools also recognize individual differences and, more often than not, accommodate them by serving several age groups. In practice, then, services to "young" children include at least three- and four-year-olds. Currently, the trend is to define even infants and toddlers as young children and offer services for them. To many early childhood–child developmentalists, "young" means birth to age five, although for others it connotes birth to age eight. Current legislation reinforces the murkiness of age distinctions: some is targeted to four-year-olds only, some to three- and four-year-olds, and some to children from birth to age five. We simply haven't agreed on how young *is* young.

Another ambiguity surrounding the concept of "young children" concerns the use of the word *children*. Typically, because of the importance of the family in the life of a child, professionals serving young children almost automatically include their families in the programs they offer. But their vocabulary rarely reflects this commitment, for they seldom mention the family explicitly. There are notable exceptions. The states of Missouri and Minnesota, for example, have instituted a program of parent education and an early childhood family education program, respectively. And the Connecticut Four-Year-Old Committee thought the inclusion of families to be so important that it adopted the new name, the Committee on Four-Year-Olds,

Their Families, and the Public Schools. Professionals should be as careful to include families in their vocabulary as they have been to include them in their programs and services.

The term *schooling* is no less troublesome, and certainly no less important. As used currently, *schooling* is equated with both an instructional process and a delivery mechanism. As an instructional process, schooling refers to the nature and content of what goes on in the classroom. Is the emphasis more on didactic instruction than on experiential learning? On workbooks and pencils than on workbenches and pegs? A heavily didactic orientation, widely opposed by some early childhood educators, can seem merely like kindergarten pushed down a year. Or, schooling for young children can offer a program of care and education that is suitable for the age group and that attends to the youngsters' physical, emotional, cognitive, and behavioral development. From this perspective alone, then, there are ambiguities in what early childhood specialists and child developmentalists imply by the word *schooling*.

The term *schooling* is equally ambiguous when used to refer to the delivery mechanism. In this context, the term may suggest funding, sponsorship, or housing. If, by schooling, we are referring to funding, we may be implying that schools should be fiscally responsible for educating young children below the age of five, just as they are for children aged five to seventeen, or that the schools should act as a conduit for funds generated at the community or federal level. Whatever we are arguing, we need to disentangle the terms and be explicit when funding issues are discussed.

Sponsorship, another issue that can be implied by the term *schooling*, is also weighted with multiple meanings. Sponsorship may mean that programs for young children are monitored by and accountable to the schools. It may imply close control in terms of teacher certification and salary and benefit options. Or sponsorship may imply a more casual alliance, without heavy bureaucratic involvement. The nature of sponsorship is highly idiosyncratic—thus the word's multiple interpretations.

Finally, when schooling implies housing, it suggests that programs for young children are physically housed in school buildings. Yet this tells us little about the precise nature of the relationship between the school and the program. The program may be housed in the facility but remain sequestered from the fabric of school life. Or the program may be fully operated by the school district and hence be required to adhere to school policies. Even if the word *schooling* is disentangled from *housing*, ambiguity prevails because of the uncertain link between location and accountability. And further, if a program is accountable to a school because of its location, it may be unclear to what extent this implies its programs should be "school-like."

Use of the term *schooling* is also problematic for other important reasons. Usually *schooling* connotes an academic orientation, suggesting that when early childhood programs are located in public schools, they are oriented toward school readiness. Further, because of the universal availability of schools, the term *schooling* is particularly onerous to private providers of preschool services: it raises the fear that all services for young children will take place *only* in schools. Of course, this is not realistic; one need only think of the abundance of nonpublic education for elementary and high school students that exists in the nation. The term *schooling*, then, is unfortunate not only because it is ambiguous and misleading but also because it can be threatening to non-school-based providers of preschool services.

But although these definitional problems are complex, we cannot allow them to mask the real issues at hand. The concept of early schooling raises some of education's most perplexing questions: What is the appropriate function and scope of schooling? How does schooling differ from education and how *should* it differ? What is the appropriate balance between equity and excellence? How should effective standards for programs and personnel be created and monitored? Who is responsible for the care and education of young children in America? It is to these issues that we turn now.

The Physical Grounds: Issues of Auspices

Debate about where young children should be served hinges on two main points: first, the actual capacity of schools to serve youngsters adequately, and second, the consequence for other providers of care if the majority of young children are placed in schools.

Positions on the schools' capacity to serve young children and their families fall generally into two camps. Those against placing young children in schools sometimes question the overall competency of American education: "Why give young children to the schools anyway? They haven't done such a terrific job with children in kindergarten through the twelfth grade." Others, including many conservatives, feel young children should be cared for by their parents, and still others object to the increase in responsibility and cost that including a younger generation in the schools would entail. Some skeptics think that schools are too bureaucratic to be responsive to the needs of young children, whom they see as requiring more parental involvement, comprehensive services, and continuity than the schools can deliver. They ask whether unions and schools can countenance teachers' eating lunch with young children, whether curriculum planners can tolerate "play" as a curricular strategy, and whether the motivation for early childhood programs is the genuine needs of children and families or merely more jobs for unemployed teachers. Finally, advocates for minority children express concern that schools dominated primarily by white middle-class values cannot reinforce the social and emotional development that begins in the minority home (National Black Child, 1985).

On the positive side, those who favor the placement of young children in the schools argue that schools are uniquely qualified for this task for several reasons. First, they are readily available throughout the United States and are fully accessible to all children and parents. Thus, the problem of limited accessibility, particularly for low-income youngsters, is minimized. Advocates also contend that schools have had education as their mission for centuries and that because they have served children just one year older (five-year-olds), they can easily adapt to serving younger children. These advocates further argue that because schools have regularly administered large sums of money, their fiscal and accounting procedures are well established, making them suitable recipients for any large-scale federal, state, or local funds (Shanker, 1976). Others contend that schools are desirable places for young children because they have professional standing, certification standards, and salary schedules, as well as a vested interest in having better prepared students at kindergarten entry (Schweinhart & Koschel, 1986, p. 22).

But regardless of one's perspective on the capacity of schools to serve young children, the early schooling debate is being waged on another front—between the nonsubsidized providers of services and subsidized providers. Those who serve young children in private for-profit and voluntary nonprofit sectors raise legitimate questions about the consequences of expanded publicly funded services, asserting that if children are served in the public domain, their services will be less in demand. What would happen then to private investments in the industry? This concern is based on solid experience. When, in the southern states during the sixties and seventies kindergartens were added to public school systems, and in New York City in the eighties an all-day kindergarten program was instituted, the nature of private and voluntary nonprofits changed dramatically. In all likelihood, expansion of publicly supported early childhood services would have similar results.

Although complex, these problems are not insoluble. Clearly, the issues they raise point toward the necessity for a careful, well-planned implementation strategy, one that will give schools time to assess their individual capacities in light of the unique needs of young children and to make the necessary changes. Similarly, since the expansion of publicly funded services will probably alter the nature of nonsubsidized services, ideally ample planning time and training supports must be made available to the affected agencies.

Although anticipating institutional changes occasioned by the expansion of services to young children is helpful, this is only a small part of providing better services. We also need to understand that no matter on which physical grounds—under whose auspices—programs for young children are established, more difficult pedagogical and philosophical issues persist.

The Pedagogical Grounds: Issues of Image and Content

Diverse Images: Diverse Services

Although we speak of a single early childhood field, historically it has served two functions: care and education. These functions arose from different traditions, serve different needs, and are offered by different institutions. Nowhere is the dichotomy more obvious than in questions related to pedagogy: What shall be taught? By whom?

One conception of early childhood services is rooted in the social welfare orientation that has led to the establishment of many of America's child-care facilities for young children. Predicated on a commitment to provide care for children while parents work or are trained, child care (and federally subsidized child care in particular) may be associated with custodial care, which, it is assumed, will provide the minimum level of care necessary to alleviate parents' anxiety while they are employed outside the home. In contrast to this orientation, which focuses on serving adult needs, many services have been established with the primary goal of benefiting the children. Programs established by middle-class parents, mostly through the voluntary sector, have focused on providing opportunities for children to develop socialization skills, whereas those for low-income youngsters have focused on providing comprehensive services and opportunities to expand cognitive and social competence. Although different in orientation, both types of programs were nevertheless child-centered.

The field of early childhood and child development grew up within this dual tradition, and unfortunately the field today retains some of its contradictory images. Each October, for example, the Current Population Survey includes questions about preprimary enrollment. Parents are asked to identify the kind of services (if any) their youngsters are receiving. Is their child enrolled in "a group or class that is organized to provide educational experiences for children, and that includes instruction as an important and integral phase of its current program of child care" (Chorvinsky, 1982, p. 18)? Or is their child in custodial care? That the question is so phrased perpetuates the custodial-educational dichotomy of the past.

In spite of this historical background, early childhood programs are changing and the custodial-educational split is narrowing. Educated parents of today consciously look for care that is attuned to their children's development. Just as important, few child-care centers and programs perceive themselves to be less than educative in intent. In a recent Connecticut survey of child-care programs, not a single center saw itself as anything but educative and developmental in its goals and practices (Kagan & Newton, 1986).

Vestiges of the split are also evidenced in the dual image of providers. Child-care workers in custodial centers are often seen as unskilled workers who need little more than a "loving way." But early childhood teachers, who often work with children of the same age, are required to have teacher certification and/or to meet state standards. The roles defined in the *Dictionary of Occupational Titles* (U.S. Department of Labor, 1977) reinforce these disparate images: a child-care worker is described as one who helps children remove outer garments; teaches them simple painting, drawing, and songs; and directs them in eating, resting, and toileting. In contrast, a prekindergarten teacher plans group activities to stimulate learning, instructs children in activities designed to promote social and intellectual growth, and prepares children for primary school.

In reality, though, like the programs themselves, the caretaker-educator distinction among workers is diminishing. Now, the early childhood field is a specialization with programs ranging, as in other fields, from A.A. to Ph.D. levels. Individuals who work with young children may also pursue an innovative competency-based credential, the Child Development Associate; others may seek more formal, theoretical training. In some communities, such as New York City, teacher certification is a requirement whether individuals are employed by the Board of Education or by federally subsidized child-care or Head Start programs.

Thus in the past twenty years, early childhood education has become a professional field with standards, criteria, and certification, even though the earlier image as less than professional persists. It is this continuing denigration of day care that heightens the split between schools as educative and day care programs as custodial—an especially damaging opposition at a time when integration of the two is needed. Before the early childhood field is expanded, it must take giant steps toward common ground—toward eradicating the custodial versus educational and care giver versus teacher dichotomies.

The Content Issue

Early childhood education gained legitimacy when experts told America that intelligence was elastic: it could be expanded and preschool was the time to do it (Bloom, 1964; Hunt, 1961). With high hopes of improving children's cognitive and academic performance, Head Start and Head Start–like programs emerged in the mid-sixties. Curriculum models were developed and tested. For example, a national curriculum experiment called Planned Variation implemented and tested different curriculum approaches to ascertain if they affected children differentially (Miller, 1979). The nation became interested in getting preschoolers "ready"—in giving them a real cognitive head start.

The legacy of Head Start persists, and with it the debate about whether academic programs are appropriate in early childhood environments. This question is debated not only among early childhood educators but between early childhood and elementary educators as well. Differing views may be rooted in the distinctive orientations of psychology and education, the two academic disciplines that shaped the early childhood field. Those oriented toward psychological principles, or principles of child development, generally advocate less emphasis on structured academics; other educators, particularly those trained for elementary or upper-grade instruction, advocate more emphasis on academics, on the grounds that even preschool children are able to learn and enjoy the intellectual stimulation of learning.

Not only do the goals of instruction differ, but so do methods and approaches. Stress on academics connotes the mastery of basic facts, colors, numbers, and shapes, whereas cognition refers to the process of learning and of comprehending, for example, not just the number "one," but the "oneness of one." Concerns abound that elementary school teachers may be preoccupied with helping children master basic concepts essential to later academic achievement. Child developmentalists fear that under the rubric of readiness not enough attention will be paid to cognitive processes and to helping children foster dispositions toward learning: motivation, curiosity, inquisitiveness, spontaneity. They are concerned that "pre-kindergarten programs may reinforce a downward extension of formal education into the preprimary years" (Morado, 1986, p. 63).

The concern of early childhood specialists within and outside schools is whether an elementary school setting, attuned to academic achievement with its system of fixed schedules and its emphasis on achievement and evaluation (and hence, advancement and failure), can break out of its traditional mold sufficiently to accommodate the special learning needs of young children. Can an institution established to foster the acquisition of academics restructure itself to accommodate important cognitive, social, and dispositional factors within the early childhood curriculum? In spite of these doubts, some child developmentalists concede that early childhood personnel who understand the developmental needs of young children not only exist in public schools but regularly fight to maintain environments that are sensitive to these needs.

Although it is appropriate to ask questions concerning what the schools can and cannot do, it is also important for early childhood specialists to examine their own standards for developmental appropriateness. The National Association for the Education of Young Children (NAEYC) has taken leadership in this area and developed a set of standards that is helping to clear up confusion about what constitutes quality in early childhood (Bredekamp, 1986).

Comprehensiveness: The Nature of the Curriculum

Head Start helped not only to foster cognitive instruction in the field but to make it more comprehensive as well. Before Head Start, the public had conventional notions about preschool that focused on the classroom and did not include expanded services such as parental involvement or attention to health or nutrition. Although a few programs, such as parent cooperatives, provided rich opportunities for parental involvement, comprehensive services were not expected as part of a quality preschool program. But research on Head Start and other efforts has reminded professionals that children do not exist in isolation: they are part of a family and community that shape their being (Bronfenbrenner, 1979). Gradually, in the past twenty years, the vision of what constitutes quality early childhood programming has been expanded beyond the classroom and the child; it now includes the provision of a full array of services to the child and the family.

The degree to which public schools can accommodate the profession's commitment to comprehensive services is a matter not simply of interest but of perceived responsibility and pragmatics. Some educators have questioned how far the school's responsibility extends beyond the academic education of its students. Is it really the school's job to feed and clothe youngsters? Other educators acknowledge the importance of good health and nutrition if students are to learn, but realize that structurally most schools aren't set up to handle the services a holistic orientation requires. For example, eating with young children and engaging them in conversation at meal and snack times are critical components of the early childhood curriculum and services. Yet often this is not sanctioned by union contracts.

Although there are no absolute rights and wrongs, schools and child-care settings do have a record of past differences in philosophy of learning and commitment to the total child and family. Because of these differences, incorporating services to preschoolers in a setting that isn't intensely sympathetic to the unique requirements of early childhood programming is problematic operationally and often a source of real conflict. In order to be on educationally firm ground, schools must understand and be willing to accommodate holistic and comprehensive programming if an early childhood program is to be a successful part—even a small part—of public school services.

The Philosophical Grounds for Early Schooling: Issues of Equity, Standards, and Values

Equity for Children

Inequity of access to quality programs has been a nemesis of early childhood programs for decades. Programs usually are not available to all children equally, and, even when they are, they are typically segregated by income: poor children are enrolled in subsidized programs, and middle- and upper-class youngsters attend fee-based centers. Even those who champion high-quality Head Start and Head Start–like programs recognize that the economic segregation of children is a critical programmatic weakness (Zigler, 1986). This commonplace economic segregation is particularly troublesome because it flies in the face of research and our national ethos. Numerous scholars have investigated the effects of desegregation, and although reviews of their research on its relationship to pupil achievement indicate that desegregation will not necessarily close the white-black achievement gap (St. John, 1975), nevertheless positive effects have been documented. Weinberg (1975) noted such an effect on minority achievement levels, and Crain and Mahard (1978) showed that mixing college-bound middle-class students with minority low-income youngsters has a positive effect on the poorer minority children. In the most comprehensive assessment of desegregation in the United States initiated under the auspices of the Office for Civil Rights and the National Institute of Education, Hawley (1981) and his team presented a favorable picture of the results of desegregation in terms of both its impact on children and its relative success as a social intervention. But beyond what research has shown, integration is the law of the land, inherent in our commitment to public education. The Supreme Court fortified this commitment to integration in *Brown* v. *Board of Education* in 1954. Serving all children, and serving them together once they reach the age of five, is mandatory.

It is a paradox that an opposing ideology characterizes our services to children just a year younger. Preschoolers from disadvantaged families, far from experiencing the heterogeneous ideal advocated for five-year-olds, are sequestered into publicly funded programs for poor children. On the other hand, middle- and upper-class children are almost completely served in the private sector, in either profit or nonprofit programs. Thus, social stratification is publicly sanctioned for preschool children.

As we grapple with new options, the early childhood community must ask to what extent this approach to early education perpetuates class inequities. Will a universal approach to early education expand opportunities for low-income youngsters, or will limited funding mean that in the name of integration slots previously assigned to low-income youth will be allocated to middle- and upper-class children? Does *provision* of universal services mean *consumption* of services universally and equitably? Does equity mean equality? Or to achieve equity might we need unequal services?

Equity for Adults

Just as equity is an issue for children, so it is for adults in the field. As new responsibilities are expected of providers, and as efforts are made to attract new people to the field, the equity issue takes on even greater significance. Early childhood providers, mostly women, earn less than men and less than care providers in other service industries, such as hospital workers and social worker aides. In addition to the interfield issue of salary and benefit parity, inequities exist within the field itself. The perceptual differences between teachers and care givers are manifest in their training, wage and benefit levels, and employability. There are grave disparities between salaries and benefits from one type of early childhood sponsor to another. For example, teachers in public school settings may earn more than twice the salary and receive significantly greater benefits than child-care workers in other settings. And parity is absent not just between the education and child-care communities but within each community itself. For example, even within one funding stream—that of the government—vast discrepancies exist in the amount of teacher support that is offered. Head Start employees, for example, have had access to rich training opportunities; many have not had to pay for their Child Development Associate (CDA) training, whereas federally funded child-care providers have no such benefit. There is a lack of equal access to CDA, a reality that impedes the CDA from becoming a truly national credential, and a reality that exemplifies the lack of adult equity in the field.

Every comprehensive report on early education has called for coordination among providers of services, regardless of funding auspices. But given decades of salary, benefit, and training inequities, how realistic are the prospects for coordination? Perhaps, as a correlate of cooperation, the profession needs to look at ways to redress some of the inequities.

Standardization

Analogous to the question of equity for individuals is the question of program equity—the question of standardization. How much standardization across different funding streams and different programs is necessary and desirable? Should emphasis be placed on developing parity across funding streams or on developing quality programming within a funding stream?

Curriculum research shows that different curriculum types and programs provide richness and variety, as well as the possibility of tailoring local programs to local needs and desires. Researchers have generally agreed that a standardized curriculum is not desirable, but that a standardized level of quality is needed. The problem then becomes how to achieve a standard level of quality without endorsing specific curricula or regulations. For example, in child-care centers licensed by the state, typically care giver–child ratios and group size are established, ensuring some uniformity on these variables within individual states. But schools are traditionally exempt from day-care licensure requirements. While schools may adhere to some requirements, rarely are they as stringent as day-care standards. Consequently, even within a given state, criteria as important as ratios vary considerably. Early childhood educators must decide if programs, because they are located in one type of physical facility, should be exempt from regulations to which comparable programs located in other types of facilities are accountable.

As long as school-based prekindergarten functioned in isolation, and as long as so few children were cared for in these programs, these issues were not prominent. But, as dialogue among early childhood providers increases across sectors, and as parents become more knowledgeable consumers of early childhood services, dysfunctional cross-sector distinctions will become more apparent. How to reconcile these differences, and how to decide which areas call for standardization, are questions to be resolved in the eighties and nineties.

High-Quality or Good-Enough Care?

Related to standardization is the question not of *what* should be standardized but at what *level* that standard should be set. Is "high quality" necessary or is "good-enough" care and education sufficient? Scholars in both child care and education have raised the good-enough issue (Lightfoot, 1983; Rambusch, 1985; Willie, 1982). Essentially a resource distribution question, some scholars suggest that when needs far outdistance available services and resources, the system might well consider a slight falling-off from the ideal of quality to services that are good enough—that it might just be a wiser policy to serve *more* children with services that are good enough than fewer children with quality services. It should be noted that "good enough" in this context does not mean "mediocre," but rather connotes services that are sufficient for the requirements of the situation (Willie, 1982). Although admittedly this notion dashes idealistic aspirations, it may resolve the overpromise-and-underfinance syndrome that characterized early childhood programs of the 1960s and 1970s.

But yet another question arises: what constitutes good-enough care? Although early childhood specialists know much about quality care and some about poor care, they know little about less than optimal care. Is the profession willing to explore such an option? Can it go on record as advocating something less than optimal? Are the cost savings significant enough to warrant reductions in quality?

Two examples of the good-enough ideology are already in place, one in Texas and another in Florida. Both states adopted sweeping reforms in early childhood education, Texas in 1984 and Florida in 1986. From reviews so far, both efforts are generally promising. The Texas legislation (1984 Texas Education Reform Bill, House Bill 72) specified that any school district may offer prekindergarten classes, but such classes must be offered if the district identifies fifteen or more eligible children—"eligible" meaning four-year-olds who are unable to speak and comprehend the English language or are from a family whose income is at or below subsistence level.

But when the Lyndon B. Johnson School of Public Affairs conducted an evaluation of the legislation, it was found that districts will implement the new program only because they *must*, not because they are enthusiastic about preschool education. Attitudes ranged from an emphatic "we'll only offer it if we have to!" to what one administrator called "neutral enthusiasm" (Texas School Finance Research Project, 1985, p. 112). Several administrators also expressed concern that the state may be in the process of redefining the role of the public schools to include child raising, a responsibility some thought more appropriate to parents. "Are we going to begin taking them from the cradle?" asked a superintendent from a small district (p. 112). Perhaps the gravest concern cited in the report was the teacher-child ratio of 1:22 (the same required for teachers of kindergarten through second grade). Two points emerge: First, although Texas passed and implemented landmark legislation, it may, in its implementation, be yielding programs that are barely good enough. Second, within the legislation itself, the 1:22 ratio (in a field that recommends 1:10 as the appropriate practice) is a severe handicap to achieving even good-enough service.

The Florida legislation, more recent and more innovative than the Texas bill, grants money to organizations that emphasize parental involvement and education, adequate teacher training, and health screening. The bill ensures curriculum continuity through the elementary grades and requires grantees to develop plans for coordinating their programs with those for disabled preschool learners and district kindergartens. The legislation offers money to any public school, Head Start program, or private nonprofit or for-profit facility that enrolls at least 50 percent educationally and economically disadvantaged children. Grant money is to be used for disadvantaged enrollees; other children must pay on a sliding schedule (Chapter 228.0615, Florida Statutes). Such an approach is a long step toward solving the problems of programmatic segregation of young children by income. But the legislation has one important omission: it makes no mention of ratios, and Florida's ratio in programs for four-year-olds is 1:20 (Department of Health and Rehabilitative Services, 1986). Is Florida's a quality effort, as parts of it appear to be? Or is it simply good enough because the unsuitable ratio will negate many of the law's intended positive effects?

In fairness to Florida, the law does call for examining the state's current ratio standards. Thus, in time and given sufficient motivation and information, future legislation could improve the law. In this case, good enough might be useful as an interim strategy. Others, however, would argue that once good enough is in place, it's good enough for good; their skepticism implies that the early childhood profession shouldn't settle for anything less than quality standards.

Issues of Responsibility

The question of who is ultimately responsible for the care and education of young children is broader than the issues discussed above and is perhaps the most perplexing. As a nation, we've had a difficult time determining whether the family, the government, or the private sector is most responsible. This is evidenced by the fact that there is no coherent family policy (Bane, 1978). Others contend that the very absence of a family policy is itself a policy (Marmor, 1983; Zigler, Kagan, & Klugman, 1983). Whichever ideological stance is taken, it is clear that the lack of direction by the federal government on children's issues has caused unnecessary fluctuations in service, a waste of resources—human and financial—and a lack of equity in service distribution.

Certainly issues of family privacy and family rights need to be considered when assessing appropriate involvement for governmental and nongovernmental sectors. But the fact that opinions differ is not sufficient cause to halt discussion of responsibility. In order to explore the issues presented in this chapter and throughout the book, we need to focus on the development of a consistent governmental stance on early education. Leaving it to the states yields only fragmented services. Is it appropriate or right that children in one state have greater access to quality services than children in others?

Clearly, the elaboration of responsibility must take place in three domains: first, among three broad sectors—the family, the government, and the voluntary sector; second, among levels of government—federal, state, and local; and third, among agencies of government—education and health and human services. Although it will not be an easy task, addressing the issue of early schooling from the perspective of shared responsibility might help elucidate, if not settle, the national debate.

Conclusion

Throughout this volume certain questions recur concerning the physical, pedagogical, and philosophical grounds on which early schooling should be based. It should not be surprising that concrete answers will not be readily apparent. But how the issues are resolved will reflect our society's attitudes toward its youngest citizens, our agility at problem solving, and our values. Through vigorous and thoughtful debate, we as a nation should be able to stand more resolutely and more firmly convinced of the grounds on which developmentally appropriate care and education will be rendered.

REFERENCES

Bane, M. J. (1978). *Family policy in the United States: Toward a description and evaluation* (Working Paper No. 52). Cambridge, MA: Joint Center for Urban Studies of the Massachusetts Institute of Technology and Harvard University.

Berrueta-Clement, J., Schweinhart, L., Barnett, W., Epstein, A., & Weikart, D. (1984). *Changed lives*. Ypsilanti, MI: High/Scope Press.

Bettleheim, B. (1987, March). The importance of play. *Atlantic Monthly*, pp. 35–46.

Blank, H., & Wilkins, A. (1985). *Child care: Whose priority? A state child care fact book*. Washington, DC: Children's Defense Fund.

Bloom, B. S. (1964). *Stability and change in human characteristics*. New York: Wiley.

Bredekamp, S. (1986). *Developmentally appropriate practice*. Washington, DC: National Association for the Education of Young Children.

Bronfenbrenner, U. (1979). *The ecology of human development: Experiences by nature and design*. Cambridge, MA: Harvard University Press.

Brown v. Board of Education. 347 U.S. 483 (1954).

Chorvinsky, M. (1982). *Preprimary enrollment 1980*. Washington, DC: National Center for Educational Statistics.

Crain, R. L., & Mahard, R. E. (1978, Summer). Desegregation and black achievement: A review of research. *Law and Contemporary Problems*, *42*.

Gesell, A. (1940). *The first five years of life: A guide to the study of the preschool child*. New York: Harper & Row.

Hawley, W. D. (Ed.). (1981). *Effective school desegregation: Equity, quality and feasibility*. Beverly Hills, CA: Sage.

Hunt, J. McV. (1961). *Intelligence and experience*. New York: Ronald Press.

Kagan, S. L., & Newton, J. W. (1986, October 9). *Profit and quality in child care: Preliminary results of a Connecticut study*. Presentation to Program on Non-Profit Organizations, Yale University, New Haven, CT.

Lightfoot, S. L. (1983). *The good high school: Portraits of character and culture*. New York: Basic Books.

Marmor, T. R. (1983). Competing perspectives on social policy. In E. F. Zigler, S. L. Kagan, & E. Klugman, (Eds.). *Children, family and government* (pp. 35–36). New York: Cambridge University Press.

Miller, L. B. (1979). Development of curriculum models in Head Start. In E. Zigler & J. Valentine, (Eds.). *Project Head Start: A legacy of the war on poverty* (pp. 195–220). New York: Free Press.

Morado, C. (1986, July). Prekindergarten programs for 4-year-olds: Some key issues. *Young Children*, *41*(5).

National Black Child Development Institute, Inc. (1985). *Child care in the public schools: Incubator for inequality?* Washington, DC: Author.

Rambusch, N. (1985, April 8). *Reconceptualizing quality* (Cassette Recording). Presented at the Child Care Colloquium, Bush Center in Child Development and Social Policy, Yale University, New Haven, CT.

Salholz, E., Wingert, P., Burgower, B., Michael, R., & Joseph, N. (1987, February 2). Kids need time to be kids. *Newsweek*, pp. 56–58.

School at 4: A model for the nation. (1985, February 20). *The New York Times*, p. 22.

Schweinhart, L. (1985). *Early childhood development programs in the eighties: The national picture*. Ypsilanti, MI: High/Scope Early Childhood Policy Papers.

Schweinhart, L. S., & Koschel, J. (1986). *Policy options for preschool programs*. Ypsilanti, MI: High/Scope Early Childhood Policy Papers.

Shanker, A. (1976, June 5). *Public schools and preschool programs: A natural connection*. Testimony presented to a joint meeting of the House Select Subcommittee on Education and the Senate Subcommittee on Children and Youth. Item #627. Washington, DC: American Federation of Teachers.

Should 4- and 5-year-olds be in school? (1986, March 28). *Christian Science Monitor*, p. B7.

St. John, N. (1975). *School desegregation: Outcomes for children*. New York: Wiley Interscience.

Texas School Finance Policy Research Project. (1985). *The effects of House Bill 72 on Texas public schools: The challenges of equity and effectiveness (#370)*. Austin, TX: Lyndon B. Johnson School of Public Affairs, The University at Austin.

U.S. Department of Education. (1986). *Pre-school enrollment: Trends and implications* (Publication No. 065-000-00276-1). Washington, DC: U.S. Government Printing Office.

U.S. Department of Labor. (1977). *Dictionary of occupational titles* (4th ed.). Washington, DC: U.S. Government Printing Office.

Weil, J. (1986). *One third more: Maine Head Start expansion with state funds*. Ellsworth, ME: Federal-State Partnership Project, Action Opportunities.

Weinberg, M. (1975). The relationship between school desegregation and academic achievement: A review of the research. *Law and Contemporary Problems*, *39*, 240–270.

Willie, C. (1982). Educating students who are good enough. *Change*, *14*(2), 16.

Zigler, E. (1986, May). Should four-year-olds be in school? [Special Report: Early Childhood Education]. *Principal*, *65*(5), 10–17.

Zigler, E. R., Kagan, S. L., & Klugman, E. (Eds.). (1983). *Children, families and government: Perspectives on American Social Policy*. New York: Cambridge University Press.

PART II

Policy and Practice: Points of View

CHAPTER 2

Formal Schooling for Four-Year-Olds? No

EDWARD F. ZIGLER

A developing momentum is moving our nation toward universal preschool education (Zimiles, 1985). Many decision makers are advocating the downward extension of public schooling to four-year-olds. New York's Mayor Koch not only made all-day kindergarten mandatory but also appointed a commission charged with reorganizing and broadening access to all early intervention and preschool programs in New York City. A *New York Times* editorial entitled "School at 4: A Model for the Nation" hailed Koch's initiative as the most sensible way to "save the next generation" (1985, p. 22). American Federation of Teachers president Albert Shanker also endorsed preschool education. So many positive voices have been heard that it is easy to assume that schooling for four-year-olds is an uncomplicated issue that has met only with popular support and enthusiasm. Indeed, the commissioner for education in New York State, Gordon Ambach (1985), stated that it was impossible to find anyone to uphold the negative side of the issue.

There are some negative voices, however, and they are beginning to be heard. Herbert Zimiles (1985), a leading thinker in the field of early childhood education, has argued that the movement toward universal preschool education is characterized more by enthusiasm than thought. The commissioner of education for the state of Connecticut, Gerald Tirozzi, another champion of public education for four-year-olds, established a committee to study the issue within the general context of children's services. In their recommendations, this committee concluded that "under no circumstances do we believe it appropriate for all four-year-olds to be involved in a 'kindergarten-type' program within the public schools" (Kagan, 1985, p. 3). In this chapter, I will add my voice to those who have argued that the issue of universal schooling for four-year-olds requires more thought than it has been accorded.

The current impetus for earlier schooling has two sources. The first is the concern generated by the increasing criticism of our public secondary schools. The National Commission on Excellence in Education report, *A Nation at Risk* (1983), detailed the failures of secondary schooling in America. Similar studies (for example, Boyer, 1983; Sizer, 1984) soon followed. These reports emphasized the need for higher academic standards, more attention to basics, more rigor in teaching, and longer school days and years. Few of them proposed earlier schooling as a solution to our educational problems.

An ostensible exception, Mortimer Adler's thoughtful *Paideia Proposal* (1983), did link school reform and early childhood education. Adler stated: "preschool deprivation is the cause of backwardness or failure in school. . . . Hence at least one year—or better, two or three years of preschool tutelage must be provided for those who do not get such preparation from favorable environments" (pp. 37–38). Too often, however, Adler's caveat with regard to the purely remedial nature of preschool for the disadvantaged is ignored. It is not Adler's opinion, nor is it mine, that the more advantaged children in our society require a year of preschool education at the state's expense.

A second source of the momentum toward universal preschool education is the inappropriate generalization of the effects of some excellent remedial programs for the economically disadvantaged. Several preschool intervention programs—such as Head Start (Lazar & Darlington, 1982), the New York University Institute for Developmental Studies (Deutsch, Deutsch, Jordan, & Grallo, 1983), the Ypsilanti-based Perry Preschool Program (Berrueta-Clement, Schweinhart, Barnett, Epstein & Weikart, 1984), the New York State prekindergarten program (Ambach, 1985), and the Brookline Early Education Program (Pierson,

Tivnan, & Walker, 1984)—have succeeded in spurring the developmental and cognitive growth of economically disadvantaged three- and four-year-old children. But extrapolation to all children from these programs is inappropriate for two reasons. First, benefits were obtained only for economically disadvantaged children. Second, these intervention programs differ from standard school fare in a number of important ways, since they provide primary health and social services. In addition, unlike conventional schooling, this assistance is provided to the family as a whole, not simply to a target child. These are vital differences, as many theorists believe that preschool programs are most successful when parents participate and that the basic needs of children and their families must be met before schooling can have any effect (Bronfenbrenner, 1974; Deutsch, Deutsch, Jordan, & Grallo, 1983; Radin, 1969; Slater, 1971; Sparrow, Blachman, & Chauncey, 1983; Valentine & Stark, 1979; Waksman, 1980).

Public preschool education shares few of these services and concerns, nor can they become the primary focus of the educational establishment. It is an open question whether early school-based programs will result in the same increases in social competence found by the Cornell Consortium (Royce, Darlington, & Murray, 1983) following early intervention programs for the economically disadvantaged, increases which may well be a consequence of services having very little to do with formal education. It was precisely those differences between Head Start and formal schooling that I have outlined here that led many of us to oppose President Carter's proposal to move Head Start into the new Department of Education, and that in the end prevented its inclusion.

The Perry Preschool Program

Other differences, too, must be considered when interpreting the benefits of the Perry Preschool Program in Ypsilanti, Michigan, an intervention program involving either one or two years of half-day preschool for seven months each year and periodic home visits for high-risk four- and five-year-olds. This well-known exemplary intervention effort achieved remarkable success, and it deserves the praise it has received from many quarters. It is one of the few intervention efforts that attempted to assign participants randomly to experimental and control groups. Further, it is one of the few intervention efforts that have met my dictum that the assessment of early intervention efforts should include a cost-benefit analysis (Zigler & Berman, 1983). But generalizing from the results of this unique effort to typical public programs is highly problematic for three reasons.

First, it is very unlikely that a preschool program mounted in the typical public school will be of the quality represented by the Perry Preschool Project. The program's experimental character ensured that it would be exceptionally well planned, monitored, and managed. Further, the very fact that staff members are participating in an experiment can stimulate and motivate them. For example, researchers worked extensively with the direct child care givers in analyzing and constructing the program (Barnett, personal communication, 1985), and visiting experts held weekly seminars for the entire preschool staff (Weikart, 1967). Although the consequences of these aspects of the program were not analyzed, their potential effect on program outcome may well have been substantial.

Second, there are questions concerning the Perry sample. It was not only nonrepresentative of children in general; there is some doubt that it was representative of even the bulk of economically disadvantaged children. The sample was limited to black youngsters, when in fact the majority of low-income children are white (U.S. Bureau of the Census, 1984); it is even problematic as to whether the sample was representative of low-income black children. The Perry Project was limited to children with IQs between 61 and 88. Yet the median IQ of black children in the United States was 80–85 in the early 1960s (Kennedy, Van de Riet, & White, 1963). A further argument against generalization from the Perry Preschool Project lies in the fact that participation was fully voluntary, which introduced a self-selection phenomenon (how families that did not choose to volunteer differed from the final project sample is an open question).

Finally, the Perry Project poses a number of methodological difficulties. First, to be assigned to the intervention group, children had to have a parent at home during the day, resulting in a significant difference between control and intervention groups on the variable of maternal employment. Second, as noted by Haskins and Gallagher (1984) assignment to experimental and control groups was not wholly random. Although this departure from random assignment is probably of minor consequence, it does render interpretation of program effects problematic. Finally, criticisms have been advanced that the Perry program's cost-benefit analyses overestimated the benefits attributed to the intervention (Hanke & Anwyll, 1980).

I concur with the Gottfrieds (1984) and Larsen (1985) that caution should be exercised in generalizing from one group to another. (I would like to see the outcome of the High/Scope model when mounted by people with less expertise than those employed in the Perry project.) Furthermore, evaluations of any intervention should be conducted by researchers not involved in the development of the model being evaluated (Zigler & Berman, 1983). Given the pervasiveness of self-fulfilling prophecies (Rosenthal & Jacobson, 1968; Merton, 1948), this is merely a commonsense concern. I should note, however, that Campbell (in press) has recently argued that it is appropriate for those who mount programs to do their own evaluations in order to retain their qualitative subjective insights in their analyses.

Appropriate Candidates for Intervention

The High/Scope data generate the intriguing hypothesis that preschool intervention is particularly effective for the most economically disadvantaged children, a view supported by the New York State evaluation of its experimental preschool program (Irvine, Flint, Hick, Horan, & Kikuk, 1982). The New York study indicated that the only cognitive gains that lasted beyond the preschool period were among children whose mothers scored extremely low on measures of education.

This view has apparently not escaped the attention of educational decision makers. Almost all the states that now provide school-sponsored programs for four-year-olds limit enrollment to low-income, handicapped, and, in some cases, non-English-speaking youngsters (Kagan, 1985). Even the Ypsilanti group recognized that these are the children who can most profit from intervention (Berrueta-Clement et al., 1984, p. 7). Although Pierson et al. (1984) have made some claims for the effectiveness of preschool programs for middle-class children, their criterion for this status is questionable. In any case, the gains made by children of educated parents in their study were far less than those made by the children of less educated parents. What is more, such differences as were found may turn out to be short-lived, as no long-term assessment of the intervention and control groups has been carried out.

In contrast, there is a large body of evidence indicating that there is little if anything to be gained by exposing middle-class children to early education (see Adler, 1982; Caruso & Detterman, 1981; Clarke, 1984; Darlington, Royce, Snipper, Murray, & Lazar, 1980; Swift, 1964). For example, the only advantage Swift (1964) could find as a result of preschool education was a small degree of enhanced social development when the children entered school; those not involved in preschool reached the same level of social adjustment in less than two years. Similarly, Abelson, Zigler, and DeBlasi (1974) found that while an extensive four-year intervention program benefited low-income children, it had no effect on middle-class youngsters. In his review of research on preschool intervention, English specialist on child development and education Martin Woodhead (1985) states:

> Three main considerations affect the validity of drawing general conclusions for early education policy. First, the populations served by these projects were severely disadvantaged, mainly black children, and the evidence for wider replicability is inconclusive. Secondly, the projects all featured a carefully designed, well-supported programme with low ratios of children to teachers. Finally the effectiveness of pre-school may also be conditional on features of the educational and family context in which intervention took place. (p. 133)

American schools are already under great financial pressure and must make the most efficient use possible of limited economic resources. I have long been an advocate of cost-benefit analyses for all types of social programs (Zigler & Berman, 1983). As previously stated, our best thinking suggests we can make the most effective use of limited funds by investing them in intervention programs that target three overlapping groups: (1) the economically disadvantaged child, (2) the handicapped child, and (3) the bilingual child (Casto & Mastropieri, 1984; Kagan, 1985; White & Casto, 1984). Spreading education budgets to include all four-year-olds would spread them too thin. Such an extension would not only have little effect on the more advantaged mainstream, but would diminish our capacity to intervene with those who could benefit the most.

There is, however, one potential advantage to universal preschool education. A weakness of Head Start and Head Start–like programs is their built-in economic segregation of children. Poor children go to Head Start, while more affluent children go elsewhere. Universal preschools would better integrate children across socioeconomic lines and, as Zimiles (1985) has noted, would introduce equity into early childhood programs. Although this would waste funding on children who have little to gain from early education, it would also guarantee its availability to those who could not otherwise afford it. Furthermore, Abelson et al. (1974) and Coleman et al. (1966) suggest there are educational advantages to mixed socioeconomic and racial groupings. Nevertheless, although we would be well-advised to promote the integration of children from diverse social and ethnic backgrounds, the cost of doing so through universal preschool education outweighs its potential benefits.

The Real Need: High Quality Child Care

Educators in several states point to parental pressure for all-day kindergarten as evidence of the value parents place on early education, but I believe that they have misread this demand. What many parents are expressing is less a burning desire for preschool education than their desperate need for quality day care. Fifty-nine percent of the mothers of three- and four-year-olds are now employed outside their homes, and many of these mothers have enrolled their children in child-care programs that provide organized educational activities (Chorvinsky, 1982). Yet, ironically, not even all-day kindergarten programs are able to fill the day-care needs of families with both parents working outside the home. Schools tend to adjourn around 3:00, two hours before most working days end. Thus, the day-care problem has only been partly solved, and this token improvement may actually lead parents to take fewer precautions, given the relatively short period of time children are alone.

Day care can be prohibitively expensive for many families, and it is not surprising that many would prefer to shift the cost to the public school system. The Perry Preschool Project was estimated by its originators to cost approximately fifteen hundred dollars per year per child in 1963. Given the number of three- and four-year-olds in the nation today, and adjusting the figures for inflation, the total cost of a universal child development program would be many billions of dollars per year. Unfortunately, advocates of universal preschool education continue to behave as though these vast sums will magically appear. Fiscal reality demands we target populations who can most benefit from care and provide them with the more general programs best suited to their particular needs.

We must also listen to those families who neither need nor want their young children placed in preschool. The compulsory aspect of many of the proposed early education plans has angered many parents and set them in opposition to school officials—a poor beginning to the positive home-school relation that is vital to the educational process (Bronfenbrenner, 1974; Lazar & Darlington, 1982). Decision makers must be sensitive to the individual needs of children and parents and recognize that, whenever the family situation permits it, the best place for a preschool child is often at home.

We must strive also to be sensitive to the individual differences among young children. Some four-year-olds can handle a five- or six hour school day. Many others cannot. Whenever it is best for the children to be at home with their parents, we should not needlessly deprive families of valuable time they could spend together. This is not to ignore the fact that home may be a place of abuse or neglect, a welfare hotel, or a confusing and insecure environment without what we have come to accept as adequate resources. For these children, day care may be the best available alternative. Yet many competent, caring parents who are at home resent school administrators' proposals to keep their preschool children in a full-day early education program. In fact, recent work by Tizard and her colleagues has demonstrated that the conversations children carry on at home may be the richest source of linguistic and cognitive enrichment for children from all but the most deprived backgrounds (Hughes, Carmichael, Pinkerton, & Tizard, 1979; Tizard, Carmichael, Hughes, & Pinkerton, 1980; Tizard & Hughes, 1984; Tizard, Mortimore, & Burchell, 1981; Tizard, Hughes, Carmichael, & Pinkerton, 1982, 1983). This body of work highlights the vast scope of information and ideas that are transmitted at home, as opposed to the circumscribed agenda of the school. The fact that parent and child share a common life and frame of reference allows them to explore events and ideas in intimate, individualistic conversations with great personal meaning. At a time when universal early education, the earlier the better, is being advocated, the Tizard work reminds us of other, equally important roots of cognitive development.

A Time for Childhood

I concur with Elkind (1981) and Winn (1983) that we are driving our young children too hard and thereby depriving them of their most precious commodity—their childhood. The image of the four-year-old in designer jeans and miniature executive briefcase in hand may seem cute, but rushing children from cradle to school denies them the freedom to develop at their own pace. Children are growing up too fast today, and prematurely placing four- and five-year-olds into full-day preschool education programs will only compound this problem.

Those who argue in favor of universal preschool education ignore evidence that indicates early schooling is inappropriate for many four-year-olds and that it may even be harmful to their development (Ames, 1980; Collins, 1984; Elkind, 1981; Gesell, 1928; Yarrow, 1964; Zimiles, 1985). Marie Winn (1983) notes in *Children without Childhood* that premature schooling can replace valuable playtime, potentially slowing or reducing the child's overall development. This is an especial danger given the present cognitive thrust in education, increasing the possibility of an overemphasis on formal and highly structured academics (Ames, 1980; Zimiles, 1985). The supervision of very young children must be a distinctive form of care suited to the rapid developmental changes and high dependency of these children, not a scaled-down version of a grade-school curriculum.

At the same time we must remember that although early childhood is an important and sensitive time, it is not uniquely so. In the 1960s we believed early childhood was a magic period during which minimal intervention efforts would have maximal indelible effects on the child. In the current push toward early formal education we can see the unfortunate recurrence of this idea.

Every age in a child's life is a magic age. We must be just as concerned for the six-year-old, the ten-year-old, and the sixteen-year-old as we are for the four-year-old (Clarke & Clarke, 1976). In fact, the proposed New York plan is especially troubling in that it includes a suggestion to add a year of education at the beginning of formal schooling and to drop a year at the end of high school. The work of Feuerstein (1970; Feuerstein, Rand, Hoffman, & Miller, 1980) and Hobbs and Robinson (1982), to name but a few scholars in this area, has demonstrated that adolescence is itself a sensitive and fluid period in the life of the child. We must guard against shortchanging one age group in our efforts to help another.

The Easy Way Out

This is not the first time universal preschool education has been proposed. Wilson Riles, then California state superintendent of schools, advocated early childhood education ten years ago, as school superintendents in New York and Connecticut are doing today. Then, as now, the arguments in favor of preschool education were that it would reduce school failure, lower drop-out rates, increase test scores, and produce a generation of more competent high school graduates. I have reached the same conclusion in interpreting the evidence as did the state of California finally: preschool education will achieve none of these results. I am not simply saying that universal preschool education will be a waste of time and money. Rather there is a positive danger in asserting that the solution to the poor school and later life performance of the disadvantaged will be solved by a year of preschool education. The nation is on the verge of falling into the over-optimistic trap that ensnared us in the mid-sixties, when expectations were raised that an eight-week summer program could solve all the problems of the poor. If we wish to improve the lives of the economically disadvantaged, we must abandon the short-term "solutions" of the sixties and work for much deeper social reforms (Zigler & Berman, 1983). The purely symbolic function served by relying on educational innovations alone to solve the problems of poor children has been noted by historian Marvin Lazerson:

> Too often discussions of educational reform appear to be a means of avoiding more complex and politically dangerous issues. . . . Education is . . . cheaper than new housing and new jobs. We are left with greater school responsibility while the social problems which have the greatest effect on schooling are largely ignored. The schools—in this case, preschool—are asked to do too much, and given too little support to accomplish what they are asked. A variety of interest groups, however, are satisfied: educators, because they get status and funds, social reformers, because they believe in education, and government officials because they pass positive legislation without upsetting traditional social patterns. (1970, p. 84)

We simply cannot inoculate children in one year against the ravages of a life of deprivation. Even champions of early childhood education have made sobering statements warning us not to expect too much while doing too little. Fred Hechinger wrote, "Part of the problem is to overpromise and underfinance. The hard fact is that there are no educational miracles for the effects of poverty" (1985, p. C10). In an incisive analysis, Sen. Daniel Patrick Moynihan agreed, warning that exaggerated reports of success in the field of early childhood education lead inevitably to near nihilism when these extravagant hopes are unfulfilled: "From finding out that not everything works, we rush to the judgment that nothing works or can be made to work" (1984, p. 8). Moynihan noted that the Ypsilanti researchers were restrained in their claims of the benefits of early childhood education, stating that such programs are "part of the solution, not the whole solution" (quoted in Moynihan, 1984, p. 13). In editorializing these results, however, Moynihan unabashedly stated, "Yes, after all the years of experiment and disappointment, American society does know one sure way to lead poor children out of a life of poverty" (p. 13). Moynihan's point that research is threatened when results are exaggerated in this fashion is well taken. Just as the credibility of researchers can be damaged, so too can the credibility of educators if they insist on promising more than they can possibly deliver. Barbara Tizard states:

> Insofar, then, as the expansion of early schooling is seen as a way of avoiding later school failure or of closing the social class gap in achievement, we already know it to be doomed to failure. It would perhaps be sensible for research workers to point this out very clearly to public authorities at an early stage. This is not, of course, to say that such an expansion has no value—no one would agree that a young child should not be fed well, because his present diet may not affect his adult weight and height. Nursery schooling, or particular forms of it, may help to develop the child's social and cognitive skills as well as add to the happiness of both child and mother. What seems certain, however, is that without continuous reinforcement in the primary school or home, pre-school education has no long-term effect on later school achievement. (Tizard, 1974, p. 4)

A Realistic Solution

Educators must realize they cannot reform the world or change the basic nature of children. The real question is how to provide the best experience during the day for a four-year-old—specifically for those who cannot remain at home with a consistent, competent care giver. Parents do not need children who read at age four, but they do need affordable, good-quality child care. The most cost-effective way to provide universally available—again, not compulsory—care would be to work through the school. I am advocating a return to the concept of the community school as a local center for all the social services required by the surrounding neighborhood. These full-service schools would, in addition to supplying other programs, provide full-day, high-quality child care for four- and even three-year-old children in their facilities, since they are already present in the community. Although such preschool programs would include a developmentally appropriate educational component, they would be places primarily for recreation and socialization—the real business of preschoolers. In-school day care could also easily accommodate older children after school is dismissed. Another investigator summarizes the need in this way: "We must . . . align the goals of programs for infants, preschoolers, and early elementary school-aged pupils so that such programs become components of an integrated, consistent plan for educating young children" (Weinberg, 1979, p. 915).

Such a program, although operating on school grounds, should not be staffed solely by teachers. Instead I propose that we staff school-based day-care programs with teachers in a supervisory capacity and with Child Development Associates (CDAS), the certified care givers currently employed in our nation's Head Start program. The National Day Care Study (Ruopp, Travers, Glantz, & Coelen, 1979) found that the one background characteristic of teachers that related to program quality was their training for early childhood programs. Certification of CDAS is based on both educational attainment and proven competence in meeting all the needs of children.

Finally, in thinking of three- and four-year-olds, let us not neglect the needs of five-year-olds. I believe that a full day of formal schooling is too much even for these children. Instead, I would propose a half-day kindergarten program to be followed by a half day in school day care for those who need it. The extra cost could be borne by parents on a sliding-fee basis, with financial assistance available to needy families. Licensed qualified teachers would teach a half day in the morning and certified CDAS would care for the children in the afternoon. A half day of education is plenty for a five-year-old. Again, let me emphasize that the day-care element should be strictly voluntary; no parent who wants his or her child at home after school ends at noon should be denied this. Furthermore, such a program would do well to adopt a whole-child approach, recognizing the child's socio-emotional needs in the course of development, as exemplified by Biber (1984) in her Bank Street model, rather than treating kindergarten like a miniature elementary school with a heavy cognitive-academic orientation. New York University's Institute for Developmental Studies educational enrichment program is another excellent example of a program using a sound whole-child approach.

On a larger scale, many aspects of the funding issue will have to be addressed, such as the tax base and licensing procedures. Federal support might be expected to subsidize costs for economically disadvantaged children. Cost containment would also be enhanced by making use of existing school facilities.

In short, we must ask ourselves—what would we be buying for our children in universal preschool education programs, and at what cost? The family-oriented, multiservice community school could meet the many different needs of preschoolers and their families with a variety of programs from which parents could select to suit their needs and desires. Such services could include comprehensive intervention programs, health and nutrition components, and high-quality, affordable day care, to name only a few possibilities. Our four-year-olds do have a place in school, but it is not at a school desk.

REFERENCES

Abelson, W., Zigler, E., & DeBlasi, C. (1974). Effects of a four-year Follow Through program on economically disadvantaged children. *Journal of Educational Psychology*, *66*(5), 750–771.

Adler, M. (1982). *The Paideia Proposal*. New York: Macmillan.

Ambach, G. (1985, March). *Public school for four year olds; yes or no?* Paper presented at the American Association of School Administrators, New York, NY.

Ames, L. B. (1980, March). Kindergarten—not for four-year-olds! *Instructor*, pp. 32, 37.

Berrueta-Clement, J., Schweinhart, L., Barnett, W., Epstein, A., & Weikart, D. (1984). *Changed lives*. Ypsilanti, MI: High/Scope Press.

Biber, B. (1984). *Early education and psychological development*. New Haven: Yale University Press.

Boyer, E. L. (1983). High school: A report on secondary school in America. New York: Harper & Row.

Bronfenbrenner, U. (1974). Is early intervention effective? In M. Guttentag & E. L. Struening (Eds.), *Handbook of evaluation research* (Vol. 2). Beverly Hills, CA: Sage.

Campbell, D. (In press). Problems in the experimenting society in the interface between evaluation and service providers. In S. L. Kagan, D. R. Powell, B. Weissbourd, and E. Zigler (Eds.), *America's family support programs: Perspectives and prospects*. New Haven: Yale University Press.

Caruso, D., & Detterman, K. (1981). Intelligence research and social policy. *Phi Delta Kappan, 63*, 183–186.

Casto, G., & Mastropieri, M. (1984). *The efficacy of early intervention programs for handicapped children: A meta-analysis*. Logan: Utah State University, Early Intervention Research Institute.

Chorvinsky, M. (1982). *Preprimary enrollment 1980*. Washington, DC: National Center for Education Statistics.

Clarke, A. M. (1984). Early experience and cognitive development. In E. W. Gordon (Ed.), *Review of research in education. Volume II*. Washington, DC: American Educational Research Association.

Clarke, A. M., & Clarke, A. D. B. (Eds.). (1976). Early experience: Myth and evidence. New York: Free Press.

Coleman, J. S., Campbell, E. Q., Hobson, C. J., McPartland, J., Mood, A., Weinfeld, F., & York, R. (1966). *Equality of educational opportunity*. Washington, DC: U.S. Department of Health, Education, and Welfare, U.S. Government Printing Office.

Collins, G. (1984, September 4). Experts debate impact of day care. *The New York Times*, p. B11.

Darlington, R. B., Royce, V. M., Snipper, A. S., Murray, A. W., & Lazar, I. (1980). Preschool programs and later school competence of children from low-income families. *Science, 208*, 202–204.

Deutsch, M., Deutsch, C., Jordon, T., & Grallo, R. (1983). The IDS program: An experiment in early and sustained enrichment. In The Consortium for Longitudinal Studies (Ed.), *As the twig is bent* (pp. 377–411). Hillsdale, NJ: LEA.

Elkind, D. (1981). *The hurried child*. Reading, MA: Addison-Wesley.

Feuerstein, R. A. (1970). A dynamic approach to the causation, prevention and alleviation of retarded performance. In H. C. Haywood (Ed.), *Social cultural aspects of mental retardation*. New York: Appleton-Century-Crofts.

Feuerstein, R., Rand, Y., Hoffman, M. B., & Miller, R. (1980). *Instrumental enrichment: An intervention program for cognitive modifiability*. Baltimore, MD: University Park Press.

Gesell, A. (1928). *Infancy and human growth*. New York: Macmillan.

Gottfried, A., & Gottfried, A. (1984). Home environment and cognitive development in young children of middle-socioeconomic-status families. In A. Gottfried (Ed.), *Home environment and early cognitive development: Longitudinal research* (pp. 57–115). Fullerton, CA: Academic Press.

Hanke, S. H., & Anwyll, J. B. (1980). On the discount rate controversy. *Public Policy, 28*, 171–183.

Haskins, R., & Gallagher, J. (1984, August). *The voices of children project: A report to the Carnegie Foundation*. Chapel Hill: University of North Carolina at Chapel Hill, Bush Institute for Child and Family Policy.

Hechinger, F. (1985, April 23). Schools and the war on poverty. *The New York Times*, p. C10.
Hobbs, N., & Robinson, S. (1982). Adolescent development and public policy. *American Psychologist*, *37*, 212–223.
Hughes, M., Carmichael, H., Pinkerton, G., & Tizard, B. (1979). Recording children's conversations at home and at nursery school: A technique and some methodological considerations. *Journal of Child Psychology and Psychiatry*, *20*, 225–232.
Irvine, D. J., Flint, D. L., Hick, T. L., Horan, M. D., & Kikuk, S. E. (1982). *Evaluation of the New York State experimental preschool program: Final report*. Albany, NY: State Education Department.
Kagan, S. L. (Ed.). (1985). *Four-year-olds—who is responsible?* Unpublished report presented to the Connecticut Board of Education by the Committee on Four-Year-Olds, Their Families, and the Public Schools.
Kennedy, W., Van de Riet, V., & White, J. (1963). Normative sample of intelligence. *Monographs of the Society for Research in Child Development*, *28*(6, Serial No. 90).
Larsen, J. (1985, April). *Family influences on competence in low-risk preschool children*. Paper presented at the biennial meeting of the Society for Research in Child Development, Toronto, Canada.
Lazar, I., & Darlington, R. (1982). Lasting effects of early education: A report from the Consortium for Longitudinal Studies. *Monographs of the Society for Research in Child Development*, *47*(2–3, Serial No. 195).
Lazerson, M. (1970). Social reform and early childhood education: Some historical perspectives. *Urban Education*, *5*, 84–102.
Levine, M., & Levine, A. (1970). *A social history of helping services*. New York: Appleton-Century-Crofts.
Merton, R. (1948). The self-fulfilling prophecy. *Antioch Review*, *8*, 193–210.
Moynihan, D. P. (1984). *On the present discontent*. Paper presented at the convocation for the 140th anniversary of the School of Education, State University of New York, Albany.
National Commission on Excellence in Education. (1983). *A nation at risk* (A Report to the Nation and the Secretary of Education, U.S. Department of Education). Washington, DC: Author.
Pierson, D., Tivnan, D., & Walker, T. (1984). A school-based program from infancy to kindergarten for children and their parents. *Personnel and Guidance Journal*, *4*, 448–455.
Radin, N. (1969). The impact of a kindergarten home counseling program. *Exceptional Children*, *36*, 251–256.
Rosenthal, R., & Jacobson, L. (1968). *Pygmalion in the classroom*. New York: Holt, Rinehart, & Winston.
Royce, J., Darlington, R., & Murray, H. (1983). Pooled analysis: Finding across studies. In The Consortium for Longitudinal Studies (Ed.), *As the twig is bent* (pp. 411–461). Hillsdale, NJ: LEA.

Ruopp, R., Travers, J., Glantz, F., & Coelen, C. (1979). *Children at the center* (Final report of the National Day Care Study, Vol. 1). Cambridge, MA: Abt Books.
School at 4: A model for the nation (1985, February 20). *The New York Times*, p. 22.
Schweinhart, L., & Weikart, D. (Winter, 1985). What do we know so far? A review of the Head Start synthesis project. *High/Scope ReSource: A Magazine for Educators*, 1–17.
Sizer, T. (1984). *Horace's compromise: The dilemma of the American high school*. Boston: Houghton Mifflin.
Slater, B. R. (1971). Perceptual integration. In H. Mitzel (Ed.), *Encyclopedia of educational research* (Vol. 4 1613–1618). New York: Macmillan.
Sparrow, S., Blachman, B., & Chauncey, S. (1983). Diagnostic and prescriptive intervention in primary school education. *American Journal of Orthopsychiatry*, *53*, 721–729.
Swift, J. W. (1964). Effects of early group experience: The nursery school and day nursery. In M. L. Hoffman & L. W. Hoffman (Eds.), *Review of child development research*. (Vol. 1, pp. 249–289). New York: Russell Sage.
Tizard, B. (1974). *Early childhood education: A review and discussion of current research in Britain*. Atlantic Highlands, NJ: Humanities Press.
Tizard, B., Carmichael, H., Hughes, M., & Pinkerton, G. (1980). Four-year-olds talking to mothers and teachers. In L. A. Hersov, M. Berger, & A. R. Nichol (Eds.), *Language and language disorders in childhood* (pp. 49–76). Oxford: Pergamon Press.
Tizard, B., & Hughes, M. (1984). *Young children learning*. Cambridge: Harvard University Press.
Tizard, B., Hughes, M., Carmichael, H., & Pinkerton, G. (1982). Adults' cognitive demands at home and at nursery school. *Journal of Child Psychology and Psychiatry*, *24*, 269–281.
———. (1983). Children's questions and adults' answers. *Journal of Child Psychology and Psychiatry*, *24*, 269–2281.
Tizard, B., Mortimore, J., & Burchell, B. (1981). *Involving parents in nursery and infant schools*. London: Grant McIntyre.
U.S. Bureau of the Census (1984, March). Unpublished data from the current population survey.
Valentine, J., & Stark, E. (1979). The social context of parent involvement in Head Start. In E. Zigler & J. Valentine (Eds.), *Project Head Start: A legacy of the war on poverty* (pp. 291–315). New York: Free Press.
Waksman, M. (1980). Mother as teacher: A home intervention program. *Interchange*, *10*(4), 40–52.
Weikart, D. (1967). *Preschool intervention: Preliminary results of the Perry Preschool Project*. Ann Arbor, MI: Campus Publishers.
Weinberg, R. (1979). Early childhood education and intervention: Establishing an American tradition. *American Psychologist*, *34*, 912–916.
White, K., & Casto, G. (1984). *An integrative review of early intervention*

efficacy studies with at-risk children: Implications for the handicapped. Logan: Utah State University, Early Intervention Research Institute.
Winn, M. (1983). *Children without childhood*. New York: Penguin.
Woodhead, M. (1985). Pre-school education has long-term effects: But can they be generalized? *Oxford Review of Education, 11*(2), 133–155.
Yarrow, L. J. (1964). Separation from parents during early childhood. In M. L. Hoffman & L. W. Hoffman (Eds.), *Review of child development research* (Vol. 1). New York: Russell Sage.
Zigler, E., & Berman, W. (1983). Discerning the future of early childhood intervention. *American Psychologist, 38*(8), 894–906.
Zimiles, H. (1985, April). *The role of research in an era of expanding preschool education*. Revised version of paper presented at the meeting of the American Educational Association, Chicago, IL.

CHAPTER 3

The Case for Public School Sponsorship of Early Childhood Education Revisited

ALBERT SHANKER

Early childhood education has had a long and bumpy history in the United States, much of it spent debating whether it would undermine the "natural" order of mothers' staying at home to care for their young children. The idea that early childhood education is unnatural or un-American has not entirely died, but reality has overtaken ideology. Now that the majority of American mothers of preschool children work outside the home, it has become harder for policymakers to be indifferent to the lack of affordable, quality child care available to families. It is therefore not surprising that early childhood education is making a comeback as a national issue.

Early childhood education is also enjoying a new respectability. The idea that the early childhood years have a profound impact on human development is an ancient one, but modern social science findings have confirmed that young children who are deliberately exposed to stimulating experiences fare better than children who are not. Although many still would prefer that these experiences take place at home under the loving tutelage of a mother, the accumulating research findings about the positive effects of educationally sound preschool programs have dissipated much of the fear of institutional child care. The latest and most dramatic evidence of the benefits of such programs, particularly for disadvantaged youngsters, comes from the Perry

Preschool Project. Not only has this news heartened child advocates, it also has broadened the potential constituency for early childhood education. Usually identified only with the needs of working mothers and the interests of educators, early childhood education now also engages policymakers and citizens concerned about the costs and consequences of the large numbers of disadvantaged children who grow up to become liabilities to themselves and to society.

Early childhood education ought therefore to be a political winner. It bridges the interests of parents from all economic levels, of married and single mothers, of mothers who work and those who need or want to work. It has implications for nonparents and for the elderly who also bear the costs if other people's children grow up to become dependent or deviant adults. It obviously touches education, welfare, health, and other social service professionals. Slowly but steadily, and with a recent push from the National Governors' Association, the political community is indeed rousing itself to the issue of early childhood education. Not since the 1960s has the potential for developing a coherent and caring policy toward preschoolers seemed so bright.

Yet despite the signs of popular and political support for early childhood education, it is not at all clear that a consensus surrounds the issue. What exactly do we mean by early childhood education? The dominant image now comes from the Perry Preschool Project, a high-quality, high-cost educational program for disadvantaged youngsters in a public school setting. But the more usual model of early childhood education is a low-quality, low-cost proprietary program. Similarly, the rhetoric of some policymakers focuses on the custodial needs of working parents, which implies full-day, year-round child-care programs. Yet the rhetoric of others concerns the developmental needs of youngsters, which denotes preschool programs of half a school day or less. Some conceptualize early childhood education as an academic readiness program. Others prefer a whole-child approach that involves attending to the social, emotional, cognitive, and health needs of preschoolers and often includes a parent education component. Differences of opinion (and cost) also exist over whether programs should be compulsory, universally available, or targeted only to the poor and disadvantaged.

Less philosophically complex but even more controversial than questions about the nature and purpose of early childhood education is the issue of sponsorship. Historically, the battles over turf have been between the public schools and community-based organizations, between elementary educators and early childhood educators. The transcendent interest in restoring early childhood education to the national agenda has submerged these differences, but the attacks on public schools heard at the 1986 annual meeting of the National Association for the Education of Young Children suggested that a renewal of old antagonisms is not out of the question.

Some of these differences over early childhood education may not be as intractable as they appear or as they once seemed. Ignoring them, however, or acting as if all early childhood education programs or sponsorship arrangements are equal surely will do nothing to reconcile these differences. Indeed, the failure to revisit these issues may mean that in the name of developing a coherent and caring policy toward young children and promoting equity, policymakers will instead be further institutionalizing our present patchwork of policy and exacerbating inequalities. The challenge we now face is to expand both the quantity and the quality of early childhood education. That means insisting on standards while avoiding standardization. It involves promoting flexibility while ending fragmentation. And it means equalizing the opportunity for disadvantaged youngsters to be integrated into the mainstream of American life without further segregating them in poverty programs.

The Sources of Demand and the Failure of Supply

Recent arguments on behalf of expanding early childhood education are fueled by a number of sources, but chief among them is the influx of mothers of preschool-age children into the labor force. In 1975, 38.8 percent of mothers with children under the age of six were employed. Five years later, the proportion had climbed to 46.8 percent. In the early 1980s, the 50 percent mark was reached, and by 1986 it was 54.4 percent. Almost 60 percent of women with children between the ages of three and five are now in the labor force (U.S. Bureau of Labor Statistics, 1986; Grubb, 1986).

The rise in the proportion of working mothers cannot be explained solely by the increase in single mothers. In fact, whether because of women's liberation or, more demonstrably, the need for a second income, the increase in labor force participation of married mothers of preschoolers has been particularly dramatic. In 1948, the proportion of married mothers who worked outside the home was 13 percent. By 1965, the figure had almost doubled to 23 percent, reaching 37 percent a decade later. In 1986, it was 54 percent, with no sign of abating (U.S. Bureau of Labor Statistics, 1986; Grubb, 1986).

Not surprisingly, the proportion of young children enrolled in child-care programs has also increased. Although it is difficult to sort out participation by type of program, we know that between 1970 and 1983, the enrollment rate of three- and four-year-olds in some kind of program increased from 21 to 38 percent. Seven out of ten children of working mothers are cared for in their own homes or in the homes of others. Two out of five children are minded by relatives. Fifteen percent are in day-care centers, and nearly one out of ten accompanies the mother to work (Hechinger, 1986).

Although what falls under the category of preschool education varies from study to study, it is clear that preschool attendance is highly associated with family income. The preschool enrollment rate for families earning below twenty thousand dollars a year is 46 percent and drops to 29 percent for families with annual incomes below ten thousand dollars. In sharp contrast, the preschool enrollment rate for families earning over twenty thousand dollars annually is 64 percent. Viewed from the perspective of parents' educational attainment, the unequal access to preschool is also apparent. Whereas the enrollment rate for three- and four-year-old children of elementary school dropouts was 23 percent, it was 58 percent for children of college graduates (Hechinger, 1986; Schweinhart & Koshel, 1986).

Not only is the supply of child care inadequate and strongly associated with ability to pay, but the quality of many programs fails to live up to the rhetoric about our devotion to children. Many experts have warned about the detrimental effects of substandard child care. Mere custodial care, even in well-maintained facilities, does not provide a child with the experiences necessary for sound cognitive, social, and emotional development. As suggested by a recent headline, "Fatal Fire Renews Debate on Child-care Standards" (*Education Week*, Dec. 3, 1986), when facilities and staffing quality or ratios do not meet even minimal standards, the problem may go beyond the quality of life to life itself. As late as 1986, child advocates were still pressing not only for the enforcement of the Federal Interagency Day Care Requirements but also for a more adequate set of standards.

The low-quality custodial model of early childhood "education" owes its existence in no small part to the ill-repute with which the very people child care was supposed to help were regarded for much of American history: working mothers. Although women's participation in the labor force has been steadily increasing since the turn of the century, it was not until recently, when the proportion of mothers who worked outside the home approached 50 percent, that this condition was viewed as something other than a symptom of pathology. To be sure, concern for the welfare of poor children of working mothers was certainly evident from the beginning of American history. But compassion could not overcome the prejudices against these children's poverty-stricken families nor the prevailing view that women, no matter how desperate their circumstances, ought not to put paid work over their child-rearing responsibilities. As a result, the few model programs earlier in this century that accounted for both a child's developmental and custodial needs either disappeared or degenerated into solely custodial programs branded by the perceived deficits of working mothers.

While mothers working and therefore institutional child care were viewed as a perversion of a healthy mother-child relationship, the obverse situation also came to be regarded as true. If the mother-child relationship was "abnormal," for reasons either of poverty or of family breakdown, then institutional child care could be an antidote to "bad" mothers; it could even be a means of allowing poor mothers to get out of the house and work. But whether mothers were damned if they worked or damned if they didn't work, the legacy of child-care programs as essentially baby-sitting operations remained the same. Only twice, during the Great Depression and during World War II, was the stigma attached to most working mothers lifted and an effort made, at the federal level, to provide educationally sound care for their children. The effort was feeble indeed. At the end of each crisis, the scales again tilted toward mere custodianship.

The custodial model was next elaborated as part of the War on Poverty during the 1960s. Child care again became a part of federal policy, but as a provision of welfare legislation it was again primarily intended to enable poor mothers to receive training or get work, not to provide for the educational needs of their youngsters. The Federal Interagency Day Care Requirements that regulated the policy did mandate an educational component to the programs, but this was honored more in the breach than in the promise.

Throughout the 1960s, federal spending for children increased significantly. Yet, with the exception of Head Start, federal policy reinforced a by-then unequal system of services in which the poor received low-cost, low-quality custodial day care, the affluent patronized private nursery schools, and those families who fell in neither category were left to fend for themselves. There is no evidence to suggest that this pattern has changed (Grubb, 1986).

Quality Early Childhood Education

In contrast to the traditional custodial model of early childhood programs is the educational or developmental model most commonly associated with good preschools but also characteristic of good day care.[1] Indeed, if the major demographic

1. Although my characterization of the custodial model of early childhood education is clearly pejorative, it should in no way be construed to denigrate either the function of custodianship or day-care programs in a generic sense. Clearly, meeting a child's custodial needs is very important. Equally clearly, many day-care programs offer developmentally sound activities, while many preschools do not. But although the difference between day-care and preschool programs is frequently only nominal, the distinction between the custodial and developmental models is historical and real. By custodial model, then, I mean low-quality programs that are no more and sometimes less than mere baby-sitting operations, indifferent to or ignorant of the unique developmental needs of preschoolers.

influence on the revival of interest in early childhood education has been the increased labor force participation of mothers of young children, then another significant influence has been the steadily accumulating research findings about the benefits of educationally sound preschool programs.

The notion that the preschool years are crucial to a child's emotional and intellectual development is, of course, not novel. Even before the research confirming this perception was available, and as early as the 1920s, some middle-class and affluent families availed their children of the enriching experiences offered by nursery schools. Initially open only part time, nursery schools steadily increased their hours of operation as even their clientele began to work outside the home. Although they became more similar to custodial child-care programs in hours of operation, however, nursery schools' affluent clientele and quality programs meant that they escaped the stigma attached to day care (Grubb, 1986).

Researchers confirmed what nursery school advocates and wise mothers involved in full-time child rearing already knew. Within the last thirty years, the work of educators like Jean Piaget and Benjamin Bloom supported the idea that young children should have available to them a variety of guided stimulating experiences and that such early learning was implicated in children's subsequent development.

Although this line of thinking did not generally produce a reexamination of the traditional custodial model of child care, it did shape Head Start, one of the major programs of the War on Poverty in the 1960s. The inauguration of Head Start with the passage of the Economic Opportunity Act of 1964 marked the beginning of a federal recognition that child-care services for poor children, like those for the more affluent, should have educational content.

Over the past two decades, the primary source of governmental support of early childhood programs has been federal, with Head Start the flagship of this effort. Much research has been devoted to Head Start, and most of it has confirmed the expectations of the program's supporters. Yet despite the largely positive research findings about the effects of Head Start, the political shifts and budgetary vicissitudes afflicting identifiable poverty programs have meant that Head Start now serves a mere 24 percent (and probably less) of the three- and four-year-olds living in poverty (Schweinhart & Koshel, 1986).

The success of Head Start spurred a number of other experiments offering disadvantaged youngsters educationally sound preschool programs. The results thus far have been encouraging, some of them even electrifying. For example, a 1985 study of 175 disadvantaged children conducted by the University of North Carolina concluded that good preschools can raise IQs by as much as 15 points and significantly improve school achievement in later grades. Other studies also confirm that the educational model of preschool programs can help boost children's intellectual and social development (for reviews, see Berrueta-Clement, Schweinhart, Barnett, Epstein, & Weikart, 1986, pp. 30–36; Schweinhart & Koshel, 1986, pp. 6–7).

Many of the preschool programs represented by these studies have had their day in the sun. None, however, has captured as much political attention as the High/Scope Educational Research Foundation's Perry Preschool Program study (Berrueta-Clement et al., 1986). Although a few studies have analyzed the long-term results of early childhood education programs, the Perry Preschool study is the first longitudinal cost-benefit analysis of such a program. It is in no small part due to the stunningly positive outcomes of the Perry Preschool Program that there has been a growing receptivity to expanding early childhood education.

Initiated in 1962, the study examined the long-term effects of participation and nonparticipation in a developmentally based preschool program on 123 disadvantaged black youths who were at risk of school failure. Researchers collected in-depth information about the children starting at age three up to age nineteen. Of prime concern were the children's attitudes and academic and vocational accomplishments.

According to the researchers, preschool attendance altered performance by nearly a factor of two on four major variables at age nineteen. The preschoolers' subsequent rates of employment and participation in college or vocational training were nearly double those of the group without preschool. Moreover, for those who attended preschool, the rate of teenage pregnancy (including live births) and the percentage of years spent in special education classes were about half of what they were for those who did not attend preschool. Preschool attendance was associated with a reduction of twenty percentage points in the detention and arrest rate and nearly that much in the high school drop-out rate. Scores on a test of functional competence were also superior for those who attended preschool (Berrueta-Clement et al., 1986).

Considered in terms of their economic value, these benefits make the preschool program a worthwhile investment for society. Indeed, over the lifetimes of the participants, preschool is estimated to yield economic benefits with a percentage value that is over seven times the cost of one year of the program (Berrueta-Clement et al., 1986).

The key to the extraordinary individual and social benefits of the Perry Preschool Program—in fact, of all the preschool programs that have received similar evaluations—is quality. The Perry program was based on solid principles about the cognitive and social development of young children. Teachers were intensively trained, and child-staff ratios were no more than 6:1. Weekly home visits also were a part of the program. On the one hand, the program was expensive: $4,818 per child a year in 1981 dollars. On the other hand, the lifetime benefit was about $29,000 per participant. Extraordinarily, just the savings realized from the program participants' reduced need for special education placements in school were sufficient to reimburse taxpayers for the cost of running the program for one year.

Still, the short-term costs of the Perry Preschool Program have had an astringent effect on some of the enthusiasm initially expressed about its results. This is not entirely surprising. Americans are becoming habituated to looking to the immediate bottom line and ignoring the future. The question is, in being penny-wise are we becoming pound-foolish? Do we prefer to be niggardly when it comes to expenditures on young children and instead incur the high economic, social, and, potentially, political costs associated with our high rates of school failure and drop-outs, teenage pregnancy, youth unemployment or underemployment, delinquency and criminal behavior, and welfare dependency?

Society's answer thus far is that we do. High-quality preschool programs are not the magic bullets that will wipe out poverty. But the evidence is powerful indeed that they can significantly and even permanently revise the grim life sentence stamped on so many children of poverty.

Contradictions and Inequalities

On the face of it, the two major reasons for the resurgence of interest in early childhood education—the fact that a majority of mothers of young children work and the growing body of research about the short- and long-term benefits of good preschools—should be compatible. After all, parents who have to find child care want the best possible arrangements for their youngsters; serving the interests of children through the availability of quality child care serves the interests of their parents. Surely no one wants public policy to pit the economic needs of young children against their developmental needs.

Unfortunately, although there is no theoretical or moral contradiction between serving the needs of working mothers and those of their young children, practically speaking there is. The legacy of our hostile or ambivalent attitudes toward mothers who work is the persistence of low-quality child-care programs that do not benefit youngsters and can do harm to them: the purely custodial model. Some of these so-called programs are a product of public policy. Many others are private and owe their existence to the failure of public policy to respond to the growing need for quality child care—and to the opportunities for greed and hucksterism this vacuum abets. Whatever their sponsorship, purely custodial early childhood programs do not serve the interests of children.

At the opposite extreme is the legacy of high-quality programs initially associated with nonworking middle-class or affluent mothers and more recently extended to a limited degree to disadvantaged youngsters: the educational model, the only one with demonstrable benefits to children. Some of these high-quality preschool programs are also a product of public policy, Head Start being the major example. Most others are private and owe their existence in part to an implicit public policy that states that the ability to offer one's child quality preschool experiences should be conditioned on one's ability to pay for it.

One result of both the overt and implicit public policies on early childhood education is that the supply of neither public nor private programs of high quality is adequate to the demand. The other, related result is a series of inequalities: access to child-care programs of any sort is related to the ability to pay; access to good programs depends on the size of a family's income; and, within the category of quality programs, there is a dual system, one for the rich, the other for the poor—and catch-as-catch-can for those who fall in neither category. Clearly, too, the wealthier a mother is, the greater her opportunity to avoid the wrenching choice between meeting the need or desire to work outside the home and meeting the needs of her youngsters; both interests can be accommodated.

As a matter of public policy, the contradiction between enabling mothers to work and enabling children to thrive can, of course, be reconciled. It is, after all, a product of history and public policy, and both are shaped by human decisions. Although history cannot be undone, public policies can be. In this sense, recent public initiatives concerning early childhood education are both encouraging and discouraging. The good news is that no policymaker seems to seek the continuation of the legacy of low-quality custodial child-care programs for the poor. The discouraging news is that many of them do not recognize the difference between low-quality and high-quality programs. Indeed, in the name of exemplary programs, some states have enacted and others are in danger of enacting poor programs, in large part because they have failed to recognize and reconcile the different purposes of early childhood programs (Grubb, 1986).

The dilemmas are complex but clear. To meet the custodial needs of mothers who work full time is to enact a program that operates for eight or nine hours a day throughout the working year. Such programs typically do not provide the rich, carefully designed developmental experiences associated with the preschool programs cited by the research and touted by policymakers. On the other hand, the Perry Preschool Program and others demonstrating benefits to children usually operate for only about three hours a day and only during the school year, not the regular year. These brief hours obviously leave the child-care needs of a large chunk of families only partially resolved.

In addition to differences in hours of operation, the custodial and educational models are associated with very different staffing patterns. The custodial model may have high child-adult ratios, whereas the educational model supports no more than ten children for every adult; many quality programs have even fewer children per adult. Custodial programs are also generally indifferent to the qualifications of the staff, whereas educational programs insist on teachers with a solid education in child development principles and practices and even a trained support staff. Clearly, too, custodial programs can be run on the cheap; educational programs cannot.

That there has been a failure to recognize different purposes of early childhood education—indeed, even the differences between good and bad or indifferent programs—is best exemplified by the recent experience in Texas. In 1984, the Texas legislature enacted a preschool program as part of its education reform package. Citing the needs of working mothers and at-risk youngsters and aware of the positive findings from Head Start and the Perry Preschool Program, the legislature provided for half-day programs in which child-adult ratios of 22:1—almost three times the ratio of Head Start programs and almost four times that of the Perry Preschool Program—were permitted. The Texas Department of Education had no staff members who were experts in early childhood education, and it provided little or no guidance to the many districts that were also unfamiliar with such programs. Not surprisingly, although the legislation noted the desirability of employing teachers with credentials in early childhood, this has been ignored because of the shortage of teachers (Grubb, 1986).

There is no question that the provision of early childhood education by the state of Texas is a landmark event. A long-shut door has been opened in Texas, and the move is creditable. Whether any future evaluation will bring the program closer to its aims or lead to its abandonment because it failed to produce "Perry-like" results is an open question. As currently implemented, however, the program, at a half day, falls short of meeting custodial needs and, with its 22:1 child-adult ratio and few qualified teachers available, falls short of meeting children's developmental or educational needs.

Finally, it is important to note that research has validated the lasting benefits of good early childhood education programs primarily for disadvantaged youngsters. This is not to say that more privileged children do not benefit from such programs but, rather, that the research has concentrated on economically disadvantaged youngsters. The available evidence that preschools produce greater positive results for disadvantaged children than for more affluent children does, however, raise tough cost-benefit issues for public policy. On the one hand, it is more equitable to concentrate resources on those who most need and can least afford high-quality preschools. The fact that the benefits to this group (and to society) far outweigh the costs of such programs further underscores the prudence of this course. On the other hand, such a policy typically has meant deliberately segregating disadvantaged children in their own programs, a policy that is hardly consistent with our egalitarian principles and ideals. History also teaches us that public programs that are targeted exclusively to the poor—a narrow and powerless constituency—suffer the most from the vicissitudes of politics and budgets.

Contradictions and conflicts therefore abound in this area. For policymakers to persist in acting as if early childhood education were a unified concept, as if all programs going by that name were equal and equally beneficial for children—and as if stating that a program has a variety of purposes obviates the need for carefully designing the program to meet those goals—is to risk exacerbating and extending the worst features of early childhood programs. The opportunity to meet a growing demand for a service that at its best is manifestly beneficial will have been squandered.

Although some could argue that something poor is better than nothing, there is an alternative to this fatalism. It involves recognizing that there *are* historic contradictions and conflicts permeating the early childhood education issue, but that they are neither inherent nor inevitable. The reason is simple: the historical distinctions between custodial and developmental early childhood programs do not square with children's needs nor do they reflect current reality. Similarly, the legacy of negative attitudes that forced many mothers to compromise the best interests of their children because of their need to work should be, and is being, broken.

As Norton Grubb has eloquently stated:

> Above all, the idea that early childhood programs should be either "developmental" or "custodial" can only limit these programs. The schools, after all, are rich, multi-purpose institutions, with economic, political, moral, and vocational purposes coexisting. Early childhood programs at their best are similarly rich and multi-faceted, providing cognitive, physical, social, and emotional development for children, security and full-time care for working parents, substantial cooperation between parents and caregivers, and parent education for parents seeking different ways of interacting with their children. . . . To search for a single purpose for early childhood programs is to destroy this vision of what early childhood programs could be. (Grubb, 1986, p. 17)

Although this vision has been made manifest in a number of programs in local school districts, most of the initiatives in the states since 1979 have perpetuated the historic distinctions between the custodial and developmental models or have created new hybrids that fulfill neither purpose well (Grubb, 1986). Nonetheless, the recent report devoted to the early childhood education issue by the National Governors' Association (NGA) is cause for optimism. Some of the right questions are now being asked: "In developing early childhood programs, one of the first issues to be raised is the purpose of such programs. Will state-sponsored programs be aimed at children whose families fall within a particular income range? Will the programs include only educational or developmental components, or will they include a daycare component as well?" (National Governors' Association, 1986, p. 105).

The NGA Task Force on Readiness does not offer answers to these questions. Instead, it urges each state to study its existing early childhood programs and demographic factors to determine which programs should be given the highest priority. Given the diversity of the states, this reticence concerning answers is understandable, but, it also means a missed opportunity to publicize and reform the pattern of confusion and fragmentation now afflicting early childhood education. Moreover, although states do indeed face tough decisions about where to put their resources for maximum benefits, the danger continues to exist that they will fail to consider the choice of *not* choosing a single purpose for early childhood programs.

Put another way, we should not again miss the opportunity to meet both the custodial and developmental needs of preschoolers, to combine or coordinate day care and preschool education and make them universally available to all children. The American Federation of Teachers (AFT) has sounded that call before, in the 1970s. There is nothing that has transpired to suggest that it was mistaken. Quite the contrary: the demand, the desperation, for child care has increased; the incidences of children harmed by substandard programs have increased; the body of evidence about the benefits of quality preschools has increased; and the inequality of access to early childhood education has increased. Now, as then, the arguments on behalf of making public education the prime sponsor—although not necessarily the only site—for multipurpose early childhood education programs are the most compelling.

Public School Sponsorship of Early Childhood Education

The first advantage of this proposal is that the public education system already has in place organizations experienced in administering large and complex programs. Many state and local education agencies have child development experts on staff. Those that do not would have to hire such people to ensure that programs are age- and need-appropriate or utilize the expertise of such staff in other agencies through interagency agreements. The experience of states such as California and Connecticut suggests that education departments that use an advisory group composed of educators, child development experts, representatives from welfare departments, and other groups whose activities touch the lives of young children are particularly successful at mounting appropriate and flexible programs.

Under the sponsorship of public education and with the formal cooperation of other relevant agencies and groups, order can be brought out of the chaos and fragmentation now characterizing early childhood policies, and the divorce between day-care programs and developmental programs can be reconciled. For example, a public school can run both a preschool program, with its approximately three hours of a deliberately developmental "curriculum," and a quality day-care program whose hours account for the remainder of the working day. Parents would be free to choose whether their child attended only the preschool portion or remained throughout the working day. In some localities, this would involve a new willingness to be flexible about the hours during which school buildings are open. Although costs might increase, new efficiencies and a more rational use of school facilities would be realized.

The school system also can work with other agencies to ensure that plans for preschools are coordinated with existing or anticipated day-care programs. The point is that public school sponsorship of early childhood education does not require uniformity or rigidity. School districts would be free to expand and vary their services to meet local needs or fund other agencies or even non-profit organizations that were providing high-quality services. There is also no reason why, at the state or local level, the decision could not be made to provide incentives for home care or extended maternity leaves. The goal is quality, flexibility, and coordination.

A second advantage of this proposal is that public schools are universally available. They exist in urban, suburban, small-town, and rural areas. This means that early childhood education could be universally available, although it should not be compulsory. Ideally, of course, programs would be free of cost to all who desired to attend. Short of this ideal, it may be necessary to design a plan that is based on the ability to pay. Such a plan must enable poor children to attend free, permit the majority of families to take advantage of early childhood education services without unnecessary hardship, and be sensitive to the need for confidentiality in order to avoid stigmatizing anyone. Since a number of school districts currently charge some sliding-scale fees for child-care services, thoughtful models already exist.

Third, the public education system is best equipped to offer or coordinate the variety of services, such as health and nutrition, that support a child's development. The safety and health record of public schools is also superlative, especially in light of the millions of children they serve every day. Moreover, public schools are more ready (and willing) than other providers to respond to the special needs of handicapped and non-English-speaking children, both in the mainstream and through special services.

The public education system is also in a better position to address the problems of staffing that have characterized many programs and undercut confidence in early childhood education. For one, the licensing or credential-checking systems in place in state and local departments of education could help ensure that quality standards for early childhood education staff are both promulgated and monitored. Of course, the existence of such a machinery for enforcing standards does not necessarily mean that it will be used to that end, as the practice of "emergency" certification illustrates. But its mere existence and its public nature—that is, its ability to be called to account—offer more leverage for enforcing quality than currently exists for alternative providers. Similarly, although public education is hardly saintly in adhering to agreements about appropriate child-adult ratios, its performance is better than most child-care operations and, again, has the capacity to be rigorously monitored and called to account. And no other existing arrangement can surpass the public schools' ability to deliver in-service training, which could keep the staff abreast of current child development theory and practices.

There are those who will argue that it is tantamount to madness to call for public school sponsorship of early childhood education during a time of intense criticism of public education. The education reform movement of the 1980s has produced a stack of reports documenting the shortcomings of the public schools. My own voice as president of the AFT has been loud and clear about the necessity of fundamental reform. But, as in the past, the response to the criticisms of the last few years, although not always adequate or thoughtful, illustrates that public education is a strikingly accountable institution. We do not hear much about what goes on in other institutions of government. We know even less about the private and other organizations sponsoring early childhood education that are subject only to loose controls or no democratic controls at all. Yet we always know the condition of public education, and we have an array of democratic policy mechanisms to improve its condition.

Still, the fears about the structural and educational rigidities that would beset early childhood programs under public school sponsorship are worth exhuming. According to the charges leveled during the 1970s, particularly around the time the federally proposed Child and Family Services Act of 1975 was being considered, public schools were bureaucratic, authoritarian institutions that revolved more around the interests of educators than the needs of children and their parents. Elementary education, critics contended, was narrowly conceived in terms of basic cognitive skills imparted through fixed lessons by teachers who essentially lectured to orderly rows and columns of too numerous children in self-contained classrooms. The schedule and time clock ruled expectations about the progress of children, as well as the day. Children who did not keep pace uniformly, usually according to the criteria of standardized tests, were labeled failures. The ideals of individualized instruction were espoused, but the legacy of the factory model of schooling prevailed.

Of course, this stereotypical image of the public schools ignored some important realities. For one, only the worst schools fit the stereotype. Second, many public schools were already running exemplary preschool programs, none of which was "contaminated" by the rigidities of the upper elementary grades. And third, there were many factorylike preschool programs outside the public schools and others of such poor quality that introducing some of the worst features ascribed to the public schools would have represented an improvement. More than a decade later and with many more successful experiences with public schools sponsoring preschools, those realities are still with us.

Yet some of the groups that raised these criticisms about the rigidities of the public schools had a point. If the factory model of schooling is not pervasive, it nonetheless represents the dominant organizing principle of public education. It should under no circumstances be extended downward to the preschool level, and it should by all means be repudiated in the entire system. Given the recent report and efforts of the Carnegie Task Force on the Teaching Profession (1986) and considering the new tenor of the second stage of education reform in the 1980s, there is reason to believe that the structural and educational rigidities of the public school system will be addressed. Indeed, new models of school organization and learning are already being tried, and some of them owe much to the lessons learned from the flexible, developmental, child-centered approach that the best of the early childhood education community pioneered.

The renewed interest in early childhood education brings us another chance to reconcile the conflicts over early childhood. Our failure to do so will not stop mothers from working and needing quality child care. It will not materially harm the parties to the conflict. It will, however, hurt young children and perpetuate the problems of meeting their economic, developmental, and custodial needs. There is no reason for the lack of coordination between day care and preschool education, save a set of policies that have irrationally fragmented the planning and administration of such programs and maintained the historic and unequally applied distinctions between a child's custodial and educational needs. There is every reason to expect more incidences of fatality, abuse, and just plain neglect if we continue to be indifferent to standards and implicitly delegate our responsibility for the welfare of the nation's children to organizations concerned only for their own welfare.

It is possible to have standards without standardization and flexibility without fragmentation in early childhood education policy. The solution lies in making a variety of quality early childhood education programs universally available to all parents who want these services. A large part of the means to that end involves the early childhood education community recognizing that the public education system is the best prime sponsor. Another part involves the continuing willingness of the public school system to recognize child development–based approaches to learning and to make the structural and educational changes indicated by the best of these approaches. By drawing on their strengths rather than hurling charges about their weaknesses, child advocates might this time actually cooperate on behalf of effective, caring policies toward children.

REFERENCES

Berrueta-Clement, J. R., Schweinhart, L. J., Barnett, W. S., Epstein, A. S., and Weikart, D. P. (1986). Changed lives: The effects of the Perry Preschool Program on youths through age 19. In F. M. Hechinger (Ed.). *A better start: New choices for early learning* (pp. 11–40). New York: Walker.

Carnegie Task Force on the Teaching Profession. (1986). *Teachers for the 21st century* (A Report of the Carnegie Forum on Education and the Economy). New York: Carnegie Corporation of New York.

Grubb, W. N. (1986, August). *Young children face the states: Issues and options for early childhood programs*. Draft paper for Rutgers University, The Center for Policy Research in Education.

Hechinger, F. M. (Ed.). (1986). *A better start: New choices for early learning*. New York: Walker.

National Governors' Association. (1986). *Time for results: The governors' 1991 report on education*. Washington, DC: Author.

Schweinhart, L. J., & Koshel, J. J. (1986). *Policy options for preschool programs*. Ypsilanti, MI: High/Scope Early Childhood Policy Papers No. 5.

U.S. Bureau of Labor Statistics. (1986, August 20). *Half of mothers of children under three now in labor force*. Washington, DC: U.S. Department of Labor 86–345.

U.S. Department of Labor. *Labor force statistics derived from the current population survey: A databook* (Vol. 1, Table C-11). Washington, DC: U.S. Government Printing Office.

CHAPTER 4

From National Debate to National Responsibility

BERTHA D. CAMPBELL

Interest in early schooling comes from our professed commitment to the well-being of young children. Unfortunately, many of the programs springing up are either overly structured or purely custodial. They may serve family needs, but they fail to provide the kinds of rich, exploratory, developmental experiences with people, materials, and ideas so necessary for children's development into competent adulthood. In overly structured programs, there is a failure to recognize the difference between schooling and education. In custodial programs, there is a failure to recognize that children are learning all the time through observing, through experiencing, through feeling. The term *schooling* brings to mind formal, prescribed programs that limit children's exploration, creativity, and original thinking. It also forms a cleavage between public school and other programs, and carries the implication that all public school programs are formal.

The national debate on early schooling reflects a variety of biases. Public school people see the programs as a way of using unoccupied space; unions see them as a way of giving unemployed teachers a job; Head Start and private programs see them as a threat to their existence; and economy-minded citizens and politicians see them as bearing big dollar signs and taking money from other programs.

Whatever professionals or the public may think about early

schooling, the simple fact is that over 60 percent of all four-year-olds nationwide are already in programs. The percentage is probably much higher in heavily populated and industrial regions. According to the 1980 census data, attendance in preschool programs tripled between 1970 and 1980 and the numbers are rising daily (Bureau of Census, 1984).

Reasons for these increases are varied and complex. For the most part they reflect demographic and social trends. The increased numbers of single parents and families in which both parents work *must* have care for their children outside the home. Another strong influence is the increase in the number of middle- and upper-middle-class parents who *want* their children in programs to provide an early push into the academic world. With this growing intense interest in early schooling, the question then becomes not so much "should there be programs available for young children?" but rather "what kinds shall they be?"

Headlines in newspapers, magazine articles, and book jackets add fuel to the fire with such statements as "Early Schooling Is the Rage," "Preschool Education Linked to Later Difficulties," "Better Late than Early," "Getting Off to a Quick Start," and *The Hurried Child.* The debate is faintly reminiscent of the blind man and the elephant fable. Each of the statements has a semblance of truth, but each may be false when taken out of context. When the dust has settled, the arguments are seen to center on three main issues: (1) who shall be served? (2) under whose aegis? and (3) what kind of program shall be provided?

This chapter describes New York State's experience with its Experimental Prekindergarten Program and examines the three issues in the light of that experience.

The New York State Experimental Prekindergarten Program

The New York State Experimental Prekindergarten Program is in the twenty-second year of what was to have been a five-year program. In 1965 the legislature voted $5 million to initiate a program for three- and four-year-olds from low socioeconomic areas. The popularity of the program resulted in annual extensions. In the 1986–87 school year a $22 million appropriation provided services to 10,500 children in eighty-two school districts. A $27 million appropriation has been approved for the 1987–88 school year.

From its inception, the prekindergarten program was intended to examine two questions: the feasibility of publicly administered programs for three- and four-year-olds, and the relative impact of a comprehensive developmental prekindergarten on the early elementary grades.

The New York State Education Department designated its Bureau of Child Development and Parent Education as program managers. Established in 1927, the bureau, as its name implies, has a history of commitment to programs that exemplify two cardinal points: all learning has its roots in sound social and emotional development with the intellect an integral part of the whole child, and the involvement of parents is an essential factor in the education of children.

Competitive grants are awarded annually to school districts that can demonstrate need (based on numbers of unserved low-income families), meet certain guidelines, and provide their local share in cash, not in kind. The local share for the first five years was 10 percent of the budget. Originally the intent was to increase the share annually until it matched the state aid formula, but action by parents and local school districts has maintained the local share at 11 percent. Schools that are in compliance with the guidelines continue to be funded. The program is still in existence because staff and parents have fought for its survival.

All programs administered by public schools, of course, must meet requirements established by law and the commissioner's regulations regarding health, safety, classroom size, and staff qualifications. The prekindergarten guidelines, however, established additional conditions.

Each classroom is staffed with two adults, a teacher and an assistant, with ancillary services provided by an assigned staff. Specialists are urged to work with teachers rather than directly with children, thus helping teachers to improve their skills and deepen their insights. Specialists who must work directly with children are encouraged to do so in the classroom with the teacher present in order to provide continuity in the child's school day.

Group size is limited to fifteen children, although it may be increased to seventeen with written approval of a bureau consultant. Final class size is set after the group is established and the teacher knows the children well enough to determine how it will function. Program quality is the overriding consideration.

Each school district's proposal must include a cost-effective budget and a narrative that describes four components and three implementation strategies in detail.

The components include:

1. Comprehensive health services covering physical, mental, dental, and nutritional health; provision of examinations, immunizations, and preventive education; and plans for treatment through referrals to proper agencies. (Public schools in New York State were not permitted to pay for treatment when the program started.)
2. Comprehensive social services aimed at helping families become independent in meeting their own needs by providing linkages with public, private, and voluntary social and health service agencies.
3. Involvement of parents in the education of their children through employment in the program, home visits by staff, parent visits to school, parent meetings that focus on child-rearing practices and parenting skills, and participation in decision making.
4. A developmentally oriented program for children that shows evidence of planning for age-appropriate activities based on children's interests and that builds on each child's strengths rather than focusing on deficits.

The implementation strategies include:

1. A staff development program to ensure orientation and commitment to the program mandates.
2. A follow-through program that provides for all components to be continued through at least the third grade.
3. A program evaluation that is not limited to test scores, but rather demonstrates that parents, staff, administrators, the community, and perhaps the children themselves are involved

in the cyclical process of planning, implementation, assessment, refinement, and revised planning.

A bureau consultant is assigned to each program, which provides continuity and results in the program staff looking upon the consultant as a member of the team, not as a monitor checking on compliance. Although the guidelines provide the framework for a good program, it is recognized that they do not ensure excellence, nor would monitoring ensure compliance. In the last analysis, any program will be only as good as the parents and the community want it to be. Depending on monitoring for compliance tends to encourage the program staff to put on a show when the monitor is visiting rather than maintaining consistently high standards.

In 1975 the New York State Legislature requested a longitudinal evaluation of the prekindergarten program. The subsequent five-year evaluation design was two-pronged: (1) five standardized measures were administered, the results of which were given in a final evaluation report (Irvine, Flint, Hick, Horan & Kukuk, 1982); and (2) an in-depth study was conducted, which was reported in *The School Lives of Seven Children* (Carini, 1982). Corroborations were provided by the findings of Lazar's Consortium (Lazar & Darlington, 1982) and the High/Scope Research Foundation (Berrueta-Clement, Schweinhart, Barnett, Epstein, & Weikart, 1984).

The in-depth study was intended to demonstrate that narrative/descriptive data are as valid as statistically oriented data and that it is possible to conduct an evaluation that continues as a process when evaluation funds are no longer available. Using the child study approach, researchers discovered a fringe benefit: the most effective staff development program that far exceeded expectations and strengthened the overall program. The process has continued in some form in many of the schools.

Teachers in the in-depth study were asked to select one child who interested them and gather extensive data in order to describe the child to the fullest (but not to explain, change, or psychologize about the child). When teachers protested they had fifteen children, it was pointed out to them that they would be in good company—Jean Piaget had maintained that to know one child well was to know all children better. The process led researchers to describe the craft of teaching as observation, nonjudgmental recording, and personalized planning for children based on data collected. Through this process, teachers began to see themselves as responsible for their own professional growth and to use one another as a support system. When they observed and saw holes in their own data, they became keener observers, and their observations led to their planning enriched activities, which, in turn, resulted in even richer observations. This cyclical process resulted in program planning focused on the child rather than content. (Others also made observations in order to confirm the validity and reliability of the teachers' data.)

As an experimental program, the prekindergarten was not intended to serve all eligible children, but the program's popularity created a demand for enrollment by both eligible and ineligible families. Through the socioeconomic mix provided for in the guidelines, it was hoped that homogeneous grouping would be avoided, but the increasing numbers of eligible families led many programs to limit enrollment to eligible children.

As the program continued, it became, in essence, a service rather than an experiment. Questions arose about the fairness of funding a limited number of school districts out of general tax monies. This led to proposed legislation for universal programs for all four-year-olds.

During the last five years he served as commissioner, Gordon Ambach and the Regents proposed universal programs for all four-year-olds whose parents wished them to attend publicly funded programs. Proposed legislation outlined voluntary half-day programs for all children one year prior to kindergarten entry, with reimbursement set according to the state aid formula, double-weighted for children from poor families. Special legislation was also proposed for handicapped children. It was specified that districts seeking reimbursement would have to meet the guidelines established for the Experimental Prekindergarten Program. Concern for working parents led to the inclusion of a provision for extended day-care services, costs of which would be borne by Head Start or Title XX, in the case of eligible families, or by parental fees. An additional proposal made the same reimbursement available to community-based programs that could meet the guidelines.

The National Debate

We turn now to discussion of the three issues in the national debate—who shall be served? under whose aegis? what kind of program shall be provided?—as they are illuminated by New York's two decades of experience with the prekindergarten program.

Who Shall Be Served?

The first question addresses the issue of enrollment: shall a program be open to all children or limited to those with special needs, such as those who are handicapped, live in poverty, or come from non-English speaking families? Arguments against universal opportunity include the high costs of serving all children and the fact that data on which to base any decision are limited to children from economically disadvantaged groups.

Costs of universal education for all four-year-olds would be very high, since good programs for young children are expensive. Per capita costs in New York State actually ranged from $1,500 to $4,000 with local monies supporting any difference between state funding and actual costs. But America does not lack money to initiate programs; it simply values other priorities more. If a country that professes to value children as its most important resource can find monies for star wars, military aid to overthrow governments, and extremely expensive election campaigns, it can provide funding to assure good beginnings for all its children. If the president can argue that military preparedness will provide jobs and improve the economy, it can be argued, too, that provision of programs for younger children will provide jobs and improve the economy, and at the same time will improve the quality of life. Perhaps we should heed the old Chinese proverb: how you live is more important than if you live.

Cost-effectiveness is a consideration if services are to be provided for all four-year-olds. One would hope that all public programs would spend money judiciously, but cost-effectiveness, in this context, is more than a matter of using monies wisely to administer a program. When spending money on young children, we are sowing the seeds for competent adulthood. (Information documenting long-term cost-effectiveness can be found in Weber, Foster, & Weikart, 1978.)

Equity is also an important issue. If one examines census data regarding the incomes of families whose children were enrolled in early childhood programs in 1980, one sees that almost 70 percent of the four-year-olds came from families with gross incomes above $25,000; only a little over 30 percent came from families with incomes below $15,000 (Bureau of Census, 1984). In other words, children from wealthier families were more than twice as likely to attend a program than those from poorer families. Aside from the impact this unequal access has on the social fabric, failure to provide universal opportunity for all four-year-olds leaves public funders vulnerable to class action suits by the excluded families. Such action, in fact, has already been threatened by some parents in New York.

The argument mentioned earlier regarding research data bears examination. The appropriateness of programs for four-year-olds is supported by a substantial body of research demonstrating they work. The fact that most research has been limited to economically disadvantaged families does not necessarily mean that other children cannot profit from attendance. Middle-class parents, in fact, have enrolled their children in private and cooperative nursery schools since the mid-1940s to provide them with opportunities for enrichment and socialization. Heterogeneous grouping would enhance learning for all children involved.

The argument that we need more research and empirical data before launching universal, publicly funded programs for four-year-olds is questionable. As Betty Caldwell (1983) pointed out, when she was president of the National Association for the Education of Young Children, this same apprehension existed when the decision of whether Head Start should be a massive service or a limited research program had to be made. The framers of the Head Start guidelines were concerned that the knowledge, experience, and resources to undertake a massive program were unavailable. Nevertheless, there are many highly qualified professionals who understand the importance of a good beginning for young children and know how to plan programs to provide it.

(We do need, however, to prepare more teachers with a developmental point of view who focus on something other than "classroom management.")

Another factor that affects plans for universal preschool programs is that of competition among service providers. The first mention of the proposed universal program in New York created a statewide stir, as private schools and day-care and Head Start programs joined forces to urge the legislature to vote against it.

There is an unfortunate perception that Head Start and day-care programs are locally controlled and belong to the people, whereas schools are bureaucratic organizations that pay only lip service to parental involvement. This perception is understandable. Many of the families enrolled in Head Start have had a history of negative relationships with the public schools. They are often intimidated by school personnel and do not feel comfortable entering the school environment to volunteer or question school practices. Such feelings may intensify as they contrast a well-equipped prekindergarten, housed in a permanent school building and staffed by well-paid teachers, with Head Start and day-care programs struggling with inadequate budgets, housed in makeshift facilities, and staffed by people with low salaries and poor benefits. Since children spend many years in public schools, ways must be found to help parents and their children gain a more positive image of school if they are to be successful there.

Another enrollment factor surfaced in the prekindergarten program. Since Head Start has a poverty index for eligibility, the program tended to enroll only families ineligible for Head Start. This tacit agreement not to compete for families resulted in the enrollment of the poorest families in Head Start, thus creating a "status" poor group in some prekindergarten programs. Some parents, either because they needed full day care or because they wanted their children to have more extensive experiences, elected to send their children to two half-day programs, the prekindergarten program and Head Start or day care. The prekindergarten staff discouraged this practice on the grounds that the children would have to relate to two sets of adults and classmates. In many communities day-care directors responded by refusing to enroll children on a half-day basis. This created problems for parents which the proposed legislation has tried to address. The intent is to provide continuity in environments and relationships for the children and options for parents. Some parents, of course, will always prefer to send children to community or private programs rather than to the public school for a variety of reasons: convenience of location, quality of programs, or a desire to keep siblings together.

Programs can be mutually beneficial, however. Head Start can help public schools become less bureaucratic and more parent oriented, and schools can help Head Start achieve some of the goals they are working toward. In some communities, staffs from Head Start, day-care and prekindergarten programs join to share experiences through joint staff development, often exchanging ideas, materials, and sometimes even children themselves. In several school districts, one director carries responsibility for both the Head Start and the prekindergarten programs.

Some school districts in New York State are already offering districtwide four-year-old prekindergartens. One Long Island community, Freeport, reports that they serve approximately 80 percent of all four-year-olds with others attending Head Start or day-care or private programs. The community makes an active effort to locate hard-to-reach families, especially those who are non-English-speaking. Publicity through the public school has resulted in greater awareness of the many services available in Freeport. Far from competing with each other, all the programs are reporting longer waiting lists, and some of the private ones have indicated they are serving more three-year-olds. Families benefit when they can choose the program best suited to their special needs.

An argument heard frequently is that poor children need enrichment through preschool programs but that middle-class children don't. This claim may have been true at one time, but modern family trends have brought many changes. Decreasing family size means less opportunity for socialization among siblings; high mobility of families robs children of continuity of experiences with friends, relatives, and neighbors; increasingly unsafe neighborhoods keep children from seeking friends around the block. In addition, busy parents have less time to enrich their children's lives with trips to the zoo, the fire station, or the grocery store; or walks to pick flowers or feed ducks. Even eating together, an activity called "the last tribal meeting place," can become an infrequent event.

Finally, universal opportunity to attend publicly funded programs does *not* imply compulsory attendance; it simply means that all parents have an option of which they may take advantage. No early childhood program should be mandatory. That would suggest that all children could learn more from attending a program than from being at home with a parent who wants to be with them. That, of course, is far from the truth.

Under Whose Aegis?

Whether programs for four-year-olds should be administered by public schools or community-based organizations is an emotional question. Proponents of the public school argue that it is the logical place to provide continuity of surroundings, staff, relationships with friends, and learning experiences in children's lives. Because some schools have space available, many of them have started their own programs or rent space to private nursery schools or day-care programs as their student populations decrease. Schools have at hand experienced administrators and such ancillary services as nurses, psychologists, and guidance and social service personnel, as well as bilingual, music, art, and physical education specialists. Services like these can enrich a good program. In addition, many administrative costs—housing, transportation, lunch and breakfast programs, telephones, duplicating facilities and other office services—can be absorbed by school budgets to the advantage of the program.

The arguments against programs in public schools center around questions of "formal schooling" and the high costs of professional salaries. Professionally trained staff members command higher wages than those who are not credentialed. But this is a two-edged argument: programs for young children warrant a staff with the best knowledge about child growth and development. If we indeed value our children, staff salaries are not the place to cut costs. Regardless of the question of salaries, no early childhood program should be without a highly competent staff.

The argument that public schools have performed so poorly with elementary-age children that they should not be permitted to administer programs for four-year-olds has not proved true in the New York State experience. Many teachers welcomed and quickly adopted the child study approach, which focuses on the child rather than the curriculum's content.

It should also be pointed out that differences always lie within groups, not between them. There are excellent and terrible public schools, and Head Start and day-care programs. No one group has a monopoly on excellence or disasters. One can always find teachers in any setting pushing meaningless academic skills in an ineffective way because they do not know how children learn or because they fail to put into practice what they do know as a result of administrative and parental pressures.

The case for the public school, then, is a strong one. Schools belong to the public. Parents and citizens who become actively involved in examining the philosophy of the school rather than the curriculum can ensure quality programs for four-year-olds, and the ripple effects can change the elementary years. The important thing is that parents and professionals find ways to develop cooperative rather than adversarial relationships.

If public schools are to provide programs for four-year-olds, however, they must assume responsibility for serving all the family's needs. There must be provision for extended full-day services before and after school and during vacations, providing continuity for children whose parents work. Schools have space that is idle for too many hours each day. Since they belong to the public, these spaces should be made available for public use without the payment of rent.

In New York State legislation has been passed to enhance the use of schools for extended child-care purposes. Small competitive grants from the State Department of Social Services provide start-up costs for child-care programs when school is not in session, with priority given to programs housed in public schools. Difficulties can arise, however, when different state agencies carry responsibility for education and child care. In New York State a joint committee representing Education, Social Services, and the Governor's Council on Children and Families worked together to avoid duplication of efforts and overlapping of services.

Problems were encountered related to payment for child-care

services. By statute, public school services must be free to all families. This was resolved through a legal opinion from the Office of Council stating that parents could pay fees to public schools for child care if the program was not "educational," education, for this purpose, being interpreted as "what goes on during the school day." There are many ways to work out problems with local school boards without violating school laws. Sometimes parents form corporations to collect fees; others donate gifts to the school. The important thing is that families should have options for part- or full-day programs with extended days available for working parents.

Finally, the point should be made that the administering agency is not as important as the quality of the program. Mayor Ed Koch in New York City and Governor Mario Cuomo have both recognized the need for coordinating public schools, Head Start, and day-care programs. The State Education Department has proposed legislation to enhance coordination, which it is hoped will minimize the differences among programs and focus on the well-being of children. Ways must be found to fund a variety of programs that work, giving parents choices that are cost neutral so that they can select programs according to personal preference and need rather than what they cost.

What Kind of Programs Shall Be Provided?

Good programs for young children do not confuse education with formal schooling or intellectual development with academic achievement. They are not concerned with raising the IQ or preparing the child for kindergarten. No stage of development is viewed as a preparation for the next stage. Good programs recognize that all learning is based on healthy socioemotional development. A child feeling secure and confident about himself and others provides the soundest basis for all future learning.

Program quality starts with a competent staff. New York State regulations require that classrooms be staffed by certified teachers. But certification documents only that the candidate has been exposed to required coursework. It has little to do with qualifications to teach. As in all professions, it provides no guarantees of excellence or even competence. Some people are qualified, but not certified; others are certified, but not qualified. Children, and often their parents, may not know who is certified, but they always know who is qualified.

Not all staff members of any one program must be professionally trained, but they must all be competent. Many adults relate to children on an intuitive basis. They instinctively know what to do, but they may not know why they are doing it. The competent professional knows the "what" and the "why." There must be a sufficient number of competent professionals to provide leadership for those who work with children by instinct.

Teachers of young children should have had experience with young children. They must have an understanding of human growth and development. They must comprehend their role as motivators. They must know how to set the stage for learning and then allow children to discover things for themselves. They must be cognizant that they teach more by the kinds of people they are than by all the formal teaching they do. They must understand that the greatest thing they teach is enthusiasm for learning. This precludes the use of prescribed programs with dull, meaningless workbooks and ditto sheets. The learner must become invested in his/her learning. It is useless to teach a child to read if he or she learns to hate reading in the process. Above all, they must know that learning can't be turned off and on like hot and cold running water; that learning is continuous, uneven, and highly personalized.

Competent staff, then, will have the knowledge, background, and experience to provide the ingredients of a successful program. They will know how to prepare environments that are conducive to learning, that will attract and delight children and lead them to discovery. Centers of interests will be planned with definite goals in mind, but children will be permitted to create their own structure for learning.

Professionals will know how to include parents in every aspect of the program, helping them build confidence in their competence as parents while raising questions that will lead them to examine their own practices with their children. They will recognize parents as the most important adults in children's lives.

Professionals will know how to enlist the support of administrators through classroom visits, public meetings, and informal discussion groups.

Professionals will understand that evaluation does not consist merely of pre/post-tests; it is a process by which growth is enhanced, not a product. Children will be assessed through observational records, teachers' notes and jottings, and reviews of the children's work, whether it be block building, creative arts, or the exploration of scientific concepts. Programs will be assessed through interviews with all persons involved including the children themselves—the source of some of the best data.

Professionals will be sensitive to children's need for continuity and stability. Uri Bronfenbrenner (1985) documents the lack of continuity and stability in many children's lives: in the home, because of divorce, separation, and frequent changes among adults who care for them; in the community, because of high family mobility and depersonalized services in large supermarkets, overspecialized clinics, and service agencies with high turnover in personnel; and in the schools, where one child may see as many as eight to ten adults in any one day. Young children need the consistency of relating to the same small number of adults and children in order to develop deep, lasting relationships so necessary for feelings of confidence.

Professionals will know how to schedule the school day, with different pacing for full- and half-day programs and provision of vigorous, active periods interspersed with quiet, relaxing ones. There will be opportunities for children to listen to stories, to participate in music and movement, and to explore materials like water, sand, and paint. And there will be time for children to reflect and ponder, and internalize what they have learned.

Some Final Considerations

The New York experience demonstrates that when programs employ quality staff, those people mobilize the community around the program to ensure its excellence. Children begin to see parents and staff as a team working in their interests. Parents and teachers come to know one another as people, not simply as professional and parent. Above all, parents feel valued and respected, and teachers recognize that parents know their own children better than anyone else ever will. Professionals must continue to learn how to put their theoretical knowledge together with the specialized knowledge of the parent in order to provide the best possible programs for the child.

Consistent quality among large numbers of programs, however, is not easily achieved. Large-scale programs run the danger of overstandardization, overspecialization, and overgeneralization, all of which can be exacerbated by bureaucratic regulations.

At a presentation to the American Education Association in Chicago, Herbert Zimiles (1985) spoke of the important questions that nursery school teachers used to raise. They focused on children's development and their evolving experiences with materials and with adults and peers. They were not concerned with standardized measures or memorized facts. Dr. Zimiles's words should be heeded since the old questions are still the most valid ones: What does it mean for a young child to live part of the day in an environment that is not his home? What are the strains and stresses associated with it? How disruptive is it of his total growth and development? And, most important, how can the programs we plan take these important issues into account?

Melvin Tumin pointed out at a conference sponsored by the New York State Education Department (1968), "The creation of capacity is continuous. It is without end. It is diverse. It is variable from child to child and within any child variable from time to time and from topic to topic. . . . It is the sense of success and a feeling of one's capacity to become capable that is indispensable to the achievement of that capacity." He stated that it is the responsibility of adults to make it possible for that capacity to be created pleasurably at all times. We must care equally for all children and be "prepared with our diversity to meet their diversity." That same creation of capacity applies to parents, if at a slower, less spontaneous rate.

History buffs will observe that the ferment about early schooling resembles that about kindergarten not too long ago, before it was accepted into the educational family. The same arguments prevailed. Resolution of the issues will require thoughtful study of children, recognizing that though they may be more alike than different, each is unique. Programs must be planned to fit their needs; children should not be expected to fit into the program.

We all want children to be smart and good and competent; the disagreements lie in how they become that way. On one hand are the behaviorists who believe that you can get a person to do anything if the reward is right; on the other are the naturalists who believe we should just leave children alone. In between these two extremes are the maturationists, the developmentalists, the cognitionists, the cognitive developmentalists, the social theorists—to mention only a few. The old quip may indeed be true that when you get five psychologists together you have twelve theories. This is confusing for parents, and it often leaves professionals themselves in a quandary. We need to start with the child and study his learning style rather than trying to fit him into an established theory.

Children are great mimics. They will learn anything we value, but they learn best from those who care for them and care about them. Parents and professionals have to agree on their goals for children, and those goals should not be limited to high marks on standardized measures. They should include the acquisition of wisdom, compassion, moral and ethical values, and appreciation of beauty, not merely cognitive performance. Given the pace of change in the world, we have no notion of what children will need to know when they reach adulthood. The best we can do is help them become self-confident, self-disciplined, self-propelled autonomous learners.

It is paradoxical and sad to note that, at a time when the body of knowledge about children's growth and learning has expanded greatly and is more generally available to the public, that knowledge is not being put into practice to benefit children and their families. Knowledge gleaned from industrial and management research, rather than that from the study of human growth and development, has pervaded the planning and administration of many publicly funded programs. The cry for accountability is warranted, but the kind of accountability required by the use of standardized measures is questionable. Younger children are less predictable and more vulnerable, which makes standard assessments less reliable. Teachers' observations and parents' comments provide the most valid data.

It would be good if decisions about preschool programs could be based on benefits to young children and their families rather than on emotional generalizations that create dissension among planners. We should focus our attention on which ingredients are necessary for good programs and on how we can convince policymakers that this is a wise use of public monies. Children are our biggest voiceless minority; they need staunch, articulate, knowledgeable, committed advocates. Working together, it may be possible to raise a generation of adults fit to live with young children.

REFERENCES

Berrueta-Clement, J., Schweinhart, L., Barnett, W., Epstein, A., & Weikart, D. (1984). *Changed lives*. Ypsilanti, MI: High/Scope Press.

Bronfenbrenner, U. (1985). The three worlds of childhood. *Principal*, *65*(5), 7–11.

Bureau of Census, U.S. Department of Commerce. (1984). Detailed population characteristics, *1980 Census of Population*, PC 80-1-D, pp. 1–38. Washington, DC: U.S. Government Printing Office.

Caldwell, B. (1983). Should four-year-olds go to school? *Young Children*, *38*(4), 48–50.

Carini, P. (1982). *The school lives of seven children: A five-year study*. Grand Forks: University of North Dakota Press.

Irvine, D. J., Flint, D. L., Hick, T. L., Horan, M. D., & Kukuk, S. E. (1982). *Evaluation of New York State Experimental Prekindergarten Program* (Final Report). New York: State Education Department.

Lazar, I., & Darlington, R. (1982). Lasting effects of early education: Report from the Consortium for Longitudinal Studies. *Monograph of the Society for Research in Child Development*, *47* (Serial No. 195).

Tumin, M. (1968, February). *Early education: The creation of capacity*. Paper presented at the conference of the State Education Department, Albany, NY.

Weber, C. U., Foster, P. W., & Weikart, D. (1978). *An economic analysis of the Ypsilanti Perry Preschool Project* (High/Scope Monographs No. 5). Ypsilanti, MI: High/Scope Press.

Zimiles, H. (1985, April). *Four-year-olds in public school: What research does and does not tell us*. Paper presented at the meeting of the American Education Association, Chicago, IL.

CHAPTER 5

Child Care in the Public Schools: Public Accountability and the Black Child

EVELYN K. MOORE

The need to secure affordable, convenient, reliable child care has become a problem of crisis proportions in white and black communities across America. Both communities should be wary, however, of new efforts to "solve" the child-care crisis by using the most attractive immediate option. A rush to judgment in this public policy arena could have devastating effects on our children for years to come.

This chapter will examine black Americans' concerns as they relate to the public debate over placing early childhood education in the public schools. It will attempt to articulate a black perspective on this debate by exploring the context in which new proposals are evaluated by blacks, and by offering new ways of looking at those proposals. Finally, it will suggest a number of critical criteria that, if adopted by all child-care providers, would meet the demands of black child-care experts and advocates.

In January 1986, the National Black Child Development Institute (of which I am executive director) issued a report entitled *Child Care in the Public Schools: Incubator for Inequality?* (1985a). This report analyzed one popular solution to the day-care crisis and outlined the Institute's concerns regarding the ability of public schools to adapt various aspects of their curriculum and administration to the needs of a new constituency, that of very young children.

The conclusions of this report, which will be discussed in this chapter, must be evaluated in context. Although we keep an open mind on all issues of concern to black children, we make no claims of scholarly distance. We are a grass-roots organization with a long history of activism in the area of day care and early childhood education. Certainly this experience and our mission have colored our attitude toward this subject. It is imperative, therefore, that I preface this analysis with a candid statement of our biases.

The National Black Child Development Institute (NBCDI) is a nonprofit educational organization dedicated to improving the quality of life for black children. Through an extensive affiliate network, located in thirty-three major urban centers throughout the United States, NBCDI relies on committed volunteers to monitor public policy, advocate for a better quality of life for black children, and provide needed services in their communities.

Today, the Institute focuses on three major policy areas: child care, child welfare, and education. The issue of child care has been central to the organization's mission from the very beginning. The Institute was founded in 1970 by people intimately involved in day care: parents, pediatricians, psychologists, and others who met at a national conference to discuss child development from a black perspective. That discussion has continued for fifteen years.

In 1985, the Institute decided it was again time to infuse the national debate with some awareness of a black perspective. At a fall 1985 Public Policy Training Institute held in Washington, D.C., NBCDI members discussed with experts in the field and national policymakers the pros and cons of the movement toward placing early childhood education in the public schools. At the end of this session, NBCDI members urged their national office to study the issue further and to compile a report detailing the potential impact of this movement on black children. An advisory committee of child development experts worked through the fall and winter to prepare the report that was ultimately released at a January 1986 news conference in Washington. Subsequently, another task force set out to amplify and refine the report's recommendations so they would be of even greater specific help in planning.

Thus, it is clear that this report is indeed biased by its compelling concern for the welfare of black children. When we chose the title *Child Care in the Public Schools: Incubator for Inequality?* we were very careful to put a question mark at the end to signal our hope to stimulate debate. It was our expressed purpose to question an idea that was quickly putting down roots as conventional wisdom. We were, and remain, deeply troubled by the rush to form public policy on the basis of expedience. No matter how desperate the need for new child-care systems, which is driving the movement for early childhood programs in the public schools, the stakes are too high to let our children get caught in the rush to a quick solution.

Assumptions and Obligations

The Institute released its report with an assumption and an obligation. As an organization of long-time public school advocates, it assumed the right to question the schools' ability to adapt to the needs of a new constituency, the very young. The report should not be misconstrued, however, as another knife in the back of public school education. Rather, it is an effort to identify the legitimate concerns of black people who question the ability of our public schools to transform themselves, effortlessly and overnight, to meet the needs of very young children.

As an organization, the Institute has a record of support for public schools and their teachers. As black people, we must support public schools, as it is here that the vast majority of black students will be found long into the twenty-first century. But the public schools need help. They are underfinanced, they face a shortage of new talented teachers, and they are increasingly viewed as society's cure-all for unresolved social problems from teen pregnancy to substance abuse. It is little wonder, then, that our public schools feel under attack. Our mission must be to improve the schools, not to add to their problems.

We released our report with a sense of obligation as well. As black people, we see the discussion of this issue within the context of past public policy disasters that have affected our lives and the lives of our children. In many of our nation's cities, blacks have inherited the failures of public policy: decrepit housing, inadequate public services, and empty municipal coffers. In urban public schools, once again, blacks stand to inherit institutions and programs taxed beyond their limits. Our cities' schools are already struggling under the weight of their charge: to do more with less. Can we expect them to serve our younger children well without the prospect of significant new resources?

We are sympathetic to the public schools' dilemma, but we are also impatient to see our schools improve their track record with black students. Today, 40 percent of minority youth are functionally illiterate (NBCDI, 1985b). Black children are twice as likely as whites to be suspended from school or to suffer corporal punishment (NBCDI, 1985b). Black children are three times as likely as whites to be placed in classes for the educable mentally retarded, where they make up 40 percent of all children (NBCDI, 1985b). Finally, only one in four (27 percent) black high school graduates go on to college (U.S. Department of Commerce, Bureau of the Census 1984, 1985). This is not an impressive record upon which to build new programs for black preschoolers.

As advocates for black children and their parents, we feel an obligation to voice our concerns about placing early childhood care in the public schools. These concerns are the logical extension of our experience. How can we reassure ourselves that the public schools will develop the skills and techniques necessary to nurture black talent at its most fragile and formative stage? Will public school–based child-care programs adopt the methods and procedures of elementary education that have operated in many cases to segregate blacks and to label them as nonachievers?

The Institute did not have the answers to these questions when it first set out to examine the issue. We were determined, however, to find the answers before public policy became reality. No one has the answers to prove that the public school solution is a viable one. No one has given this issue the scrutiny and research it deserves.

The Changing Debate

Some confusion is evident even in our definition of terms. In some respects, the very goals and definition of quality day care have changed so markedly that even those who are actively engaged in the debate over what constitutes a responsive day-care system are often talking about apples and oranges. There has been a noticeable change in the nature of this discussion among advocates of day-care policy over the last decade. The child-care proposals of the early seventies focused on community-based programs to complement and aid the social and economic development of the family and the community. Early testimony from advocacy groups stressed the importance of relying on parents and community leaders to define the community's needs, to set policy, and to operate the community-based child-care program (Roby, 1973).

Today, however, child-care proposals focus primarily on expedient methods of increasing the availability of day-care slots to meet the demand. We strongly support the creation of more slots. We urge, however, that other factors be considered as well, including the diversity of delivery systems and the responsiveness to individual communities and to parents. We are concerned, in sum, that expedience is rapidly replacing quality as a primary goal. This is a fundamental change in the nature of the child-care discussion.

We know there are new economic reasons for pushing the public school solution, for other options are being systematically destroyed by budget cuts. For example, the elimination of the specific earmark for child care within the federal program for social services to the states, Title XX, has further weakened the existing child-care system by forcing child care into competition with all other social service needs for fewer federal dollars. Today, child-care services that once relied on state funds and states that relied on Title XX funds have to search elsewhere for funding sources.

We know, too, that many schools themselves are badly in need of new clients. Declining enrollments threaten neighborhood schools, and for some, preschool child-care programs could be viewed as the salvation of their school.

Moreover, black parents, like white parents, are being pressured into early childhood programs by the threat that their children will lag behind those with preschool credentials. Black parents who desperately seek a route out of poverty for their children are especially susceptible to this promise. Yet few have examined the difference between the kind of high-quality early education program represented by the High/Scope experiment and the nature of the programs to be provided their child in their local public schools.

Despite the clear interest in placing early childhood education in the public schools, virtually no one is discussing the pedagogical implications of this major age change in the group served by the public schools. The Institute believes that it is time to concentrate on the fundamental question: can public school–based early childhood programs be adapted to meet black children's pedagogical, social, and developmental needs? And if so, what would it take to do this? Although these questions are especially pertinent to blacks, they are also applicable to the majority population as well. In truth, all families should be raising these questions about our education system in order to ensure that the schools are prepared to teach their children equitably and sensitively.

Institutional Characteristics in Conflict with Individual Achievement

A number of factors stands in the way of a successful transition from the current scope of public school education to the inclusion of early childhood programs. First, the conflict between the traditions of early childhood education and those of public education is significant. Early childhood education has traditionally focused on the developmental needs of the child in the context of the social welfare of the family. By encouraging the involvement of parents and by reinforcing their central position in the child's life, traditional programs have always operated with a two-client focus: the parent and the child. Yet public schools traditionally focus on parents exclusively as agents to bring about a child's cooperation and socialization. Extensive family involvement is most often in direct opposition to public school procedures, despite its importance to the young child's development.

Second, current public school curricula and teaching methods also conflict with those appropriate for very young children. Young children learn in context and in episodic fashion. Much depends on individual attention. Educator Barbara Bowman has said that

> in the first six years, children come to learning with a real inner drive to make sense out of the world and, in making sense out of the world, they learn to process information. What is important is that they achieve a balance between receiving information and constructing inner cognitive structures to handle that information, to make sense out of it. Young children need to receive their information in the context of how it is used. (Bowman, 1985)

Yet, traditionally, public schools are structured primarily to impart information out of context, transmitting social content, values, and facts to children passively listening in large group settings. They are not set up to provide the young child with the opportunities to realize his or her developmental potential.

Another characteristic of public education procedure in conflict with early childhood development goals is its reliance on testing to classify children in groups. As bad as the effects of public schools' reliance on tests and tracking are for elementary school-age black children, they are worse for younger children. Preschoolers are too young to test reliably. Yet, group tests, rather than more individualized methods of evaluation, are universally used by public schools. There is something wrong when, as mentioned earlier, black children make up approximately 40 percent of the educable mentally retarded population in schools, but they are only slightly more than 10 percent of the population at large (NBCDI, 1985b). Black families are already reeling under the negative impact of testing on their children. Who is to say that the movement toward early child care in the school will not simply serve to identify and isolate these so-called nonachievers at an even earlier age?

Yet another public education characteristic in conflict with the best interests of young black children is the standard teacher education curriculum. Teacher training for public school certification is oriented toward older children and does not take account of preschoolers' different learning patterns and needs. Yet economic pressure will surely exist to fill slots for early childhood programs with teachers holding tenure. These teachers may know little or nothing about the nature of their new charges. Moreover, despite the increasing number of black children in the system and the young child's need to identify with her teacher, proportionally few teachers are likely to be black.

How can we solve the dilemma between the appeal of public schools as centers for early childhood programs and the needs of young children that conflict with public school traditions and procedures? The Institute believes the solution lies in the public schools' voluntary compliance with the basic criteria that ensure quality child care.

We are admittedly long on criticism, but we are not without positive recommendations for bridging the distance that currently separates our concerns from our dreams. Our report offered ten major safeguards that, if incorporated into the public schools, would make the schools an attractive option for black parents seeking quality early childhood education programs. These recommendations are presented below with further explanation about their potential impact.

Safeguards for Preschool Programs

> 1. Any public school–based program for preschool-age children should incorporate an effective parent education program.

If educators recognize the importance of the child's parents as a significant factor in the education process, they will be more successful in meeting the needs of the child. Parent education is invaluable in forming the critical liaison between home and school. The goal is not only to make parents more aware of the operations of the school but also to help them become increasingly more knowledgeable about the care and development of their children.

Most parents welcome the opportunity to learn more about their children, and they appreciate and greatly benefit from good parent education programs if they are offered in a sensitive, caring, professional manner. These programs must avoid creating the atmosphere of intimidation that many parents tell us they feel when they enter school facilities.

We also urge schools to avoid pscyho-clinical parent education programs. Rather, the aim is to promote an informative exchange of such information as good child-rearing practices; the normative patterns of growth; stages in physical, social, and sexual development, language, and behavior; and approaches to good discipline. Parents need to understand what characteristics to observe in their children, how to observe their children, how to use the home as a learning environment, and how to make language a positive tool for learning and expression.

Specially designated staff persons are needed to staff parent education programs. These individuals must be culturally sensitive to the environment of the children and the community served. A professional background in child development and social work is preferable, enabling them to establish good rapport with diverse groups and to organize parent education programs including forums, seminars, parent panel discussions, and child-rearing stress-relief sessions. Staff members with this level of training can help parents bone up on cognitive skills, home management, positive parental self-awareness, and other parental needs.

Ideally, parent education centers should be established at least on a district level and should include a toy lending library, videotapes on child care and development, low-cost materials for parents to use in working with their children at home, and a process for developing and distributing television guides.

> 2. Public school–based early childhood programs need to involve parents in decisions about the curriculum and policy.

Although we clearly recognize educators as professionals, some real attempt must be made to draw parents into the decision-making process if they are to acquire advocacy skills and an understanding of good programming. Parents should be included in everything from classroom participation to the review and evaluation process.

All programs need a gradual orientation process in which parents are given information on the center and its philosophy, program, and operating procedures. A well-organized structure will allow parents to become involved in day-to-day activities of the program as grade mothers and fathers, and facilitators of holiday events or other special occasions such as grandparents' day.

It is important that programs establish advisory groups on which parents could serve on a rotating basis. These groups can forge links among home, school, and public and private organizations and can serve as a tool to recruit volunteers. They can also be instrumental in developing policies and procedural guidelines.

Parents must be permitted and encouraged to visit, to observe, and to participate in classroom activities and to attend parent-teacher conferences. Parents need numerous opportunities to talk with the program staff, and they should feel welcome in the center at all times—to eat lunch, help in class, or observe unannounced.

> 3. Teachers in public school–based programs for young children should be required to have specific training in preschool education and/or ongoing in-service training, provided weekly by a qualified staff.

As public schools add prekindergarten programs to their education efforts, provisions must be made for orienting other school personnel, particularly principals, in order to raise awareness of what constitutes a quality program. It is critical that all staff members understand the goals and philosophy of the program, health and safety standards and procedures, special needs of young children, classroom management, and interpersonal relations with the children.

One option is to consider instituting an ongoing teacher preparedness program including such features as seminars, visits to other programs, classrooms, and districts, and access to resource materials and to college and technical school child development programs.

Teachers need core training in child development, and the director or coordinator of the program could benefit from additional training in management. Through staff development, teachers can continue to build a knowledge of, sensitivity to, and appreciation for the environment from which their children are drawn. An invaluable part of the teachers' training is education about the communities and home environments of their children. Home visits can be part of this training effort. Teachers should be encouraged to share among themselves pertinent information about the children in their care, which might affect their growth and participation in the program.

The experience of private and community day-care staffs is

extremely valuable. District staff development programs should be made available to them. Community people can be recertified and given proper consideration as staff in the public schools.

> 4. Public school–based early childhood programs should be subject to a regular external review by community members and early childhood development experts.

To provide opportunities for local input, external reviews can be conducted in conjunction with school personnel, parents, and community members. Affiliates of NBCDI and other voluntary organizations concerned about the health and early development of young children could serve as part of the review team. Child development experts impartial to the school district should also be part of the review process. It is important that reviews take place at least annually and that they touch on all major components of the children's developmental program.

> 5. The staff of early childhood programs in public schools should include teachers who come from the community served by the program.

Programs are strengthened immeasurably when teachers and other staff are representative of the minorities served and reflect the ethnic and racial makeup of the community from which the children come.

Researchers are constantly telling us that the number of minorities in the field of education is dwindling. At a variety of levels, then, a special effort must be made to attract blacks and other minorities to all staff levels of early education programs. So important is this to the development of the young minority child that state departments of education, school districts, and schools of education must work together and be committed to recruiting (and, in some cases, retraining) minorities to work in child development staffing positions.

> 6. The curriculum for preschool-age children in public schools must be culturally sensitive and appropriate to the child's age and level of development.

The curriculum should embody all that early childhood experts know to be sound for very young children—not a watered-down version of first-grade development strategies. The National

Association for the Education of Young Children has published a book entitled *Developmentally Appropriate Practice* which defines the best ways of caring for young children. The NBCDI supports this book's approach to early childhood care and education.

In addition, constant positive acknowledgment of the culture and heritage of the minority child is essential. This can be achieved in part through the use of well-chosen visual aids, books, records, and other learning materials in the classroom every day—not just on special days. The curriculum for minority children can then be built around the identifiable strengths they bring to the program. The cognitive learning styles of minority children should be studied and taken into account in planning and implementing activities. There are numerous ways to enrich the minority child's environment and to provide him or her with the opportunity for verbal and other creative self-expression.

If the curriculum is value-based, then personal development, appropriate behavior, a positive self-concept, and generally positive attitudes toward self and environment are nurtured. Learning should be active, not passive. Learning through discovery is essential to healthy development, and requires adequate supervision.

> 7. The public schools that house programs for very young children should meet the same health and safety standards that apply to independent preschools and center-based child-care programs.

It is imperative that the physical facility be antiseptically clean at all times. Restrooms must be cleaned and disinfected daily; equipment and classrooms should be maintained in a safe, clean condition and in good repair. Coverings used for cots or mats where children nap require regular washing.

Written plans are needed for handling health, fire, and other emergencies and first aid supplies should be readily available. First aid and emergency treatments such as CPR must be certified by a licensed health agency. At least one trained staff member should be on hand at all times, particularly if the school does not employ a full-time nurse.

Children must be under constant adult supervision. The staff should be alert to their health conditions, reporting deviations and accidents to other staff members and parents immediately. Provision should be made to notify parents of sick children, and policies should be established governing the attendance or suspended attendance of children who are ill. Restrictive guidelines for the dispensation of medicine are important.

Care givers should be constantly on guard for signs of neglect and abuse among children in the program. If evidence of either is detected, referrals must be made to the appropriate agencies immediately.

New staff members can be required to serve probationary periods during which their physical and psychological competence for work with young children is judged. Programs should require annual checkups of care givers, including tuberculin and other tests for communicable diseases. Psychological evaluation and observation can also be encouraged on an ongoing basis.

Within thirty days of entry into the program, all children should be given a health assessment and any immunizations they need. Written health records should be maintained for each child, with documented health evaluations, immunizations, and other information obtained at least three months prior to enrollment.

> 8. Just as nonprofit early childhood development programs offer nutrition services, public school–based early childhood programs should participate in federal and state programs that provide adequate nutrition for children.

Breakfast, snacks, and lunch should be standard fare for early education programs in the schools. At the minimum, half-day programs should offer lunch and one snack, with dinner included in twelve-hour programs. It is important to provide parents with information on daily or weekly menus. If food is brought from the home, suitable facilities for storing it must be secured.

Mealtime should be a warmly social event for the children and the staff. Family-style meals, where children learn to serve themselves under adult supervision, are highly desirable. They help foster good nutrition habits and acceptable table manners. Above all, wherever center food is prepared, the premises must meet the local and state health and sanitation guidelines.

> 9. Administrators of public school–based programs for preschoolers should ensure that children entering the programs have access to appropriate health care.

The district staff and the local program staff can establish close rapport with indigent and state health agencies in order to institute a ready referral system for children. The school will then be better able to assist parents in obtaining necessary health care.

> 10. In assessing children of preschool age, the administrators of public school–based early childhood programs should not limit their assessment to, or base their program planning solely on, standardized tests.

Tests used for tracking should not be allowed. It is imperative that the program staff be aware that assessments of children are to help the teachers perform better, not to stereotype or degrade children or to minimize curriculum content. Assessments should always be followed up with parent conferences. Parents have a right to be apprised regularly of their child's needs, how the center attempts to address those needs, and, through parent education programs, how they can help at home.

The National Black Child Development Institute believes that any child-care system—public or private—serving black communities should meet these criteria. Those public schools that embrace these standards voluntarily will have our blessing, as will churches and family day-care and other centers that move to incorporate these criteria. The Institute is committed to a diverse delivery system in which all providers are based in and responsive to the communities they serve. We must have public accountability from all systems that serve our children.

If we are to entrust the youngest of our children to these institutions, we must invest our resources and our leadership in working to improve them. The public schools, far from being our adversaries, must stand as our allies in an all-out battle for black achievement. That battle will be won only when parents and community leaders work with the schools to make them responsive to all our children.

REFERENCES

Bowman, B. (1985, October). *Public schools and preschool education.* Speech given at East Texas State University, Commerce, TX.

———. (1985, June 24). *Child care and public schools: Clarifying the issues from the black viewpoint.* Speech given to the 1985 Public Policy Institute of the National Black Child Development Institute, Washington, DC.

National Black Child Development Institute. (1985a). *Child care in the public schools: Incubator for inequality?* Washington, DC: Author.

———. (1985b). *Excellence and equity, quality and inequality: A report on civil rights, education and black children.* Washington, DC: Author.

Roby, Pamela. (1973). *Child care: Who cares?* New York: Basic Books.

U.S. Department of Commerce, Bureau of the Census. (1985, October). *School enrollment: Social and economic characteristics of students.* Washington, DC: Author.

CHAPTER 6

Early Childhood Education on Its Own Terms

DAVID ELKIND

Young children learn differently than do older children and adults. Because the world of things, people, and language is new to infants and young children, they learn best through direct encounters with their world rather than through formal education involving the inculcation of symbolic rules. This fact is rooted in the observations of the giants of child study, including Froebel (1904), Montessori (1912), and Piaget (1950), and is consistently supported by the findings of child development research (White, 1970). This fact was also recognized by the ancients who described the child of six or seven as having attained the "age of reason." Given this well-established fact that young children do not learn the same way older children and adults do, the educational corollary is straightforward. The education of young children must be different from that of older children and in keeping with their unique modes of learning.

Given these observations, what is happening in the United States today is truly astonishing. In a society that prides itself upon its preference for facts over hearsay, upon its openness to research, and upon its respect for expert opinion, parents, educators, administrators, and legislators are ignoring the facts, the research, and the expert opinion as to how young children learn and how best to teach them.

All across the country, programs devised for school-aged children are being extended to the education of young children. In some states (for example, New York, Connecticut, and Illinois) educational administrators are advocating that children enter school at age four. Many kindergarten programs have become full-day kindergartens, and nursery school programs have become prekindergartens. Moreover, many of these kindergartens have introduced curricula (including work papers) once reserved for first-grade children. And in books addressed to parents, several writers (Doman, 1965; Eastman & Barr, 1985; Ledson, 1975) have advocated teaching reading and math to infants and young children.

This transformation of thinking regarding early childhood education raises at least three questions that this chapter will attempt to answer. The first is why is this happening? As we have seen, both the theory and research are consistent with respect to the fact that young children learn differently than older children and adults do, and no one really questions the principle that education should be adapted to the learning abilities of the students to be instructed. Why is the special character of early childhood and of education during those years being ignored by so many people who should know better?

The second question builds upon the first. Why is the downward extension of academics harmful to young children? After all, it could be the case that we are merely coddling young children by not introducing them to a rigorous academic program at an early age. Doesn't the new research on infants and young children substantiate their eagerness to learn and the importance of the early years for intensive instruction? Not really, as we shall see.

The third question is also sequential. If it can be demonstrated that early formal instruction inflicts more harm than it incurs good, what can we do about it? After all, that is the direction in which the society as a whole is heading. Formal instructional programs for infants and young children are expanding not only in academic areas but also in sports, the arts, and computer science. To oppose these trends is to ignore the social consensus and to be countercultural.

Social Dynamics of Early Instruction

In America, educational practice is determined by economic, political, and social considerations much more than it is by what we know about what is good pedagogy for children. Until the 1960s, however, early childhood education was an exception to this general rule. Early childhood programs were, for the most part, privately run and were well adapted to the developmental needs of the children they served. Even kindergartens in the public schools had a special status and were generally free of the social pressures operating on the rest of primary and secondary education.

All that changed in the 1960s when early childhood education was abruptly shoved into the economic, political, and social spotlight. At that moment early childhood education lost its innocence and its special status. Like primary and secondary education, early childhood became a forum for social concerns that had little or nothing to do with what was good pedagogy for children. The formal symbol of this mainstreaming of early childhood education was the passage of the Head Start legislation by the Congress in 1964. For the first time, early childhood programs were being funded by the federal government.

What brought about this changed status in the 1960s? In many ways early childhood education was the panacea of the social movements of that turbulent decade. Primary and secondary education were under attack on two fronts. The launching of the Soviet sputnik in 1957, the demise of progressive education, and books like *Why Johnny Can't Read* put a critical spotlight on the quality of American education. One explanation (rationalization) was that children were poorly prepared for school and that early childhood education should be made more academically rigorous so that children could move rapidly once they entered school.

A different, but equally powerful, spotlight upon American education came from another direction—the civil rights movement that stressed the inequality of schooling for minorities. Schools for black children were considered inferior in quality than those for white children. Again, one explanation (rationalization) was that black children were poorly prepared for school. It was not so much that the schools were inferior as it was that black children lacked adequate preschools. The Head Start legislation was one response to this claim.

It is not only educational practice that is determined by the social, economic, and political tenor of the times, but the conception of the child as well. For example, a dominant image of children in the nineteenth century—dictated by the pervasiveness of our religious orientation at that time—was that of the "sinful" child. Education of the sinful child necessarily involved a "breaking of the will" by whatever harsh measures were necessary.

With the introduction of Freudian psychology in the early twentieth century, along with the continuing secularization and urbanization of American society, the concept of the sinful child was progressively replaced by a concept of the "sensual" child. Freud's (1938) depiction of infantile sexuality and his theories regarding the central role of sexuality in neuroses focused attention upon the development of a "healthy personality." Progressive education had as one of its aims the open spontaneous expression of feelings and emotions (healthy) rather than their suppression or repression (unhealthy). During the reign of the sensual child, there was little concern with the child's intellectual development, which, it was presumed, would take care of itself if the child were emotionally healthy.

During this same period, middle-class values dictated that mothers stay home to rear their children, be supportive of their husbands, and run the home (home economics was a major department for women within most colleges and universities of the time and reflected these values). Within that set of middle-class values, the concept of a sensual infant who was in need of the mother's ministrations fit comfortably.

In the last two decades, however, thanks both to the women's movement and to the shift in our society from an industrial to a postindustrial economy, the middle-class value system has changed dramatically. The women's movement has brought to the fore their right to choose between staying home or pursuing a career. At the same time, our postindustrial economy is more in need of women in the work force than was the industrial economy. By and large, factory work requires the large muscles of men. But with the miniaturization of modern technology, the small motor skills and dexterity of women are in greater demand than the large muscle strength of men. Similarly, now that we have moved to a service economy, the social skills of women are also much in demand.

And still another changed middle-class circumstance has contributed to the growing number of middle-class women in the work force. As divorce has become socially acceptable, the rates have soared and it is now expected that more than 50 percent of all marriages will end in divorce. In more than 90 percent of the cases, it is the mothers who retain custody of their children, and since alimony and child support are rarely adequate, these women are another factor in the rising number of middle-class working women.

The result of all these changing life-styles and values has been that middle-class women are entering the work force in ever increasing numbers. More than 50 percent of the nation's women are now at work, and it is estimated that by the year 2000 between 80 and 90 percent of women will be working. One consequence of this entrance of mothers into the work force, of course, is that increasing numbers of infants and young children are being cared for outside the home. Currently an estimated 6 million children below the age of six are receiving some form of out-of-home care.

Finally, in the 1960s and early 1970s, an equalitarian political ideology contributed to the demise of the notion of the sensual child. Historians like Aries (1962) claimed that the concept of childhood was a social invention of the last few centuries that was unknown in the Middle Ages and early years of the Enlightenment. Contemporary children were, therefore, not being given credit for their capacities and abilities and were being coddled for the pleasure of adults. This view of undervalued and underestimated childhood found a sympathetic resonance in those fighting for women's rights.

The intellectual importance given early childhood by the women's and the civil rights movements, by new middle-class family styles, and by a political ideology of equalitarianism was inconsistent with the concept of the sensual child. A new notion was required.

The idea that emerged to meet the needs of this new social

zeitgeist was the concept of the "competent" infant. Perhaps unwittingly, social scientists caught up in the emotions of the social movements gave impetus to this conception by unwarranted reinterpretations of established facts about the cognitive development of young children.

Jerome Bruner (1960), for example, although not trained in child development or in education, became a guru of the educational reform movement. His totally unsubstantiated hypothesis to the effect that "you can teach any child any subject matter at any age in an intellectually honest way" became a touchstone of the new conception of the infant. In the same way Bloom's (1964) ambiguous statement (based on well-known correlations between IQ scores attained at different age levels by the same subjects) that a young child attains half of his or her intellectual ability by age four was another foundation for the competent infant conception. Finally Hunt's (1961) idea of IQ malleability (an idea that had always been accepted by all reputable psychometricians) was presented as a new idea that was in opposition to the mental-testing establishment's belief in a fixed IQ.

The conception of the competent infant and young child, then, was dictated by sociopolitical forces rather than by any new data or findings about the modes of learning of young children. Whatever psychological theory or educational research was brought to bear to reinforce this conception was carefully selected and interpreted for the purpose. Contrary evidence was ignored. It was a case of forcing facts to fit the hypothesis rather than changing the hypothesis to fit the facts. In short, our conception of the child at any point in history is more determined by social, political, and economic considerations than it is by the established facts and theories of child development.

This new conception of infant competence nicely met the new importance being placed on early childhood education as a panacea for the nation's educational problems. Early education would work because young children were more competent, more able and eager learners than we had given them credit for in the past. Early education would at last enable young children to realize the full potential that had been muffled in the past by the emphasis on play and a healthy personality.

The conception of the competent infant is clearly more in

keeping with these contemporary family styles than is that of the sensual infant. A competent infant is able to cope with the separation from parents at an early age. He or she is able to adjust to baby-sitters, day-care centers, and full-day nursery schools without difficulty. And if some parents feel any residual pangs of guilt about leaving their young offspring in out-of-home care, they can place the youngster in a high-pressure academic program. If the child were not in such a program, the parents tell one another, he or she would fall behind peers and would not be able to compete academically when it was time to enter kindergarten. High-pressure academic programs, from this point of view, are for the young child's own good.

The social dynamics behind the pressure for placing young children in educational programs appropriate for school-age children now become painfully clear. The truth is that all of these transformations within our society were not accompanied by adequate provisions for the out-of-home care for all those young children who required it. As a consequence parents are putting pressure on elected officials to provide more early childhood care. This has been the motivation for full-day kindergartens, a starting school age of four, and so on. Although the avowed reasons for these proposals is new research showing the need for early childhood education, the fact is that the "new" data consists of the "old" dubious data of the sixties. The real reason for these programs is that elected officials are feeling voter pressure to offer out-of-home care for young children.

There is yet another motivation for the introduction of formal instruction at the early childhood level. This comes from our intuitive psychology regarding technology and human behavior. Much of this psychology derives from emotions and feelings rather than from reason and balanced judgment. Nonetheless such intuitions seem so obviously correct that one feels foolish even to challenge them. The so-called gambler's fallacy is a case in point. The gambler believes that the number of previous losses affects his or her probability of winning. In fact, however, the probabilities do not change as a result of preceding events.

And the intuition that human potentials are altered by technology is equally fallacious. With respect to children, this intuition is often expressed by saying that children today, thanks to such technological innovations as television and computers, are brighter and more sophisticated than children of the past. This intuition has reinforced and supported the conception of the competent infant and young child and has been used to rationalize the form of instruction for preschool children.

Technology, however, does not change human potential nor accelerate development; it merely extends and amplifies our human potentials. The telephone extends our hearing, television extends our vision, and computers extend our memory. But our capacity for hearing, our capacity for vision, and our capacity for remembering have not been altered. In the same way, modern weaponry has amplified our ability to express our aggressive impulses; it has not altered or lessened that aggression. There is simply no truth in the intuitive belief that technology alters human potentials.

There is also no support for the assumption that growing up with a technology necessarily makes one more comfortable with it. The fallacy of this assumption is perhaps best illustrated in the area of computers. In articles, advertisements, and media presentations we are continually presented with children who are computer wizards while parents or other adults stand about in bewildered amazement. In fact, the truth is quite the reverse. Computers have been assimilated into the adult workplace with astonishing rapidity. There is hardly any business today that has not been computerized to some extent. This is true not only for banking, accounting, industrial, commercial, and investment corporations but also for doctors' offices, restaurants, and gas stations.

The only place that computers have not been easily assimilated is the school. Schools are still struggling with how, when, and where to employ computers. If growing up with a technology carries with it increased adaptability to that technology, why do adults who have not grown up with the technology adapt better to it than children who have grown up with it? The answer is that it is the level of attained mental ability rather than familiarity that determines adaptability to an intellectually demanding technology like computers.

The Harm of Early Instruction

What harm is there in exposing young children to formal instruction involving the inculcation of rules? The harm comes from what I have called "miseducation" (Elkind, 1987). We miseducate children whenever we put them at risk for no purpose. The risks of miseducating young children are both short term and long term. The short-term risks derive from the stress formal instruction puts upon children with all its resultant stress symptoms. The long-term risks are of at least three kinds—motivational, intellectual, and social. In each case the potential psychological risk of early instruction is far greater than any potential educational gain.

Before turning to those risks, however, we need to look at the ways in which early childhood education is different from elementary and secondary education as well as from the kinds of education parents provide at home. Once we appreciate the unique character of early childhood education, the risks of miseducation become readily apparent. The risks of exposing young children to elementary education are comparable to the risks of exposing elementary schoolchildren to secondary education. Just as one would not send an eight-year-old to high school, one should not send a four-year-old to elementary school.

In early childhood, children's thinking is first and foremost functional. They think of things in terms of what is done with them; at this stage a hole is "to dig" and a bike is "to ride." The young child's functional mode of thinking marks a fundamental difference between the mental abilities of young children and those of older children and adolescents. The skills children need to explore their immediate world—touching, holding, putting together, observing, listening, tasting, smelling, integrating—are built-in skills that do not have to be taught. To be sure, young children need to be taught how to cut with scissors, how to hold a crayon, and so on. But most of the skills they need to learn about their immediate world are part of their makeup.

Because young children come with their learning skills in hand, the task of the early childhood educator is quite different from that of the teacher at the elementary or secondary level. In formal education—that begun after the attainment of concrete operations—the usual sequence is to teach skills such as reading, writing, and math as a necessary prerequisite to the attainment of further knowledge. Reading is necessary for most of the learning that goes on in schools, and basic arithmetic skills are required for all later math instruction and comprehension. Writing is another skill children must acquire to communicate, among other things, what it is they have learned.

But preschool children do not need to be taught learning skills! I wish I could emblazon that fact in the minds of all those who assume that early childhood education is merely a downward extension of elementary education. For example, young children do not have to be "taught" how to "match to sample." Given a set of picture cards and a large card containing duplicates of the picture cards, children hardly need to be told to put the like pictures one on top of the other. Classifying, a more extensive matching to sample, also does not have to be taught. Nor do young children have to be taught size, color, or form discrimination. Young children can make these discriminations quite well.

If early childhood educators do not teach young children skills, then what do they teach them? They begin to teach them content, the concepts and classifications of the different disciplines such as science, social studies, and history. In early childhood, the teacher also builds upon the child's inherent skills and focuses upon content. Of necessity, the content is more fundamental than that taught in the schools.

Young children have to be presented with the different colors, the different geometric shapes, the sticks of different lengths to be ordered, the buttons to be sorted according to color, and so on. Young children already have the skills to discriminate shapes and colors, to order sticks according to size, and to classify objects according to similarities and differences. The task of early childhood educators is to provide the materials upon which children can employ their skills. They also need to give children the labels to go with the discriminations they are making.

The early childhood educator's task is different in still another way from that of the elementary or secondary schoolteacher. The organization of young children's minds is horizontal rather than vertical as it will become later. Young children do not, for example, group classes and grasp that brown wooden beads and white wooden beads can be included in the larger class of wooden beads. The subject matter breakdowns, so common in the elementary school and later, are really not meaningful for young children. The distinctions among reading, math, social studies, and science are not at all clear to the young child.

It is for this reason that young children learn most from projects rather than from lessons. In a project such as stringing beads into a necklace the child can learn the different colors of the beads (vocabulary), the different geometric shapes the beads come in (geometry), the order or pattern of the beads such as one round, two square, and so on (math), and the pleasant look of the finished product (art and aesthetics). It would be rather silly to try to separate these various kinds of learning and present them as special subject matter lessons. Young children's learning is thus horizontal or permeable; they learn about different subject matters at the same time because as yet there are no sharp boundaries separating their various types of knowledge.

If early childhood education is different from that provided by formal schooling, it is also different from the education provided by parents. Parents, as their first teachers, enable children to utilize their innate skills for acquiring language and concepts of the physical and social world. And they are the central figures in children's emotional learning as well. As Erik Erikson (1950) has pointed out, parents determine whether children's basic sense of trust outweighs their sense of mistrust and whether their sense of autonomy outweighs their sense of guilt. Equally important, it is the parents who encourage the children's curiosity and motivation for learning. Children will learn a great many things in order to please their parents and win their approval.

But parents are not, by and large, early childhood educators. This is true for several reasons. In the first place, parents are biased. It is hard for them to see their children objectively without reading either too much or too little into their verbal or motor behavior. Objectivity is critical if children are to be presented with the kinds of experiences that will help them realize their intellectual potential to the fullest. Parents also lack the training in early childhood development that would enable them to assess what kinds of materials and activities are most conducive to maximum growth.

Parents can, of course, do a great deal to facilitate the child's development. It is important for parents not only to love and protect children but also to talk to them, read to them, play with them, and take them to the park, museum, and zoo. In so doing parents instill the most important factor in the child's successful education—namely, motivation and enthusiasm for learning.

Early childhood professionals can do this as well, but they will be successful only to the extent that they reinforce a motivation and enthusiasm for learning that has come from the home. But the early childhood educator has the skills, materials, and setting to channel the young child's motivation and emerging skills into the most productive directions. Most parents do not have the time, energy, skills, materials, or settings available to the early childhood educator. What parents do at home is not the same as what the teacher does in a program.

Early childhood education, then, is different both from what is provided in the schools by elementary school teachers and from what is provided in the homes by parents. When we ignore these differences and attempt to teach young children as if they were elementary school pupils, we put them at risk for short-term stress and long-term personality damage.

Short-Term Risks

Basically, stress is a demand for adaptation. In this broad sense, of course, stress is coincident with life itself. In a more narrow clinical sense, however, stress refers to any excessive demand for adaptation. What is excessive, in turn, depends upon both the individual and the demands. Elsewhere (Elkind, 1984) I have suggested that each individual has two sources of energy with which to deal with stress. One of these is what I term clock energy. It is the energy that we use up in pursuing the tasks of daily living and that is replenished with food and rest. What I call calendar energy, in contrast, is the energy involved in growth and development that is given to us in a more or less fixed quantity and that determines our total life span.

The early symptoms of stress are those associated with clock energy—fatigue, loss of appetite, and decreased efficiency. When the excessive demands continue without adequate time for replenishment, the individual has to draw upon calendar energy.

When this happens psychosomatic stress symptoms like headaches and stomachaches begin to appear that can do injury to the organism and shorten the life span. In young children exposed to formal instruction, both types of stress symptoms are frequently in evidence.

The reason for this is straightforward. Formal instruction puts excessive demands upon young children. A concrete example may help to make the point. As we have seen, the learning of young children is "permeable" (Elkind, 1987) in the sense that they do not learn in the narrow categories defined by adults such as "reading," "math," "science," and so on. At the level at which young children learn there are no sharp boundaries. The focus upon a specific learning task, as demanded by formal instruction, is thus at variance with the natural mode of the young child's learning. From the viewpoint of formal instruction, the multiple learning potential of the young child is often seen as evidence of lack of interest or motivation for learning. Adult distress at such "failures" on the part of the child contributes to child stress.

To be sure, formal instruction is but one of the many demands made upon a young child in a formal educational program. Other stresses include the child's being separated from his or her parents and being in a new place with strange children and adults, where the youngster is required to learn new rules of conduct. Although the demands of formal instruction may in themselves not be sufficient to overstrain the young child's reservoir of clock energy, the combination of stresses associated with formal schooling can be sufficient to produce stress symptoms. In contrast, young children in a sound early childhood educational program have the support of activities suited to their learning style. This eliminates the stresses occasioned by the formal curriculum and the stilted teacher-child interactions inherent in such instruction.

Long-Term Effects

One long-term danger of early instruction is the potential harm it can do to the child's motivation for learning. The spontaneous learning of young children is self-directed (Elkind, 1987) as well as permeable. Children learn their native language not because anyone is "teaching" them that language in a formal way but because the child has both the need and the capacity to learn language and uses the language models and verbal interactions in the environment to acquire this most complicated skill. Young children have their own set of learning priorities.

To be sure, there are some things young children need to be taught, such as what might be called "healthy" fears. Young children need to learn not to touch fire, not to insert their fingers in electric sockets, and not to play with appliances. Such learning is not self-directed but is necessary for survival. On the intellectual plane, however, children's natural curiosity about the world around them is a strong directive for learning the basic categories and concepts of the physical world. Sound early childhood education encourages their self-directed learning by providing an environment rich in materials to explore, manipulate, and talk about.

When adults intrude in this self-directed learning and insist upon their adult learning priorities, such as reading or math, they interfere with the self-directed impulse. Children can learn something from this instruction, but it may be something other than what the adult intended. The child may learn to become dependent upon adult direction and not to trust his or her own initiative. Erik Erikson (1950) described early childhood as the period when the balance between the sense of initiative and the sense of guilt is struck. And this balance has lifelong consequences.

A child whose self-directed learning is encouraged will develop a sense of initiative that will far outweigh a sense of guilt about getting things started. On the other hand, a child whose self-directed learning is interfered with, who is forced to follow adult learning priorities, may acquire a strong sense of guilt about any self-initiated activities. One risk of early instruction, then, is that it may encourage a sense of guilt at the expense of a sense of initiative.

A personal anecdote may help make this risk concrete. Several years ago I met a renowned psychiatrist who told me the following story. In the 1930s psychologist Myrtle McGraw (1935) carried out what has become a classic study of the contributions of nature and nurture to motor development. McGraw's study involved twin boys, Johnny and Jimmy. She trained one of the twins, Johnny, in a variety of motor tasks such as climbing and riding a tricycle. Jimmy was not trained, and Johnny soon surpassed him in these skills. On the other hand, after the training was discontinued, Jimmy quickly caught up with his brother, so that by the end of the year in which the training took place there was no difference in motor skills between the twins. In motor learning, maturation appeared to be at least as important as training.

What the psychiatrist told me, however, was that he had seen the twins several years after the investigation was complete. When he examined the two boys, he found a striking difference in their personalities and particularly their approach to learning. Johnny, the twin who had been trained, was diffident and insecure. He seemed always to be looking for adult direction and approval of his activities. Jimmy, the untrained twin, was quite the opposite. Self-confident and self-assured, he undertook activities on his own without looking to the adults in the situation for guidance and direction. Although this example is anecdotal, it does suggest the potential risk of too much adult intervention in the self-directed learning of young children.

Early instruction also puts the child at intellectual risk. Jean Piaget (1950) emphasized the importance of what he called "reflective abstraction" for the mental ability of the child. A child who is engaging in self-directed learning can reflectively abstract from those activities. The results of that reflective abstraction are to encourage the growth of new mental abilities. Piaget gives the example of a child who is rearranging ten pebbles. The child first makes them into a square, then into a circle, and then into a triangle. What the child discovers, as a result of his activity, is that no matter how he arranges the pebbles they still remain ten in number. In effect, the child has learned the difference between perception and reason. Perceptually it may appear as if there are more pebbles in one configuration than in another, but reason tells the child that they are the same.

When adults intrude upon the child's learning, they interfere with this process of reflective abstraction. What characterizes formal instruction is that it presents the child with contents to be learned. Flashcards present the child with a visual configuration the child must discriminate and memorize. Teaching young children phonics is another example of presenting them with an association they must learn without much active intervention or exploration. Rote learning and memorization, the stuff of much formal education, provide little opportunity for reflective abstraction. But reflective abstraction is essential for the full realization of the child's cognitive abilities.

The introduction of formal instruction too early puts the child at social risk as well as at risk motivationally and intellectually. One aspect of formal instruction, thankfully absent in sound early childhood education, is the introduction of the notions of right and wrong. These notions not only orient the child's thinking but also introduce social comparison. One child gets an answer right and another gets it wrong; therefore one child is smarter, better than the other. Such social comparisons are harmful enough among school-age children, but they are really damaging among preschoolers.

This damage can occur because the focus upon right and wrong orients children away from self-directed and self-reinforcing sources of self-esteem. Instead, they are directed primarily toward adult approval and social comparison as sources of self-appraisal. This is in opposition to the self-esteem a child attains from successfully completing a self-initiated and self-directed task. The danger of early instruction from a socialization point of view, then, is that it can make children overly dependent upon others for their sense of self-worth. Sound early childhood education encourages children to feel good about themselves as a consequence of their own achievements.

The foregoing descriptions of damage to motivation, intellectual growth, and self-esteem are potential risks that are not always realized in every child who is miseducated. But why put the child at risk in the first place? There is really no evidence that early formal instruction has any lasting or permanent benefits for the child, and it could well do serious and permanent damage to the youngster's emerging personality.

It is reasonable to conclude, then, that the early instruction of young children derives more from adult needs and priorities than it does from what we know is good pedagogy for young children.

What Can Be Done?

The miseducation of young children, so prevalent in America today, ignores the well-founded and noncontroversial differences between early childhood education and formal education. The first task of educators is to reassert these differences and their importance, and reeducate parents, administrators, and legislators regarding them. And it must be made clear that it is not out-of-home programs for young children that are potentially harmful but only the wrong kind of out-of-home programs.

Specialists in this field must work, first and foremost, for the recognition that early childhood education is an educational program in its own right, and that it is both unique and valuable. This value does not derive from the fact that it is "pre" something or other, or that it does or does not prepare children for formal schooling. Rather, its value lies in the fact that it is a systematic program of education, and it must be valued for the same reason primary or secondary education is valued—namely, because education contributes to a richer and fuller life.

If educators can convey this message, then the pressure to make early childhood education a miniature of primary education will diminish and true early childhood education will find its place in public schools, day-care centers, nursery schools, and home-care settings. Early childhood education has been waiting in the wings for a long time. Its appearance on the stage as an accepted part of education with its own special place in the educational cast of characters is long overdue. Giving early childhood education its rightful role in the drama of education can only enrich the whole performance.

REFERENCES

Aries, P. (1962). *Centuries of childhood*. New York: Alfred A. Knopf.

Bloom, B. S. (1964). *Stability and change in human characteristics*. New York: Wiley.

Bruner, J. (1960). *The process of education*. Cambridge, MA: Harvard University Press.

Doman, G. (1965). *Teach your baby to read*. London: Jonathan Cape.

Eastman, P., & Barr, J. L. (1985). *Your child is smarter than you think*. New York: Morrow & Co.

Elkind, D. (1987). *The miseducation of children: Superkids at risk*. New York: Alfred A. Knopf.
———. (1984). *All grown up and no place to go: Teenagers in crises*. Reading, MA: Addison-Wesley.
Erikson, E. H. (1950). *Childhood and society*. New York: Norton.
Freud, S. (1938). Infantile sexuality. In A. A. Brill (Ed.), *The basic writings of Sigmund Freud*. New York: Random House.
Froebel, F. (1904). *Pedagogics of the kindergarten*. New York: D. Appleton.
Hunt, J. McV. (1961). *Intelligence and experience*. New York: Ronald Press.
Ledson, S. (1975). *Teach your child to read in 60 days*. Don Mills, Ontario: Publishing Co.
McGraw, M. B. (1935). *A study of Johnny and Jimmy*. New York: Appleton-Century-Croft.
Montessori, M. (1912). *The Montessori method*. Philadelphia: Frederick & Stokes.
Piaget, J. (1950). *The psychology of intelligence*. London: Routledge & Kegan Paul.
White, S. H. (1970). Some general outlines of the matrix of developmental changes between five and seven years. *Bulletin of the Orton Society*, *20*, 41–57.

CHAPTER 7

Policy, Implementation, and the Problem of Change

SEYMOUR B. SARASON

Throughout this volume, various authors raise questions regarding the capacity of schools to accommodate the unique needs of young children and their families. In each case, the author cites specific issues that must be addressed if schools are to meet the developmental needs of this younger clientele. Yet, the general processes of, and strategies for, school change have not been fully addressed. The purpose of this chapter is twofold; first, to look more closely at how schools do and do not change, and second, to look at one specific strategy related to change, namely, the use of commissions as agents of educational reform. Throughout this discussion, the complexities of changing institutions will be unraveled, and the commission strategy, used so frequently to legitimize increased public expenditures in early education, will be explored.

Changing Educational Institutions: Unlearned Lessons—Unclear Goals

In a recent meeting, in informal conversation, one educator said to another: "The educational scene is really changing." The reply was: "The educational scene has already changed. It is a new ball game." Both individuals intended their statements to mean that the perceived changes should be regarded as desirable.

That interchange raises a number of questions I wish to address. The first is: is there a general factor common to these changes? Let me list a sample of changes that have been proposed or have been implemented:

1. Children's promotion through the school years should be on the basis of tested achievement and on no other grounds.
2. The curriculum, especially in the secondary schools, should be largely prescribed to ensure knowledge and competency in core subject matter, with a renewed emphasis on the scientific-technological knowledge and competency so necessary in modern society.
3. Schools should be orderly places where a serious attempt is made to meet the needs of individual students but not to the point where those who are disorderly interfere with the education of others.
4. Entrance into the teaching profession will or should no longer be possible on the undergraduate level.
5. The competency of teachers must be established before they become full-fledged teachers and will be evaluated at intervals throughout their professional career.
6. That most teachers are or will be competent should not preclude special recognition and rewards for the gifted teacher.
7. The professional development of teachers requires career-long participation in forums that expose them to new knowledge, techniques, and perspectives.
8. As in other professions, it is desirable that teachers have the opportunity to receive recognition of their competency on a national as well as local level through a process of national certification.

Is there a common factor? As I see it, the common factor is that change will take place by raising and monitoring standards of performance so that standards are higher than they are now. In the abstract, there is nothing wrong with such attempts at change. Precisely because schools are public institutions, and thus are the creation and responsibility of local and state legislative-constitutional bodies, the proclaiming of new public policies requires actions by the legislative-administrative bodies. In the past five years, these political bodies, in almost every state, have mandated the raising and monitoring of higher standards of performance by students and educational personnel. But if one applauds the desire of legislative-administrative bodies to effect change, one has to ask how successful past efforts by similar bodies have been in bringing about desired changes by putting them into effect and then monitoring them.

As I read that history, two things stand out: each new effort at changing schools seeks to undo the previous one (compare the present effort to the one in the sixties), and what in the new effort is seen as raising standards is by the previous one perceived as a corruption of standards. Restricting myself to the present decade, I have never heard any proponents for new efforts for educational change say that pendulum swings are desirable or inevitable. On the contrary, these proponents, regardless of the substance of their proposals, seem to assume that what they advocate is a permanent "solution," a kind of compass that guarantees that schools will not veer off course. When I have pointed this out to proponents, they are initially puzzled and silent because they (the more thoughtful ones) know that schools are in a transactional relationship with a society that has changed and will continue to change in significant ways, predictable and unpredictable. The relationship is bidirectional, not understandable in the usual cause-and-effect or stimulus-response way of thinking.

If you truly believe in a transactional relationship reflecting reciprocal change on the part of both, should you not be restrained in your criticism of those whose efforts you seek to undo, those who were grappling with what for them was a changing society no less than it now is for you? It is unfair, indeed mindless, to criticize educators and others because they were trying to adapt to a changing social scene, unless you believe that they were part of a grand conspiracy to foist their ideas and values on a society that saw no need to change, which certainly was not the case in the sixties when myriad groups external to schools were clamoring for change.

We must criticize—not the need and desire to change—but we must be alert to mistakes made in the past that we should try to avoid. The first mistake, still being made, is that we believe there is a mandated way of changing and structuring schools that will make future change unnecessary—that there is a way of "solving" the problem so that we never have to solve it again. But there was and is a more grievous mistake. Because we are not dealing with problems that have solutions in the natural science sense of solution, those of us in the educational arena deal with problems that must be "solved" again, and again, and again. Therefore, advocates of change are faced with a problem that is as critical as it is difficult: How do you build into the processes of change the means for recognizing and dealing with the predictable and unpredictable consequences of the rationale powering the effort? How do you build into that effort the humility that allows you and others to confront mistakes in rationale and process, or mistakes in identifying the nature and scope of societal change?

This is a difficult challenge, made all the more so because efforts to change schools have always taken place in an adversarial context in which the combatants varied widely in terms of attitudes, goals, self-interest, turf, professional status, power, and all else that makes for heated controversy. These controversies existed in and outside of schools, as well as between schools and other outside agencies. And the winners—in the sense of a particular policy being formally adopted—had the dubious satisfaction of dealing with the losers, individuals or collectivities, who usually viewed losing not as a final defeat but as a stimulus for further battle. In describing these efforts, I intend no value judgment; I am describing what I perceive the historical record documents.

The history of educational change is far more complicated than I can indicate in this chapter. But I trust that I have made clear that efforts at change that are based on certainty about rationale and outcome—that are based on the possession of "the truth" and/or complete faith in the diagnosis of societal change—are doomed either to failure or to disappointment with minimal change. It is a kind of certainty that makes examination of underlying assumptions virtually impossible and that produces the mind set: given this problem, there is *one*, and only *one*, way of "solving" it, now and forever. To act as if one is certain at the same time one accepts the fact that certainty in these arenas is a myth is no easy matter. The history of efforts at educational change suggests that it may be impossible. The need to feel and act with certainty in regard to complicated changing institutions in a changing society is as understandable as it is mischievously self-defeating.

Let me now turn to another question stimulated by the interchange with which this chapter began—the optimism and satisfaction with which both individuals viewed current efforts to change schools. What are the goals these efforts are intended to achieve that justify such optimism? Obviously, there is not one goal but several that in combination increase the chances that each will be reached. So, each of the eight proposals for change I listed earlier has a goal, and the expectation is that achieving one goal will help, directly or indirectly, to achieve the others. But now let us ask again: do these goals have a common factor, an ultimate goal, an overarching one that gives meaning to the educational enterprise? I continue to be disheartened and amazed at how hard it is for advocates of change to state an overarching goal, a vision that says that all goals are instrumental to achieving a superordinate one. Only when I have pursued this question with people in sustained and often heated argument have we agreed about a superordinate goal which, if reached in part or whole, would, to indulge understatement, justify the enterprise.

The common goal is to enable each child to be intellectually curious about the nature of self, the social world, and the natural world. That may not be the most felicitous way of putting it, but it does emphasize that the capacity to be and remain curious, to be a question asker, an answer seeker, is essential to "the good life." What do proposals for educational change say about this? How do the diverse subgoals relate to this superordinate goal? These questions are unanswered. Some might argue that there is more than one overarching goal or argue for another one, but no one would downplay the centrality of the one I stated. But if they do not downplay it, they nevertheless ignore it. Let me make this concrete by an example that has recently become a popular mechanism for promoting educational change, namely, the use of commissions as levers of reform.

The Role of Commissions in the Process of Educational Change

In 1985–86, I was a member of the Early Childhood Education Commission appointed by Mayor Koch, charged with recommending how to make educational opportunities available for four-year-olds in New York City. I agreed to be on the commission not because of my expertise, which was not all that much, but because of my interest in how changes in society, the research and theoretical literature, advocacy and lobbying groups, the political climate, and leadership combine to bring about a new public policy that will ameliorate the adverse consequences of a recognized problem.

Like many commissions, this one began with multiple agendas. Although it was clear from the beginning that any set of recommendations would be implemented over time for all four-year-olds on a voluntary basis, it was no less clear that the major target groups were those who came from economically impoverished backgrounds, a significant number of whom spoke or comprehended English only a little or not at all. Further, while the stated goal of the commission was the prevention of dropout and academic failure, the commission also needed to distinguish between near- and long-term goals, the means and the ends.

To help clarify the commission's goals, I posed the following question at meetings: what do we mean by *education* for four-year-olds? The word *education* is associated with imagery of a group of children in an enclosed space where an adult "teaches" them "something" they need to know. And what children need to know is predetermined in terms, among other things, of what the adults think children are like: their capabilities, interests, cognitive styles, and so on. What are distinguishing characteristics of four-year-olds? How well do model programs take them into account? How should our observations influence what we propose? These are the questions I kept raising.

These questions had three sources. The first was the importance I place in the fact that young children are quintessentially question-asking and question-answering organisms, curious about the nature of self, of others, and of their social and physical world. The second source was my conviction that capitalizing on and nurturing their curiosities is our most important task, especially for those children whose social world does not recognize or cannot capitalize on their curiosities. And the third was that most programs I have observed over the years have been too similar to classrooms in our schools where teachers pour knowledge *into* children, as if children are empty vessels to be filled.

In light of what I said earlier, it is not surprising that I proposed as the superordinate goal the nurturing and sustaining of a child's already existing curiosities about self and the social and physical worlds. Please note that although such a goal gives a central role to a cognitive process—a normal and ever present human capacity that has a directive and organizing function—it is one that is always associated with or embedded in social-interpersonal contexts. The questions that children and we ask always involve the social and interpersonal, the internal and external worlds. The task of the adult or the teacher is to respect, build on, and direct that cognitive capacity in ways that sustain it. Far from being empty vessels, children are full of wonder and awe about themselves and their worlds, eager to explore and understand what is palpably in and around them.

No one ever disagreed with what I said. But I was not seeking agreement—that I could count on—but rather a discussion of the means whereby we would maximize the chances that the process of implementation would be consistent with the goal. What does such a goal mean for the preparation and selection of teachers? What would we have to observe in a preschool setting to conclude that the goal was being achieved, in part at least? What roles could or should families play and what implications did that have for staffing? What kinds of support and in-service experiences would be helpful to staff? And, finally of course, what did all this mean for budget and what would be minimally acceptable compromises in the face of limited resources?

Although admittedly it was difficult to address all these issues, this commission did make one particularly significant mistake—that of minimizing the issue of continuity. Whatever benefits four-year-olds derive from participation in a program, regardless of the substantive thrust of the program, are diluted unless continuity is addressed. I emphasized the point and, more important, it was emphasized by three consultants who were brought as a group before the commission to proffer advice. The panel consisted of Irving Sigel, Sheldon White, and Edward Zigler, each of whom had vast research and practical experience with programming for preschools. They did not hold identical positions, although differences among them were far less than their areas of agreement. One point about which they explicitly and vigorously agreed was: if the transition from preschool to the traditional kindergarten classroom was, so to speak, left to chance, and there was no meaningful discussion between the personnel in the two settings, many of the developmental gains these children had made would be diluted or even lost. To go from the culture of one setting to that of another is or should be more than a matter of transportation or registration. Indeed, this position is very briefly stated in the report, but the questions it raises and its implications for programming are absent. There were too many other goals and issues that bedeviled the commission to permit its taking what I said seriously.

I do not say this critically. I have served on too many commissions to continue to expect that their reports will go much beyond the most general type of statements. In practice, the function of a commission is to confirm in broad outline what political leadership has already decided needs to be done—that is, to give a basis for specific actions as yet undecided or undescribed. Those specific actions get forged through a process involving the political system, conflicting agency interests, and formal and informal power struggles centering around status and budget. This commission was in no way unusual.

Beyond the Commission Report: The Pragmatics of Early Schooling

Creating programs for four-year-olds confronts educators with far more than theories of development and the organization of a curriculum. That task confronts them with all that is known about the cultures of the school and teacher training programs, and the changes in them the new programs may require. It forces them to pay attention to the organizational climate or ambience of the program setting—leadership, decision making, planning, problem solving, in-service education—especially if the program is embedded in a larger, bureaucratic system.

Planning for and implementing programs for four-year-olds involve more than psychology and matters of curriculum. How should their teachers be selected and prepared? How large a pool of prospective teachers is needed to make selection possible? Should their preparation be conducted *primarily* on site or, as it usually is, in a college classroom? How should the site be organized and administered to further the development not only of the children but of the staff as well? If the conditions whereby a staff learns, changes, and grows do not exist for them, can they create and sustain those conditions for the children? What should be the thrust of the relationship between the site and the schools to which the children will go? What is known, or needs to be known, about the culture of the school in developing that relationship? Faced as always with the brute fact of limited resources—the one fact we can rely on—how can our usual conception of resources be *redefined* so as to compensate in some measure for limited resources? Can we continue to proceed on the unarticulated definition that a resource is that which you pay for and, therefore, control?

Creating these programs clearly requires that our conception of resources be examined. The disease of professionalism is that professionals define problems in ways so as to require more professionals, thereby rendering the problem utterly intractable. For many years I suffered from that disease. The educational scene has changed, but the changes in no way derive from a reexamination of traditional assumptions or axioms that seem so right, natural, and proper that they are never articulated and challenged. So, for example, one of these assumptions is that the formulation of a new policy, and giving it legislative or administrative sanction, is the first and most important step toward change. How can one expect change if one does not have a new policy, a directive that explicitly states that behavioral and programmatic regularities will change? That assumption explains why we have commissions and task forces: to give force to the effort to alter regularities.

I would argue—and I have history on my side—that the formulation of a new policy is both the easiest and most dangerous step in the effort at change. It is, relatively speaking, an easy step because not only has the problem been identified but alternative "solutions" to it have already gained currency. The task is to choose among alternatives or to combine features of several in some way. I have never known of a commission that did not recommend action for change. It is the most dangerous step because those who formulate a new policy almost always are prey to what I call the "engineering fallacy": implementing a new policy is, like building a new bridge, an engineering task for which we have the appropriate knowledge, time, and resources. That is to say, it is a process of application based on tested knowledge that tells us what the problems will be and how they can be successfully overcome. When an engineering firm is given a contract to build a new bridge, we have established that it has a successful track record and, therefore, that it is capable of building the bridge we need. That, unfortunately, is not the case in the implementation of a new educational policy. Indeed, implementing such a policy in practice does not rest on basic knowledge or tested principles that we can depend on to bring about the changes we desire. The bridge builder can be regarded, among other things, as an applied physicist who can make decisions about materials and designs without undue worry about the validity of the scientific underpinnings those decisions must rest on. But the implementors of educational policy are not in that fortunate situation, and that is what the policymakers do not comprehend—which, in large measure, explains the mess we are in.

I do not say "mess" for purposes of derogation but rather to suggest that professionals' enamorment with policy has directed them and the public from confronting how poorly the process of institutional change is comprehended. This is not to say that in recent decades certain things have not been learned about that process. But what has been learned has not been assimilated either by policymakers or by implementors, and we continue to underestimate the extent of our ignorance.

These issues are salient when we consider programming for four-year-olds. Just as I earlier bemoaned the absence of an overarching vision about what we want a student to be like when schooling is over, I have to ask how programming for four-year-olds fits in to an overarching vision of *family living*? Clearly, the size, structure, and stability of families have changed (and continue to change) rather dramatically. The patterns are many and we are far from understanding what any of these portends for the young child. If it is understandable that the proponents for programming can tell us only about its benefits for schooling, nevertheless one is certainly justified in asking how such programming may alter, positively or negatively, family living. As soon as you ask such a question, you are confronted with the task of articulating what you consider to be healthy family living. Are we making the assumption that programming for four-year-olds always and inexorably has positive effects on family living? Are we also assuming that it is the case that the benefits for the child from such programming are always greater than remaining at home? If the answer to either question is in the negative, why is there so little discussion about when and why such programming is *not* indicated?

At the very least, these questions give added force to another question: in practice, what should be the transactional relationship between program and family? Frankly, I bristle when I hear people uttering the pious generalization that families should be involved in these programs, because in my experience those transactional relationships are superficial and ritualistic in the extreme. I am reminded here of Public Law 94-142 which mandated a parental role in the education of a handicapped child. Practice has made a mockery of that mandate. But at least that law was unusually specific about the rights and roles of families. Indeed, one of the people who helped write that legislation told me that the guts of it were those sections that sought to alter the meaningfulness of the relationship between school and family. In the case of programming for four-year-olds, such specificity is almost always absent. If you seek to become specific, you are forced to be clear about your conception of productive family living, a clarity that is by no means easy because it derives from the arena of the "shoulds and oughts."

Why does an intellectually serious person have to deal with a Plato, a Pestalozzi, a John Dewey, and similar figures? They gave us overarching visions of the good life in the good society, visions that stir the imagination and act as a kind of conscience, reminding us that some questions and issues are in some ultimate sense more important than others for people and society.

PART III

Research and Curriculum: Points of View

CHAPTER 8

Early Childhood Education: Developmental Enhancement or Developmental Acceleration?

IRVING E. SIGEL

The purpose of this chapter is to present the case for enrichment, not acceleration, in preschool programs. The reason for making a public statement advocating enrichment and rejecting acceleration as an early childhood education objective is because of the growing pressures by parents and educators to pressure young children to achieve academic skills in preschool. This pressure to accelerate young children is fraught with danger for their emotional health. I believe it puts children at risk for achievement anxiety. There are alternatives that would provide them with rich educational opportunities that should lead to their becoming motivated to learn and achieve with minimal anxiety.

To provide a perspective on the acceleration-enrichment issue, I shall define early childhood education, examine education efforts for preschoolers over the past thirty-five years, provide some historical overview, and then present a preschool model that illustrates how a developmentally based preschool program can enhance and enrich the lives of preschoolers without pressure to push or accelerate.

Part of the research reported in this paper was supported by the National Institute of Child Health and Human Development Grant No. R01-HD10686 to Educational Testing Service, National Institute of Mental Health Grant No. R01-MH32301 to Educational Testing Service, and Bureau of Education of the Handicapped Grant No. G007902000 to Educational Testing Service.

Early Childhood Education

Defining the Term

Early childhood education (ECE), in this context, refers to school-based educational programs for children usually from about the age of three. The education of young children is an accepted form of a professional activity that encompasses both teaching and policy-making. The organization dedicated to this activity is The National Association for the Education of Young Children. Its members contend that schooling for children as young as age three is a bona fide educational experience that can influence the course of children's intellectual, social, and emotional development. Although children from all social classes have been enrolled in such programs, in general, ECE programs have been private, and since tuitions were involved, the pupils have tended to come from privileged families.

A distinction has to be made between ECE programs and day care. The former has as its mission primarily an educational experience for the children, whereas day care provides an educational experience in the context of custodial care of children, thereby enabling parents to work. This difference in program objectives leads to different requirements for the professional staff to meet the custodial or educational objectives.

Traditional Goals of ECE Programs

Although most individuals engaged in early childhood education hold similar assumptions regarding the feasibility of teaching young children, there are vast differences in their educational orientations. It should be remembered that state and professional regulations regarding qualifications for preschool teachers do not usually specify the type of curriculum that is to be used. The major exception is the Montessori program (Evans, 1975); certification as a teacher in this program is the responsibility of the American Montessori Association. In other cases, certification varies by states. The underlying objectives among the various programs, however, tend to be very similar. This commonality is reflected in an earlier statement of mine:

> Advocating preschool as an educational experience is based on the hypothesis that children [at the preschool age] are

> ready to profit from extended educational experiences, that the home cannot maximize such opportunities, and finally, that development is cumulative where early experiences facilitate children's realization of their capabilities. To the degree that this hypothesis is valid, to that degree the child is expanding his horizons within his limits, thereby expending his efforts in successful and comprehensible activities. (Sigel, 1972, p. 14)

The goal that has traditionally characterized preschool has been the expanding-horizon concept. Providing children with opportunities to relate to other children, to become acquainted with new materials like paints and clay, and to be exposed to new adults—all in a physical environment that is child-centered—helps children expand their knowledge about themselves and others.

The rules governing preschools also have tended to be similar. Group activities, opportunities for individual free play, and rest and snack times are common. Thus, a tradition has developed that governs preschool education. The similarities in these outward forms, however, often mask the disparate goals set by various programs which define how teachers are expected to interact with the children (Kamii, 1981). For example, for some programs, like Montessori, the most important focus is self-development (Evans, 1975); for others it is learning how to work in a group setting (Biber, 1984). These variations often reflect different theories of child development and lead to differences in implementation. For example, the main focus on personal social development is an outgrowth of a developmental perspective stemming from a psychoanalytic framework. For those programs that emphasize self-development and particular ways of learning, the structure of the space and the way teachers interact are directed toward these goals and children have their own private work areas. In contrast, when programs emphasize socialization through group experiences, the space is organized to facilitate group interactions.

In spite of the differences, however, there has been a general tendency to cater to the interests and talents of middle-class children; the basic concept is to enrich their lives emotionally, intellectually, and socially.

ECE as Compensatory Education

During the 1960s, with the advent of the War on Poverty program, considerable attention was paid to the difficulties that low-income children—black, white, and Hispanic—were having in school. It was believed that these children were headed for lives of poverty unless educational intervention forestalled the problems they would have mastering academic fundamentals. Many theorists and practitioners were eager to participate in an all-out effort to provide compensatory education under the aegis of Head Start (a federally funded effort) for low-income children (Kamii, 1981). Such writers as Deutsch (1964), Hunt (1961), Piaget (1952), Sigel (1965), Weikart, Epstein, Schweinhart, and Bond (1972), and Zigler and Valentine (1979) contributed to the theory and planning or participated in some of the evaluation of these early programs. (See Evans, 1975, and Biber, 1984, for an account of these efforts.)

The programs for these low-income children had a primary goal—to intervene and to alter the course of their psychosocial development, and in so doing give them the proper start so that they could profit from regular schooling. Most of these programs were based on a deficit orientation, which holds that impoverished children are deficient in the verbal, intellectual, and social skills needed to adapt to school. The programs for them were referred to as *compensatory*, and in a sense they were an effort to accelerate the children from where they were to where they should be. The implicit norm was that of the middle-class child who had already acquired appropriate readiness to function well in school. Where middle-class children had been enrolled in preschool classes to expand their horizons and enrich their socialization experiences, low-income children needed the same opportunities, but also a more basic education in language, social skills, and play situations as well.

One consequence of this attention to low-income children was the realization that ECE educators were not ready for this program; their experience was inadequate. Consequently, various types of programs proliferated, many based on different theories but dedicated to the common goal of helping these children get ready for school (Stanley, 1973).

The outcome has been a tremendous interest in preschool

education for other groups—for example, physically and mentally handicapped youngsters—because evidence from many studies with low-income children indicated that outcomes were well worth the investment of time and money (for example, Lazar & Darlington, 1982; Miller, Bugbee, & Hybertson, 1985; Weikart et al., 1978). If early experiences influence later behavior, it follows that early intervention targeted at specific educational objectives will influence later school performance.

The success of these programs for the underprivileged and the handicapped invigorated preschool efforts in general. These successes were contagious, leading some to contend that if preschool could correct deficits, then it certainly could be advantageous for middle-class children in ways not generally accepted earlier. Disagreement still exists on this point, however. Many believe that children, by virtue of their middle-class status, do not need an enriched preschool experience. The fallacy in this argument is the assumption that middle-class children are products of a homogeneous environment. This is not the case. Rather, there is variability in the way middle-class parents participate in and direct their children's intellectual and social development.

One factor that influences middle-class children's intellectual development is maternal schooling (Laosa, 1983). Laosa's study showed that the level of parental schooling affected child rearing among Chicano families. This study was only one of many demonstrating that parents' level of schooling, as indicated by social status, is an important factor influencing children's cognitive level and school achievement (Hess, 1970; Laosa, 1982). Teaching strategies, conversation, and participation in activities are more varied among middle-class parents than is commonly assumed (Sigel, McGillicuddy-DeLisi, & Johnson, 1980). Our own data support the argument that although middle-class children overall are better prepared for school success, there are sufficient differences among them to justify the assertion that ECE can have a significant impact on their cognitive development (Sigel & McGillicuddy-DeLisi, 1984). In addition, when colleagues and I at Educational Testing Service developed a program with middle-class children, we were surprised at the wide range of abilities they showed on cognitive tasks. At the end of a year noticeable changes were found in their linguistic and thinking skills (Sigel, 1979).

Current Status of Early Childhood Programs

Although the goals of the majority of ECE programs in the past tended to focus on expanding children's horizons, the scene now is shifting, creating a more dramatic cleavage among ECE professionals. The issues have resolved into controversy over the pace of teaching academics in preschool. For some, the new role of ECE is to generate programs for all children, privileged or not, that would specifically influence the course of their academic learning. Thus, for children from impoverished families, the ECE programs would provide a service similar to that of Head Start—remediation and academics—whereas, for more privileged children not in need of remediation, preschool would provide academic education—reading, writing, and arithmetic. These subjects would be taught to both groups, but methods of instruction would vary.

This distinction, although it sounds elitist, recognizes that, for children from low-income homes, early intervention could prevent subsequent academic failure. The research of Weikart et al. (1978)—a fifteen-year followup of children who were enrolled in a Piaget-type preschool program—indicated positive outcomes in terms of grade placement and general functioning. Other reports have also revealed that intervention programs were beneficial (Lazar & Darlington, 1982). In view of these results, then, there is reason to advocate continuation of intervention efforts as a way of heading off academic failure of a large segment of the population.

To argue that preschool is therefore important for middle-class children on the basis of the outcomes reported for impoverished children is to beg the question. My argument for the remaining sections of this chapter is that preschool per se is a positive educational experience and that children of middle-class families will benefit, but only relative to their intellectual and emotional needs, which are different from those of underprivileged children.

The Acceleration Concept

Before amplifying this argument, however, I want to address the acceleration issue. What is acceleration? *Acceleration is concep-*

tualized in developmental terms as placing intellectual and emotional demands on children—demands that seem over and above their cognitive and emotional level. The concept of acceleration seems to imply that activities like play and exploratory behavior are of minimal value for a child's social, cognitive, and emotional development.

Traditionally, the age at which children began academic work was age six. But now parents want their children to be given academic instruction in preschool so that they will be prepared to meet future challenges. Interestingly, this desire for acceleration is a relatively new phenomenon. The traditional ECE professionals contended that the preschool program should provide the important social and emotional background that would equip the child for further group experiences. Academic skills would be mastered in due course. This implied the maturational concept: children on their own develop a readiness for academic work.

Although evaluation of this trend toward emphasis on academics is not documented by concrete data, it is clear to me from conversations with teachers and parents and a review of the media that ECE programs are indeed beginning to stress academics. Parents want preschools and kindergartens to prepare or teach their children three Rs. Teachers report that parents are insisting that children learn to read in kindergarten; some even want their preschoolers enrolled in reading readiness and academic programs.

Thus, in the 1980s, the climate in the preschool field has changed, and an emphasis on what is called *cognitive stimulation* is increasing. The conflict is sharp between those who would teach children academic skills in kindergarten and preschool and those who would follow the more traditional ECE programs. This conflict, of course, generates disagreements over the choice of curriculum. Can cognitive stimulation be achieved in the preschool program without focusing on skill training or is such training—for example, in reading—necessary?

Evidence for Effects of ECE

In spite of the prevalence of ECE, little research has been done evaluating the effects of the experience for middle-class children, especially when the objectives were essentially social-emotional development in a group context. There was little reason for evaluation since most of the programs were in private or university-based settings—the nursery schools at universities were often teacher training facilities or research centers in child psychology, so that there was little interest in educational outcomes.

It was simply assumed that children involved in these types of educational situations would profit both in the present and in the long term from their being away from home and having to adjust to new experiences. They would become more independent and learn how to cooperate with new adults and children (Biber, 1984; Sigel, 1986). These were often described as among the most important contributions of preschool. In addition, the children would have the opportunity to explore a variety of new materials and develop new interests. Thus, anecdotal evidence and theoretical assumptions seemed to justify the maintenance of ECE.

Since middle-class children who were not handicapped or retarded were therefore not deficient in the prerequisites for school, preschool for them was often perceived as a luxury with little long-range educational merit. These views, of course, were not shared by professional ECE educators who were convinced on an experiential basis and with very little research that ECE provided a good foundation for the subsequent development of the children enrolled.

We have come full circle to determine the role of ECE. A major fallout of earlier intervention programs (as I indicated before) has been the awareness that the course of children's intellectual, social, and emotional development can be modified (Sigel, 1972). A further influence has been the growing body of research on cognitive functioning, which has demonstrated that the intellectual competence of young children has been underestimated.

The irony is that the new research findings regarding children's intellectual competence have been interpreted as justification for targeting newly *discovered* competencies for acceleration. For example, learning that children as young as one year old categorize their experiences encourages those who want to accelerate children to create exercises for lessons in categorization. But these newly discovered competencies are *not* newly acquired skills. Infants were engaging in such activities long before psychologists were on the scene. The discoveries were the result of psychologists and educators shifting their perspectives regarding children's capabilities and interests. Where in the past the focus might have been on children's emotional life, the current emphasis is on the cognitive domain. Thus, children's competencies have not changed; it is the educator's shift in focus that has changed. Children are not now a different species. They are just sensitive individuals with the same intellectual, social, and emotional needs as before. The renewed interest in ECE for middle-class children, then, may be simply the result of a misplaced use of new research findings.

Sequelae of Research on Cognitive Development

The growing interest in studying cognitive development, some have argued, is a fallout of our competition with the Soviet Union in the nuclear and space races, but I believe this is simplistic. Major shifts in research direction are not determined by a single event. Over the past twenty years there has been strong economic and scientific competition from the Soviet Union and West Germany, as well as from the Far East. These challenges to our belief that we are superior in scientific and economic matters have generated a lot of soul searching. Scientific progress depends on the quality of our educational system. Economic growth depends on the creativity and productivity of the American system. But the news has been that we are falling behind our competition.

Aside from reflecting on our own educational efforts for preparing our young people for careers in science, manufacturing, marketing, and other aspects of the economic establishment, we have looked to our competitors to identify the sources of their success. Thus, great interest has been generated in the educational systems of these countries. If we discover how Japanese schools and industry function, for example, we may answer some questions about our own future educational policy directions. This approach, however, is naive. To assume one can isolate one part of a culture like its educational practices and thereby modify our own educational system is to deny the fact that educational systems *reflect* their cultures. We cannot replicate Japanese educational approaches nor Japanese employees in the context of our Western democratic society.

What we are really doing by taking cues from these countries is reemphasizing the value of education and more to the point, concluding that if we accelerate our children's education, this will result in "more learning" and an improvement in their cognitive skills so that they will be more effective students. This rationale, coupled with parents' competitive spirit regarding their children's academic progress, has led to accelerating young children. These efforts have ranged from the Institutes for the Achievement of Human Potential program where mothers are taught to teach infants (twelve months of age and younger) to read, count, learn names of insects, and so on (Doman et al., 1981) to the teaching of academics in preschool.

I contend that these efforts at acceleration are dangerous for children's emotional development. Acceleration places children at risk for stress-related difficulties, for developing a faulty sense of personal worth, and for intellectual burnout.

Is there an alternative? Yes, we can provide young children with educational opportunities that are intellectually enhancing and enriching but that let them explore and express their curiosity without a sense of pressure. Children can be challenged in the educational setting without being judged as "good" or "smart" only if they perform according to teachers' criteria. Young children love to explore, to invent, to engage in fantasies. They should not be channeled in these activities. Rather, they should be allowed to learn from the consequences of their own actions, as long as the activities are neither physically nor psychologically dangerous. A program following these guidelines is the model my colleagues and I have developed at Educational Testing Service (Copple, Sigel, & Saunders, 1984; evaluated by Cocking, 1979). The next section describes that program briefly. (A more detailed account is available in the Copple et al., 1984, volume. In addition, see Sigel, 1987.)

A Nonacceleration Preschool Program

Although there are a number of ECE programs that focus on a holistic approach to development, such as the Bank Street program (Biber, 1984), I will focus on one my colleagues and I developed initially at the State University of New York

(SUNY) at Buffalo (1969–73) and then at Educational Testing Service (1974–79).

In the SUNY program, a low-income group of black children as young as two-and-a-half-years old was involved, and at ETS a group of middle-class children, aged four, enrolled. The same approach was used for both, but modified to meet the developmental and experiential status of these children. The program was based on the following principles derived in part from Jean Piaget and interpreted and elaborated by my colleagues and me. The program can be categorized as a cognitive developmental one, embedded in a social context. These principles guided the development of teaching strategies and materials:

1. The individual develops by actively constructing his (her) reality.
2. Development takes place through a process of discrepancy resolution.
3. Discrepancies are only perceived in relation to an individual's current expectations or knowledge.
4. Human beings understand their world through representation of it.
5. Representational competence develops in an orderly sequence.[1]
6. Representational competence develops fully only in response to interactions with the appropriate physical and social [emotional] environment (Copple et al., 1984).

These six principles formed the basis for a preschool program located at each setting where materials and teaching strategies were constructed to enable the child to face and cope with problems in physical, social, and self-knowledge. The basic idea was to create problems and help children solve them, in science, social-affective areas, music, and art. In this way the children's experiences were enriched since they helped define the level of interaction. Play was the prime activity to which our goals were addressed.

1. Representational competence refers to the individual understanding of the rule that ideas, feelings, and thoughts in general can be transformed from one medium to another. Manipulation of symbols involves representations. Understanding and using rules in this case defines representational competence.

The teachers' task was to calibrate their responses to the child's level of intellectual and social competence. For example, a rule was established that only four children could work in the block corner at one time. But rather than simply announce this to the children, we created a discrepant situation by bringing the group to the area and asking them how many could work at the place at one time. Each number was tried out and the children discovered that the number four was the right one. The rule was then established and communicated in a number of ways. The number *4* was written on the wall and a picture with four children was posted in the area. In this way the children become aware that the same idea could be communicated in different symbolic systems. This strategy is typical of how we fostered representational competence. Whenever there was a conflict because a child could not count to four, the teacher intervened and worked it out. In this way the children came to understand the rule itself, not just mechanically applying it. This strategy was followed as much as possible.

Other situations were created where children came to the problem as active learners—their natural state. Skills like reading and arithmetic were not deliberately fostered. Rather, the children were allowed to pursue their own interests as they expressed them. Books were available. Preschoolers are usually attracted to books because of pictures, and then they begin to simulate reading words. When the children asked about words, their questions were answered, but the teachers did not pressure them to learn; they did not set up structured situations in which the children were taught reading or numbers. In effect, the children's natural inclinations to play, to engage in problem solving, to learn how to share and get along with others were all part and parcel of their everyday experience.

More specific demonstrations of the types of lessons that can provide children with rich and productive learning experiences are presented in the appendix to this chapter. The lessons are typical of the program. Reviewing them, the reader will note that the teachers gave considerable thought to the rationale of the lessons, thinking through each phase of the lesson plan—the materials to be used, the teaching strategies, and the expected outcomes for the children.

Does such intensive planning preclude the opportunity for spontaneity? Not at all. The teacher is not locked into the lesson plan; rather, she now has a sense of direction that can serve as a guideline, but that can be altered when the children's responses are different from what is expected. For example, the child may not understand the teacher's question or may find the experience uninteresting. The teacher can shift in a way that will tune her into the child's perspective. The important point here is that the conceptual base of the lesson can stay the same, but the teaching strategies can be changed. When the teacher knows the rationale she can create alternatives as to the *how* of the lesson, keeping the *why* intact.

The lessons, however, formed only a part of the program. There were ample opportunities for the children themselves to initiate activity. Spontaneous interactions among children or between teacher and child could occur during free-play periods. Thus even though teachers planned lessons and set the stage for a variety of group and individual activities, they were not explicitly dominant. Teacher control was experienced through teaching strategies and rule setting. They might set the stage for action, but their strategies were to a large measure determined by children's intellectual and emotional stages. The teachers served as facilitators of child growth consistent with the child's developmental level.

The key factor that differentiates acceleration from enhancement is how teachers engage children and the degree and quality of control children have in the classroom.

Did the Children Profit?

Our results indicated dramatic changes in the children over the course of a year. Four aspects of representational competence were assessed as the crux of the evaluation program: (1) the ability to plan and think in terms of the future; (2) the ability to reconstruct information from the past and integrate it into the ongoing present; (3) the ability to understand the basic transformational rule that ideas can be represented in a variety of symbolic ways—for example, pictures, words, movement—and still retain their meaning (referred to as *conservation of meaning*); and

(4) the ability to transcend the ongoing present by transforming current experiences into some other symbolic modes.

Those children in the ETS program that focused on representational competence were compared to children in the more traditional-type program where the emphasis was on socialization. It was found that children in the experimental program were more successful in planning and predicting outcomes. They showed greater ability to handle complex language such as negation, and they tended to be more independent and effective problem solvers. There were no indications of the children showing stress or tension-related behaviors, nor was there any evidence of their feeling pressured (Cocking, 1979; Sigel, 1987). Parents reported that one of the longer term outcomes of the experimental program was that their children showed more initiative and developed more hobbies than did those in traditional-type programs.

Implications of ECE

In an informal study I did with kindergarten teachers, I found they paid no attention to the preschool children's special experiences. As one teacher said, "Since all the children in this area go to preschool, and since all preschools are alike, there is no reason to pay particular attention to that part of the child's experience."

But preschools do vary considerably in their emphasis, and children do come prepared to extend their interests. The preschool experience should be integrated in appropriate ways to the kindergarten and the first-grade programs. Teachers should learn to talk to each other across grade levels. Kindergarten and primary grade teachers should make it a point to share information about their programs so that continuity across the grades can be created. Such vertical integration would also eliminate repetition. Redundant experiences often contribute to preschoolers' feeling bored in kindergarten. Coordinating ECE with the kindergarten and primary grades by building on ECE experiences does not necessarily lead to acceleration and pressure. The kindergarten and subsequent experiences can be gauged relative to the children's earlier accomplishments. For example, more complex stories can be read, or more opportunities can be generated for creative experiences in art, music, or science. The degree of complexity can be determined if the kindergarten teacher knows what has gone on before.

Integration across grades should contribute to the children's solidifying their previous accomplishments en route to increasing their knowledge and cognitive skills. The findings reported by our program demonstrate that children can have a profitable experience appropriate to their developmental level. There is no acceleration involved here.

"But why bother at all?" someone might ask. The answer is straightforward: the children profit on two grounds. The first is that it is interesting and fun to go to school at this age. Children find enjoyment in acquiring new knowledge and developing friendships, which in itself is a sufficient reason. Chances are such experiences enhance children's sense of confidence, mastery, and self-control, which contributes to their development. The second reason is that children can expand their horizons, thereby acquiring a solid knowledge base upon which further growth can be built.

Who Should Be Responsible for ECE?

In the course of the interest in ECE, another issue has arisen: namely, who should be responsible for the program? The responsibility for ECE should be left to the child development specialists whose training is specifically geared to preschoolers. Children of this early age have needs, interests, and abilities different from those of older elementary schoolchildren. These professionals understand the dramatic developmental difference between even four- and five-year-olds.

Possessing a more clear-cut developmental perspective, early childhood educators, while differing on the academic issue, still hold to the conviction that certain developmental principles must be adhered to in educating young children. These principles, based on a set of conceptions not usually shared by public schoolteachers, are that development proceeds by stages, not ages; that preschoolers' emotional needs differ from older children's; that intellectually they need time to learn through play and exploration; that they need more freedom of movement; and that they must come to terms with themselves as learners. For these and other reasons, it is argued, preschoolers require special conditions and equipment congruent with their developmental needs. The size of the group and the teacher-child ratio also vary for young children.

Where Should Preschool Programs Be Housed?

Should four-year-olds be housed in a public school building under the aegis of the public schools? Opinions also differ on this question. Some public schools serve four-year-old children, but little is known about the educational consequences. For some the argument is that the educational arrangement has to change so that the preschool and upper grades manifest some continuity. The vertical integration concept, however, while developmental in nature, does not mean shifting the work of the kindergarten to the four-year-olds. Rather it means that programs for four-year-olds should be appropriate for that general age group, and that the children should gradually move into kindergarten depending on their developmental readiness.

There are those who oppose placing preschool programs under the aegis of public schools, fearing that preschools will become bureaucratic and rigid. The evidence for this is unclear. This is an issue that remains to be addressed more thoroughly than I have room for here, however.

Conclusions

From both a pragmatic and a historical perspective, backed up by some available data, there are good reasons for children to participate in an educational preschool prior to elementary school entry. And the benefits can be achieved without the children being subjected to undue stress or being deprived of important developmental tasks: playing, exploring, coming to understand the world around them, and fulfilling their emotional needs. Children taking part in a preschool experience where they are valued for themselves rather than for what they can do or how well they perform on adult-valued tasks should provide them with the social, emotional, and cognitive foundations they need to assimilate and adjust to the new experiences they will encounter in later schooling.

If, however, our concept of ECE is as an accelerating experience where children are pushed to be little "performers," I think we may be creating anxious, stressed children. Although data are not available demonstrating the psychosocial effects of acceleration itself, much *is* known about the effects of stress on children. We can infer from our knowledge of development that this is a matter for concern. Are we not inducing achievement anxiety in children being pushed? Are we saying to them their value lies only in their achievement? Are we depriving these children of the excitement of self-directed play? We need answers to these questions, but, until we get the answers, let us be cautious and reflect on the negative potentials. Who, after all, is in a hurry—the children or the parents?

It will be a sad day for all of us if our youngsters are eager to perform only for the extrinsic rewards, not for the intrinsic joy of learning. I believe, however, that by using what we know of the early childhood programs that provide stimulation without stress, development of a positive sense of self and personal competence, and opportunities to grow comfortably in the cognitive role, we will provide our children with rich and rewarding experiences.

APPENDIX: SAMPLE LESSON PLANS

SAMPLE LESSON PLAN NO. 1

Name of Activity: Reading *Sally's Caterpillar*
Schedule: Large group
Curriculum area/Representational system:

Science	Social/Affective
Art—2-dimensional	Movement
Construction—3-dimensional	Music
	Language arts

Objective/Goal:

1a. To increase awareness of objects and events and one's reactions to them. *A natural phenomenon which involves striking irreversible transformations. caterpillar →*

b. To increase awareness of methods for finding out about stimuli. *cocoon → butterfly.*

2a. Elaborate/refine internal representation.
 b. Search store of internal representations (with one or more criteria in mind).
3a. Understand a single representational system as a system (perceive, know about elements, transformations, etc.).
 b. Perceive/understand how that system relates to, refers to, the world.
4a. Understand a variety of representational systems.
 b. Use diverse representational systems to communicate, to encode meanings.
5a. Generate solutions, alternatives.
 b. Seek out, perceive, or identify problems.
6. Evaluate through reasoning.

Materials and Teacher Preparation:
The book, *Sally's Caterpillar,* by Anne and Harlow Rockwell

Rationale (why those subgoals, this content, this activity? why at this time?):
Exploring a natural phenomenon—the changes of a caterpillar, in this case—to gain a greater awareness of the transformations involved, the details of appearance, etc. The choice of the caterpillar is because of the children's spontaneous interest in them (several brought them to class) and because of the marked transformations they were aware of what to watch for in the caterpillar by (a) getting the group to individually and collectively bring to mind what they may already know of caterpillars and (b) providing new information (about the stages of transformations, etc.) to aid the children in constructing a fuller notion of caterpillars in their several forms.

Activity: Procedure and Teacher Strategies (Distancing):
Teacher will introduce story by referring to the two caterpillars recently brought into the classroom by children. As the story is read, the teacher will get information the children may have about caterpillars from past experience, as well as from observing those in the classroom: "What will the caterpillar that Sally finds look like? How will it feel? How big will it be? What will its legs be like?" (I)

Teacher will point out stages of caterpillars as they are read about and ask children to predict what will happen to the caterpillars brought into class. (II)

At the end of the story, she will ask children, "How will we know what's happening to our caterpillar? Will we be able to tell when it's a cocoon? How? How about when it's a butterfly? How will we know?" (III)

Reasoning (why this procedure, these strategies?):
I. (Having the children call on what they have seen or heard of caterpillars)
Children have to call on their internal representations (mental images, memory, etc.) and express these in verbal or gestural form. Specific

questions are intended to help them *refine the internal representations* and use them as a basis for what Sally's caterpillar (and later the class caterpillars) will be like.

Reading the book is intended to heighten the children's awareness of what to watch for in the caterpillar by (a) getting the children to individually or collectively *bring to mind what they may already know of caterpillars* and (b) providing new information (about the stages of transformation, etc.) to aid the children in *developing a broader notion of forms of caterpillars.*

II. (Talking to the children about changes in the caterpillar and asking them to think about how the class caterpillar will look)

Some transformations and features to *observe* are mentioned to focus the children's attention. When children see things happening, they can relate them to what they've heard.

III. (Asking the children to predict what will happen to the caterpillar and to think about how one can tell when it's a cocoon, etc.)

Being asked to think about the points in between the caterpillar, the cocoon, and the butterfly helps the child *decenter from the end states,* which is hard for young children. In so doing, they will be likelier to really understand the process. The how-does-one-know questions are good for scientists of any age to specify—what are the identifying earmarks of X? How can you be sure what you are observing in an X? and so on.

SAMPLE LESSON PLAN NO. 2

Name of Activity: Using rhythm instruments to help tell *Peter Pan*
Schedule: Large group
Curriculum area/Representational system:

Science	Social/Affective
Art—2-dimensional	Movement
Construction—3-dimensional	Music
	Language arts

Objective/Goal:

1a. To increase awareness of external stimuli and one's reactions to them.
 b. To increase awareness of methods for finding out about stimuli.
2a. Elaborate/refine internal representation.
 b. Search store of internal representations (with one or more criteria in mind).
3a. Understand a single representational system as a system (perceive, know about elements, transformations, etc.). The elements of speed and rhythm.
 b. Perceive/understand how that system relates to, refers to, the world. Speed, rhythm in music in relation to speed/rhythm of movement.
4a. Understand a variety of representational systems.
 b. Use diverse representational systems to communicate, to encode meanings.

5a. Generate solutions, alternatives.
 b. Seek out, perceive, or identify problems.
6. Evaluate through reasoning.

Materials and Teacher Preparation:

Children are each given a rhythm instrument, including, if they desire, those which they made themselves. They have already had experience using and caring for these and thinking about the musical elements of speed.

Rationale (why those subgoals, this content, this activity? why at this time?):

In this activity children are using one specific element of music to represent specific events and transformations in the storyline. Later on they will be introduced to other elements and at some point combine multiple elements.

Activity: Procedure and Teacher Strategies (Distancing):

I. After selecting instruments, group will examine ways to vary the speed at which they play their instruments. Then teacher tells them that they will be using the instruments to tell parts of *Peter Pan* in which the characters do things faster and slower.

II. During the story, at specific points, teacher tells children to use instruments and tells story in such a way that children can represent speed changes. For example, "They started to fly but Wendy was a little frightened. So first she flew very, very slowly, then she went a little faster, then a little more . . . until she was flying as fast as she could."

III. Rather than just encouraging representation of slow and fast, teacher stresses the gradual change from one to the other. She may have them stop in the middle of one of these transformations and have children go back to starting point, then start again. Story is completed using this method of representation.

Reasoning (why this procedure, these strategies?):

I. Introduction to activity and review of speed variations. This helps children orient their thinking toward this element of music.

II. Children are required to mentally represent situation verbally described by teacher and transform that into sounds created by musical instruments.

III. Emphasis on transformational aspect of representation requires that children become aware of dynamic changes involved in one state becoming another. This is important for their understanding of how transformations work in the world.

REFERENCES

Biber, B. (1984). *Early education and psychological development*. New Haven: Yale University Press.

Cocking, R. (1979, June). *Preschool education and representational thinking: The impact of teacher "distancing" behaviors on language and cognition*. Paper presented at the Fifth Biennial Conference of the International Society for the Study of Behavioral Development, Lund, Sweden.

Copple, C., Sigel, I. E., & Saunders, R. (1984). *Educating the young thinker: Classroom strategies for cognitive growth*. Hillsdale, NJ: Lawrence Erlbaum Associates. (Original work published 1979).

Deutsch, M. (1964). Facilitating development in the pre-school child: Social and psychological perspectives. *Merrill-Palmer Quarterly*, *10*, 249–263.

Doman, G., Harvey, N., Doman, J., Kerr, G., Heggestad, J., MacRury, L., Okabayashi, M., & Doman, D. *The institutes' philosophy*. Philadelphia: Better Baby Press, Institutes for the Achievement of Human Potential.

Evans, Ellis D. (1975). *Contemporary influences in early childhood education* (2nd ed.). New York: Holt, Rinehart & Winston.

Hess, R. D. (1970). Social class and ethnic influences on socialization. In P. H. Mussen (Ed.), *Carmichael's manual of child psychology* (Vol. 2). New York: Wiley.

Hunt, J. M. (1961). *Intelligence and experience*. New York: Ronald Press.

Kamii, C. (1981). Application of Piaget's theory to education: The preoperational level. In I. E. Sigel, D. M. Brodzinsky, & R. M. Golinkoff (Eds.), *New directions in Piagetian theory and practice* (pp. 231–265). Hillsdale, NJ: Lawrence Erlbaum Associates.

Laosa, L. M. (1982). Families as facilitators of children's intellectual development at 3 years of age: A causal analysis. In L. M. Laosa & I. E. Sigel (Eds.), *Families as learning environments for children* (pp. 1–45). New York: Plenum.

———. (1983). School, occupation, culture, and family: The impact of parental schooling on the parent-child relationship. In I. E. Sigel & L. M. Laosa (Eds.), *Changing families* (pp. 79–135). New York: Plenum.

Lazar, I., & Darlington, R. (1982). Lasting effects of early education: A report from the consortium for longitudinal studies. *Monographs of the Society for Research in Child Development*, *47*(2–3, Serial No. 195).

Miller, L. B., Bugbee, M. R., & Hybertson, D. W. (1985). Dimensions of preschool: The effects of individual experience. In I. E. Sigel (Ed.), *Advances in applied developmental psychology* (Vol. 1, pp. 25–90). Norwood, NJ: Ablex.

Piaget, J. (1952). *The origins of intelligence in children*. New York: International Universities Press.

Sigel, I. E. (1965). Developmental considerations of the nursery school experience. In P. B. Neubauer (Ed.), *Concepts of development in early childhood education* (pp. 84–111).

———. (1972). Developmental theory and preschool education: Issues, problems and implications. In I. J. Gordon (Ed.), *Early childhood education: The seventy-first yearbook of the National Society for the Study of Education*, Part II (pp. 13–31). Chicago: University of Chicago Press.

———. (1979). On becoming a thinker: A psychoeducational model. *Educational Psychologist, 14*, 70–78.

———. (1986). Early social experience and the development of representational competence. In W. Fowler (Ed.), *Early experience and the development of competence* (pp. 49–65). New Directions for Child Development, No. 32. San Francisco: Jossey-Bass.

———. (1987). Educating the young thinker: A distancing model of preschool education. In J. L. Roopnarine & J. E. Johnson (Eds.), *Approaches to early childhood education* (pp. 237–252). Columbus, OH: Charles E. Merrill.

Sigel, I. E., & McGillicuddy-DeLisi, A. V. (1984). Parents as teachers of their children: A distancing behavior model. In A. D. Pellegrini & T. D. Yawkey (Eds.), *The development of oral and written language in social contexts* (pp. 71–92). Norwood, NJ: Ablex.

Sigel, I. E., McGillicuddy-DeLisi, A. V., & Johnson, J. E. (1980). *Parental distancing, beliefs and children's representational competence within the family context* (ETS RR-80-21). Princeton, NJ: Educational Testing Service.

Stanley, J. C. (Ed.). (1973). *Compensatory education for children, ages 2 to 8: Recent studies of educational intervention*. Baltimore, MD: Johns Hopkins University Press.

Weikart, D. P., Epstein, A. S., Schweinhart, L., & Bond, J. T. (1978). *The Ypsilanti Preschool Curriculum Demonstration Project: Preschool years and longitudinal results*. Ypsilanti, MI: High/Scope Educational Research Foundation.

Zigler, E., & Valentine, J. (Eds.). (1979). *Project Head Start: A legacy of the War on Poverty*. New York: Free Press.

CHAPTER 9

Early Education: What Should Young Children Be Doing?

LILIAN G. KATZ

Ideally the question of whether young children should be in the public schools could be answered by inspecting a substantial body of empirical studies on the subject. Some of these studies would show which children seem to benefit, which are unaffected, and which suffer from early experience in the schools. Ideally the data would indicate the long-term as well as short-term effects on children of different kinds of schools, of varying curricula and teaching methods, and of teachers of different backgrounds, training, and experience. Some of the studies in our ideal research world would indicate the comparative effects on children of public school, Head Start, profit, nonprofit, community-based, cooperative, and other kinds of programs. And some would tell us in detail what experiences youngsters are having when provisions are *not* made for them in the public schools.

Regrettably, however, a body of studies focused directly on the topic of young children in the public schools is not yet available. In its absence we must turn to the general data on preschool-aged children's development and learning and make reliable and valid inferences from them. This is not a simple matter. I have suggested elsewhere that it is a general principle that any field characterized by a weak data base has a vacuum which is filled by ideologies (Katz, 1977a). The field of early childhood education has an inherently weak data base, partly because it would be unethical as well as impractical to perform the definitive experiments necessary to produce strong data and settle major disputes, and partly because children are studied during a period of such rapid development it is difficult to discriminate among change effects by treatment versus maturation alone. Thus many of the contentious issues concerning young children in the schools are debated from ideological positions that are fairly resistant to change, and often accompanied by a tendency to dismiss counterevidence as deficient or inappropriate.

There are clearly many different issues surrounding the question of whether or not young children should be in public schools, and most are addressed elsewhere in this volume. The one I want to discuss in this chapter is the question of what young children should be doing wherever they are—whether at home, with siblings or grandma, with a sitter, or in a licensed family day-care home, a Head Start class, a franchised day-care center, the Yale Child Study Center, or a rural or urban public school. I propose to address in two ways the issue of what young children should be doing. The first is a brief overview of current research on children's development and learning; the second part is a discussion of the implications of the research for educational programming for young children, no matter who is the sponsor.

In the first section, developmental issues regarding what we know about the ways in which children learn, and how they develop interest and communicative and social competence are discussed; this is followed by a discussion of research evidence relating to risks associated with academic pressures. In the second section, I'll discuss how research on these aspects of development can inform early childhood education practices, suggesting specific pedagogical strategies that build upon the research evidence.

Child Development and Preschool Education

Although there is as yet no body of specific research that directly examines the effects of public schooling on young children, there is important information to be gleaned from what has been reported to date. Furthermore, although the requisite data on the effects of schooling on young children are not yet sufficient for drawing reliable conclusions, there is an abundance of research on their intellectual and social development and learning that is rich with implications for the kind of teaching and curriculum that should be provided for them. Of course, all research is open to varieties of interpretations and inferences. The discussion below presents my own views of what can be learned from recent research on children's development and learning.

Four Categories of Learning

In drawing inferences from research concerning programming for young children, I find it helpful to think in terms of four types of learning goals: knowledge, skills, dispositions, and feelings. *Knowledge* during the preschool period can be broadly defined as information, ideas, stories, facts, concepts, schemas, and other such contents of mind that make up much of the material to be covered in a curriculum. *Skills* can be defined as brief and small units of action or behavior that are relatively easily observed, for example, walking along a balance beam or writing one's name. Included in this category are mental skills that can be fairly easily inferred from observed behavior that occurs in small units of time or on a given single occasion, such as counting the fingers on one's hand. Mental processes difficult to infer from observed behavior might include skills and many other kinds of information processing as well. *Dispositions*, usually omitted from lists of educational goals, are broadly defined as relatively enduring habits of mind, or characteristic ways of responding to experience across types of situations, for example, curiosity, generosity, quarrelsomeness, and so on. *Feelings* include the sense of belonging, self-confidence, and the feeling of unlovability (Katz, 1985). It is not clear which feelings are learned from experience. Surely many of them—such as anger, sadness, and frustration—are temporary reactions to situations and experiences. But feelings of competence and incompetence or acceptance or rejection in the school or classroom situation could be said to be learned in that they are the feelings typically aroused in that context.

These four categories of goals are achieved in different ways. Children can be helped to acquire knowledge by being informed about and alerted to relevant phenomena. Skills may be learned partly from observation, imitation, trial and error, instruction, and optimal amounts of drill and practice. Lessons and workbooks can be used to aid the acquisition of skills. Dispositions, on the other hand, are not likely to be learned from lessons, instructions, or lectures. Children are most likely to learn dispositions from observation and emulation of models; the dispositions are then shaped and strengthened by being appreciated and acknowledged. A general principle related to strengthening dispositions is that they must be manifested or expressed in some way. These expressions must then be followed up by being responded to positively. If, for example, we wish to strengthen children's dispositions to be curious, it will be necessary to provide opportunities for them to act upon or otherwise express their curiosity. We must then convey our appreciation of the disposition with appropriate responses. Of course, not all dispositions are desirable, and some have to be responded to in such a way that they are weakened.

Some Risks of Academic Pressures on Young Children

Among the issues surrounding whether young children should be in the public schools is the fear that they will be introduced to the kind of formalized instruction and academic schoolwork associated with the elementary grades. At issue is not whether preschool children *can* start school work early. Observation of young children in many preschool settings indicates that they can certainly be given instruction in phonics, counting, and other academic tasks. But the fact that children can do something is not sufficient justification for requiring it of them. There is no compelling evidence to suggest that early introduction to academic work guarantees success in school in the long term, but there are reasons to believe that it could be counterproductive.

Damaged-Disposition Hypothesis. The damaged-disposition hypothesis suggests that the early introduction of academic or basic skills may undermine the development of children's dispositions to use the skills thus acquired (Katz, 1985). This hypothesis seems to be a reasonable interpretation of some of the results of longitudinal studies (for example, Karnes, Schwedel, & Williams, 1983; Miller & Bizzell, 1983; Schweinhart, Weikart, & Larner, 1986; see also Walberg, 1984). Thus, although it seems possible to teach academic skills to most preschool children, it is also possible to damage their dispositions to use them. Young children can be successfully instructed in beginning reading skills, for example, but the risk of such early achievement is that in the process of instruction, and given the amount of drill and practice required for success, children's dispositions to be *readers* will be undermined.

The pressure on young children to perform academic tasks (like workbooks, ditto sheets, practice in phonics) appears harmless, or even beneficial, in the short term. But developmentalists are obliged to take into account the potential long-term consequences of early experiences, no matter how benign they appear to be at the time they occur. Results from longitudinal studies suggest that curricula and teaching methods should be approached so as to optimize the acquisition of knowledge, skills, and desirable dispositions and feelings, and that these are mutually inclusive goals; each type of learning to be given equal weight. It is clearly not very useful to have skills if in the process of acquiring them the disposition to use them is lost; on the other hand, having the disposition without the requisite skills is also not a desirable educational outcome. The challenge for educators—at every level—is to help the learner with *both* the acquisition of skills and the strengthening of desirable dispositions.

Homogeneity of Treatments. Another risk of preschool programs with academic or basic skills emphases is that such programs tend to use a single teaching method and curriculum. The principle of relevance here is that use of a homogeneous treatment like this with a group of children of diverse backgrounds and developmental patterns must produce heterogeneous outcomes. Needless to say, we want some outcomes of education to be heterogeneous. But it is reasonable to hypothesize that for those outcomes that we wish to be homogeneous, such as all children having the disposition to be readers, the treatment is likely to have to be heterogeneous. We can safely assume that when a single teaching method is used for a diverse group of young children a significant proportion of them is likely to fail. It also seems a reasonable hypothesis that the younger children are, the greater should be the variety of teaching methods used (Durkin, 1980; see also Nelson & Seidman, 1984), although for reasons of stability and practicality there are likely to be limits upon how varied they can be. This hypothesis is derived from the assumption that the younger the group, the less likely they are to have been socialized into a particular and standard way of responding to their environment, and the more likely that children's background experiences related to their readiness to learn is unique and idiosyncratic rather than common and shared.

Academically focused curricula typically adopt a single pedagogical method dominated by workbooks, drill, and practice. Even though such approaches often claim to "individualize" instruction, what typically varies is the day on which an individual child completes a task rather than the task itself! I suspect that very often "time on task" for the children in such programs could be called "time on deadly task"; after a year or two of such schooling the effect is likely to be deadening.

Learned Stupidity. Another risk that may attend introducing young children to academic work prematurely is that for those children who cannot relate to the content or tasks required of them, their likely reaction is to *feel* incompetent. When the contents or tasks of a lesson for college students are difficult to grasp or perform, the student is very likely to fault the instructor, as many teachers well know! In the case of young children however—perhaps older ones as well—repeated experiences of being unable to relate to schoolwork, are likely to lead to the self-attribution called "learned stupidity." Such children are then very likely to bring their behavior into line with the attribution.

Interaction as a Context for Early Learning

One of the most reliable principles implied by developmental research is that young children's learning is enhanced when they are engaged in interactive processes (see Brown & Campione, 1984; Glaser, 1984; Karmiloff-Smith, 1984; Nelson, 1985; Rogoff, 1982). It now seems clear that in addition to learning through trial and error and through observation, young children gain a great deal cognitively as well as socially in the course of interacting with each other, with adults, and with aspects of their environment. This trend in research also implies that children's learning is best served when they are involved in active rather than passive activities. One of the weaknesses of the conventional academic tasks in the "pushed-down" first grade and kindergarten curriculum is that it typically reduces the extent to which children are engaged in interactive processes.

The Development of Communicative Competence. Virtually all who are concerned with children in the early years recognize that it is a critical period in the development of communicative competence—namely, competence in self-expression and in understanding others. Contemporary insights into the development of this competence in young children indicate that all three basic functions of language (communication, expression, and reasoning) are strengthened when children are engaged in conversation rather than when they are simply passively exposed to language (Wells, 1983).

Conversations are a very special type of interaction in which each participant's responses are contingent upon the other's in a sequential string of responses. It may very well be that *contingency* of responses to children in and of itself has a powerful effect on the development of their minds. Also, conversation is more likely to be prolonged when adults make comments to the children rather than when they ask them questions (Blank, 1985).

The work of Bruner (1982) and others suggests that conversation is most likely to occur when children are in small groups of three or four, with or without an adult present. Most teachers of young children recognize the difficulty of encouraging conversation during a whole group session; they expend much effort reminding children that another child is still speaking or that their turn has not yet come! It seems reasonably clear that children are most likely to engage in conversation when something of interest occurs in context (Bruner, J. 1982; Clark & Wade, 1983). I am reminded of watching a kindergarten teacher attempting to engage a class of five-year-olds in a discussion by asking each in turn the question, "What is your news today?" Each child struggled to find something headline-worthy to report to his or her disinterested squirming classmates! Perhaps some of these children were learning "to listen," as the teacher intended; but many appeared to be learning "to tune out" their stammering classmates.

The Development of Interest

One of the important dispositions of concern to educators of young children is their *interest*, or their capacity to lose themselves in an outside activity or concern. Interest refers to the ability to become deeply enough absorbed in something to pursue it over time and with sufficient commitment to accept its routine as well as its novel aspects. Sometimes called "intrinsic motivation" (Morgan, 1984), "continuing motivation" (Maehr, in press), or "self-directed learning" (Benware & Deci, 1984), this disposition appears to be present in the normal human at birth and is affected by a variety of social-psychological processes throughout childhood.

Recent research has illuminated the effects of different kinds of feedback on learners' intrinsic motivation or what I refer to as the disposition called interest. Research on the so-called overjustification effect suggests that when children are rewarded for tasks in which they have initially shown interest, they subsequently lose interest in the tasks. Thus, rewards undermine their interest in such cases. The overjustification effect refers to metacognitive processes that are assumed to be occurring in children's minds, suggesting that they respond to such rewards by saying to themselves, as it were, "It must be wrong to like doing X, or I would not be given a reward for doing it" (Deci & Ryan, 1982). Since this effect applies especially to those activities children originally find interesting, it suggests that teachers should exercise special care not to offer rewards for those activities young children spontaneously enjoy or are readily attracted to.

A parallel line of research on related processes suggests that, when the positive feedback given to children is general in nature, it may serve to increase productivity but not interest (deCharms, 1983). This kind of feedback includes vague comments on the part of the teacher like "very good," "well done," and the "happy face" or gold star. If, on the other hand, the positive feedback is specific rather than general, particularly if it includes information about the competence of the performance, it serves to strengthen interest. The latter is called a "tribute"; the former, an "inducement." A tribute is associated with increasing interest in the task, whereas an inducement leads to loss of interest once the positive feedback becomes unavailable. Academically oriented programs typically emphasize general positive feedback, ostensibly to give children feelings of success. This strategy appears to work very well to induce young children to keep working at disembedded, decontextualized, and often very trivial tasks.

As I have suggested elsewhere (Katz, 1977b), curricula and teaching methods that attempt to provide children with constant amusement, fun, and excitement also risk undermining the development of children's disposition for interest. Thus the teacher's role in strengthening children's dispositions to be interested in relevant and worthwhile phenomena is a complex and highly critical one.

Children's dispositions toward sustained interest and involvement can be strengthened if they are encouraged to engage in projects that call for effort and involvement over time, and that provide contexts for extension, elaboration, and continuation of work and play (Rosenfield, Folger, & Adelman, 1980).

Social Competence

Although definitions of social competence vary on some of the details, they usually include the capacity to form and maintain satisfying relationships with others, especially those in their age group. Social competence does not require that a child be a social butterfly. It suggests that the child be capable of finding interaction and cooperation with others satisfying. It is not a source of concern if a child chooses to work or play alone, as long as he or she is capable of interacting successfully with another when desired.

If a child has not acquired minimal social competence by the age of six, however, contemporary research indicates that the youngster is more likely than others to be a school dropout (Gottman, 1983; Parker & Asher, 1986) and to be at significant risk in young adulthood in terms of mental health, marital adjustment, and other aspects of social life in which interpersonal competence is required (Asher, Renshaw, & Hymel, 1982).

The acquisition of social competence involves many complex

processes beginning in early infancy. It should be noted that inappropriate as well as appropriate social responses are learned through interaction. Weaknesses in social competence may be intensified during such interactions unless adults help the child alter maladaptive patterns. In the preschool period, such weaknesses are unlikely to be improved through formal instruction or even coaching, but they can be helped by the intervention of a knowledgeable teacher (see Katz, 1984). Fortunately, a range of techniques that teachers can use to foster the development of social competence is now available (Burton, in press; Katz, 1984).

It is useful to think of social competence as having the characteristics of a *recursive cycle*. The principle of the recursive cycle is that, once an individual has a given behavior or characteristic, reactions of others tend to increase the chances that he or she will display more of that behavior or characteristic. For example, children who are likable, attractive, and friendly tend to elicit positive responses in others fairly easily, and because they receive such positive responses, they become more likable, attractive, and friendly. Similarly, children who are unattractive, unfriendly, and difficult to like tend to be avoided or rejected by others, and in response, they tend to behave in ways that make them even more unattractive. This in turn increases the likelihood that they will more often be avoided or rejected, and the cycle becomes well established. This general principle can be applied to many kinds of behavior and learning, but especially to social behaviors (see also Patterson, 1986). The principle of the recursive cycle confirms the point made earlier—that young children should be engaged in interactive processes, especially in the company of teachers with specialized training and competencies.

Experience suggests that if we respond to children's needs for help with the development of their social competence in the early years, we can prevent them from having to suffer from social difficulties and set them on a positive cycle. If we wait until a child is nine or ten years old and is having difficulties with friendships, we may need substantial resources from a mental health agency to intervene, and it still may be too late. These recent insights from research suggest that preschool teachers' concern with children's social development is well placed and should be given as much weight in planning and teaching as their intellectual development.

Specific Implications for Preschool Programs

Curriculum Options

Many people within and outside the field of early childhood education think that the choice of a curriculum lies between either an academic or a socialization focus. Some of the risks of introducing academic tasks to young children have already been indicated. But the alternative is not simply to provide spontaneous play, although all children up to eight years of age can probably benefit from it. Rather, the data on children's learning seem to suggest that what is required in preschool and kindergarten is an *intellectually* oriented approach in which children interact in small groups as they work together on a variety of projects that help them make sense of their experiences and that strengthen their dispositions to observe, experiment, enquire, and reconstruct aspects of their environment.

In addition to the insights drawn from research on specific aspects of development, studies on the impacts of different kinds of early childhood curricula support the view that young children should be in preschool and kindergarten programs that provide interaction with others, active rather than passive experiences, and ample opportunity to initiate activities that interest them (Koester & Farley, 1982; Fry & Addington, 1984). The benefits of informal teaching methods are especially striking in the *long term* and notably discouraging in the *short term* (Miller & Bizzell, 1983; Schweinhart et al., 1986). According to Walberg (1984), a synthesis of 153 studies of open education, including 90 dissertations, indicated that

> the average effect [size for open education] was near zero for achievement, locus of control, self-concept, and anxiety (which suggests no difference between open and control classes on these criteria); about .2* for adjustment, attitude toward schools and teachers, curiosity, and general mental ability; and about a moderate .3* for cooperativeness, creativity, and independence. Thus students in open classes do no worse in standardized achievement and slightly to moderately better on several outcomes that educators, parents and students hold to be of great value. (Walberg, 1984, p. 25)

*This statistic, derived from a meta-analysis, represents a modest positive effect on the variables listed for open compared with traditional formal classes.

In sum, insights derived from developmental and related curriculum research support the view that a significant proportion of the time children spend in preschool and kindergarten classes should be allocated to the kind of project or unit work characteristic of pedagogical methods that are intellectually oriented and informal—the sort known in the 1960s as open education.

The Value of Project Work for Young Children

The project approach is a particularly promising strategy for fostering children's interactions and choice as suggested by contemporary research. A project is a group undertaking, usually around a particular theme or topic. It involves a variety of kinds of work over a period of several days or weeks. There are three basic kinds of projects, although some are combinations of two or more kinds. During the preschool period the most common type consists of *reconstructions* of aspects of the environment within the preschool or primary school setting. Another type of project consists of *investigations* of aspects of the environment and includes developing various ways of reporting the findings of the investigations to classmates. A third type consists largely of *observations* of aspects of the environment and includes the preparation of ways to present or report what was learned from the observations to others in the class.

A theme for a project may be introduced by the teacher or children or evolve from discussions they have together. There may or may not be a project leader who coordinates the activities of the group. On some occasions the membership of the project group may fluctuate; at other times, it may be beneficial to require stability of group membership or to encourage the members to see a task through to completion.

Projects usually have three rough phases that are likely to blend into each other. First is a planning phase during which children and staff discuss the elements of the project, develop plans and procedures for obtaining the materials, building the elements, or carrying out the investigations and observations. It would also include discussions about what information to obtain during field trips or site visits. There are ample opportunities in this phase for rich discussion and for children to display and generate interest in the project.

A second phase consists of constructing or building the parts of the project, gathering information, making observations, or drawing pictures by which to let others in the class know what has been learned. A third phase includes role playing or taking the roles appropriate to the various elements of the project. During this period extensions and elaborations on elements of the project may be undertaken. Almost any aspect of the environment can become the focus of a project. Many opportunities for cooperative social interaction occur in all three phases.

I recently heard indirectly of a group of kindergartners who undertook a detailed study of their own school bus! Although I have no direct knowledge of the scope of their project, it is easy to see what kinds of activities the children might have undertaken. One small group could study the driving mechanism including the motor and gear shifts, brakes, accelerator, steering wheel, and so on. Another could study the variety of lights inside and outside the bus; another the gauges and dials and the information they yield. Another group could take measurements of the width of the bus, count the number of seats and the number of wheels and learn something about air pressure in the tires. Perhaps two could examine the inside and outside rearview mirrors. The door of a school bus is unlikely to resemble those inside children's homes or their school and doors might become a topic for extended study. It is not difficult to imagine what kind of vocabulary building can accompany such a study—terms like *ignition*, *emergency door*, *fuel*, *dial*, *gauge*, *air pressure*, *accelerator*, *rearview mirror*, *gears*, and so on. Study could extend to the route taken by the bus, how many board at which stop, what traffic signs and signals are passed en route, and so on. According to my informant, following the detailed examination of their bus, the children built one in their classroom and then acted out a variety of roles associated with transporting children from home to school.

There is no special virtue to studying a school bus in the sense that someday some important test will examine the knowledge children gained from the project. What recommends it is that the bus was part of the children's own daily environment and they learned a lot about it—the correct names of its various parts, a simple understanding of how it worked, and which of its features contributed to their safety. But especially important was the fact that the project provided a context in which their dispositions to observe, inquire, and become interested and involved in a sustained group effort could be strengthened.

In a project of this type the teacher alerts children to a wide range of interesting aspects of a topic that will take several days or weeks of probing and exploring, asking questions of adults and looking up facts in reference books of appropriate levels of difficulty. The fact that children are expected to explain what they have learned to others in their class is likely to encourage persistence in obtaining information and reaching for adequate understanding (see Benware & Deci, 1984). The use of adults other than teachers as sources of information can be launched through this kind of project. Furthermore, for many of the children this particular project was likely to strengthen their disposition to observe all kinds of other vehicles more closely than they had before, perhaps making useful comparisons and reporting them to their classmates from time to time.

In sum, the project approach can be valuable for young children because it challenges their minds and can strengthen a variety of important dispositions, provide subjects for conversation, and create a situation in which cooperative effort with their classmates makes sense. Projects are also culturally relevant in that they stem from the children's own interests and environments. And yet another virtue of this approach is that it can make teaching interesting—something very unlikely to be characteristic of the more formal academic approaches to early childhood education.

Conclusion

Many educators, as well as parents, express the fear that programs for young children provided in public schools will inevitably offer experiences that too closely resemble the formal academic approach appropriate for the elementary school years. Indeed, there is some concern also that many programs for young children outside of the public schools are oriented toward academic goals. Although research bearing directly on these issues is scant, educators have learned much from developmental studies bearing indirectly on curriculum issues. The alternative to an academic approach is not simply to provide endless but pleasant spontaneous play; the appropriate contrast is an *intellectual* one.

The inclusion of project work in the curriculum is consistent with the intention to engage young children's minds in improving their understanding of their environment and to provide a context in which the development and application of their social competencies is strongly encouraged. Both intellectual and social development can be well served by the project approach, whether it is offered in a public or private group setting.

The project approach is not only developmentally appropriate; it is also culturally appropriate, and since it can make teaching interesting it provides a context in which children can observe adults intellectually engaged and interested in what they are doing!

REFERENCES

Asher, S. R., Renshaw, P. D., & Hymel, S. (1982). Peer relations and the development of social skills. In S. Moore and C. Cooper (Eds.), *The young child: Reviews of Research*, Vol. 3. Washington, DC: National Association for the Education of Young Children.

Benware, C. A., & Deci, E. L. (1984). Quality of learning with an active versus passive motivational set. *American Educational Research Journal*, *21*(4), 755–765.

Blank, M. (1985). Classroom discourse: The neglected topic of the topic. In M. M. Clark (Ed.), *Helping communication in early education*. Education Review Occasional Publications, No. 11: pp. 13–20.

Brown, A. L., & Campione, J. C. (1984). Three faces of transfer: Implications for early competence, individual differences, and instruction. In M. E. Lamb, A. L. Brown, & B. Rogoff (Eds.), *Advances in developmental psychology* (Vol. 3). Hillsdale, NJ: Lawrence Erlbaum Associates.

Bruner, J. (1982). *Under five in Britain* (Vol. 1). Oxford Preschool Research Project. Ypsilanti, MI: High/Scope Foundation.

Burton, C. B. (in press). Problems in children's peer relations: A broadening perspective. In L. G. Katz (Ed.), *Current topics in early childhood education* (Vol. 7). Norwood, NJ: Ablex.

Carnegie Corporation of New York. (1984, December). *Child care and the role of the public schools: Report of a conference*. New York: ERIC Document Reproduction Service, ED 264 013.

Carpenter, J. (1983). Activity structure and play: Implications for socialization. In M. B. Liss (Ed.), *Social and cognitive skills: Sex roles and children's play*. New York: Academic Press.

Clark, M. M., & Wade, B. (1983). Early childhood education [special issue]. *Educational Review, 35*(2).

Consortium for Longitudinal Studies. (1983). *As the twig is bent . . . Lasting effects of preschool programs.* Hillsdale, NJ: Lawrence Erlbaum Associates.

deCharms, R. (1983). Intrinsic motivation, peer tutoring, and cooperative learning: Practical maxims. In J. M. Levine & M. C. Want (Eds.), *Teacher and student perceptions: Implications for learning.* Hillsdale, NJ: Lawrence Erlbaum Associates.

Deci, E. L., & Ryan, R. M. (1982). Curiosity and self-directed learning. In L. G. Katz (Ed.), *Current topics in early childhood education* (Vol. 4). Norwood, NJ: Ablex.

Donaldson, M. (1983). Children's reasoning. In M. Donaldson, R. Grieve, & C. Pratt (Eds.), *Early childhood development and education.* London: Guilford Press.

Durkin, D. (1980). *Is kindergarten reading instruction really desirable?* Ferguson Lectures in Education, National College of Education, Evanston, IL.

Fry, P. S., & Addington, J. (1984). Comparison of social problem solving of children from open and traditional classrooms: A two-year longitudinal study. *Journal of Educational Psychology, 76*(1), 318–329.

Glaser, R. (1984). Education and thinking: The role of knowledge. *American Psychologist, 39*(2), 93–104.

Gottman, J. M. (1983). How children become friends. *Monographs of the Society for Research in Child Development, 48*(3, Serial No. 201).

Haskins, R. (1985). Public school aggression in children with varying day-care experiences. *Child Development, 56,* 689–703.

Karmiloff-Smith, A. (1984). Children's problem solving. In M. Lamb, A. Brown, & B. Rogoff (Eds.), *Advances in developmental psychology* (Vol. 3). Hillsdale, NJ: Lawrence Erlbaum Associates.

Karnes, M. B., Schwedel, A. M., & Williams, M. B. (1983). A comparison of five approaches for educating young children from low-income homes. In Consortium for Longitudinal Studies, *As the twig is bent . . . Lasting effects of preschool programs.* Hillsdale, NJ: Lawrence Erlbaum Associates.

Katz, L. G. (1977a). Early childhood programs and ideological disputes. In L. G. Katz (Ed.), *Talks with teachers.* Washington, DC: National Association for the Education of Young Children.

———. (1977b). Education or excitement. In L. G. Katz, (Ed.), *Talks with teachers.* Washington, DC: National Association for the Education of Young Children.

———. (1984). The professional preschool teacher. In L. G. Katz (Ed.), *More talks with teachers.* Urbana: ERIC Clearinghouse on Elementary and Early Childhood Education, University of Illinois.

———. (1984, July). The professional early childhood teacher. *Young Children,* pp. 3–9.

———. (1985). Dispositions in early childhood education. *ERIC/EECE Bulletin, 18*(2).

———. (1986, Winter). Current perspectives on child development. *Council for Research in Music Education Bulletin* No. 86, pp. 1–9.

———. (in press). Current perspectives on child development. In L. G. Katz, *Professionalism, development and dissemination: Three papers*. Urbana: ERIC Clearinghouse on Elementary and Early Childhood Education, University of Illinois.

Koester, L. S., & Farley, F. (1982). Psychophysical characteristics and school performance of children in open and traditional classrooms. *Journal of Educational Psychology*, *74*(2).

Maehr, M. L., & Archer, J. (in press). Motivation and school achievement. In L. G. Katz (Ed.), *Current topics in early childhood education* (Vol. 7). Norwood, NJ: Ablex.

Miller, L. B., & Bizzell, R. P. (1983). Long-term effects of four preschool programs: Sixth, seventh, and eighth grades. *Child Development*, *54*(3), 727–741.

Morgan, M. (1984). Reward-induced decrements and increments in intrinsic motivation. *Review of Education Research*, *54*(1), 5–30.

Nelson, K. (1985). *Making sense: The acquisition of shared meaning*. New York: Academic Press.

Nelson, K., & Seidman, S. (1984). Playing with scripts. In I. Bretherton (Ed.), *Symbolic play: The development of social understanding*. New York: Academic Press.

Parker, J., & Asher, S. (1986, March). *Predicting later outcomes from peer rejection: Studies of school drop out, delinquency and adult psychopathology*. Paper presented at the annual conference of the American Educational Research Association, San Francisco.

Patterson, G. R. (1986). Performance models for antisocial boys. *American Psychologist*, *41*(4), 432–444.

Prescott, E., & Jones, E. (1972). *Day care as a child rearing environment*. Washington, DC: National Association for the Education of Young Children.

Rogoff, B. (1982). Integrating context and cognitive development. In M. E. Lamb, & A. L. Brown (Eds.), *Advances in developmental psychology* (Vol. 2). Hillsdale, NJ: Lawrence Erlbaum Associates.

Rosenfield, D., Folger, R., & Adelman, H. F. (1980). When rewards reflect competence: A qualification of the overjustification effect. *Journal of Personality and Social Psychology*, *39*(3), 368–376.

Schweinhart, L. J., Weikart, D. P., & Larner, M. B. (1986). Consequences of three preschool curriculum models through age 15. *Early Childhood Research Quarterly*, *1*(1), 15–46.

Walberg, H. (1984). Improving the productivity of America's schools. *Educational Leadership*, *41*(8), 19–30.

Wells, G. (1983). Talking with children: The complementary roles of parents and teachers. In M. Donaldson, R. Grieve, & C. Pratt (Eds.), *Early childhood development and education*. London: Guilford Press.

CHAPTER 10

Curriculum Quality in Early Education

DAVID P. WEIKART

Reports of the effectiveness of early childhood care and education are appearing in newspaper editorials and articles throughout the country. Business leaders, such as those on the Committee for Economic Development, quote its power to reduce the taxpayers' burden. Education leaders, such as Mary Hatwood Futrell, president of the National Education Association, comment on its ability to improve children's educational achievement. State legislators throughout the nation are funding new programs worth a third of a billion dollars in 1985–87 alone.

Two forces have combined to make early childhood care and education a national priority. Both stem from major shifts in society. The first is the gradual movement of women from the home and farm into the paid work force, initially into low-wage and often part-time unskilled jobs and, more recently, into higher paying full-time positions. The second force is the intensifying national search for effective ways to improve the lives of disadvantaged youth.

Broad general programs for children are a fact, and they are in place nationally. While Head Start is of special note, dependent-care tax credits supporting family expenditures for care represent a large national investment. Many small-scale, private, local programs, especially those based in churches, provide the most service.

More subtle is the development of curricula to guide the services and to ensure that support to young children is not ignored or that the necessary transmission of knowledge, essential to their future performance, is not neglected. It is this issue that this chapter addresses: what curriculum approach should be employed? First, I will review the basic research on disadvantaged children that supports the value of early childhood education. Next, I will outline the outcomes of a study of the relative effects of different theoretical approaches to education. The chapter concludes with a discussion of what directions education should take.

Research in Early Education

When studies of the effects of early childhood education began in the 1960s, the basic question under investigation was: does early childhood education make a difference in the lives of children? Fears at that time were that early education would be harmful to their development and their relationships with their families. Several longitudinal studies initiated in the 1960s, some before the advent of Head Start—such as those directed by Susan Gray in Tennessee (Gray, Ramsey, & Klaus, 1982), Martin Deutsch in New York (Jordan, Grallo, Deutsch, & Deutsch, 1985), and David Weikart in Michigan (Berrueta-Clement, Schweinhart, Barnett, Epstein, & Weikart, 1984)—addressed this question by establishing designs in which experimental groups participated in preschool education and control groups did not. As these studies and others, such as those included in the Consortium for Longitudinal Studies (1983), reported their long-term results, the answer to the basic question became clear: high-quality early childhood education for disadvantaged children is a highly effective way of improving their life chances.

As might be expected, many studies addressed the short-term effects of preschool child development programs, whereas only a handful have been able to examine effectiveness ten years or more after the program's end. Yet the weight of the evidence from all these studies points in the same direction.

As shown in table 10.1, these studies and others—such as the New York State Department of Education's Experimental Pre-

Table 10.1: Documented Effects of Good Preschool Programs for Poor Children

Finding *Study*	Program Group	Control Group	Probability of Error
Intellectual ability (IQ) at school entry			
Early Training	96	86	<.01
Perry Preschool	94	83	<.01
Harlem	96	91	<.01
Mother-Child Home	107	103	—
Special education placements			
Rome Head Start	11%	25%	<.05
Early Training	3%	29%	<.01
Perry Preschool	16%	28%	<.05
New York Prekindergarten (age 9)	2%	5%	<.01
Mother-Child Home (age 9)	14%	39%	<.01
Retentions in grade			
Rome Head Start	51%	63%	—
Early Training	53%	69%	—
Perry Preschool	35%	40%	—
Harlem	24%	45%	<.01
New York Prekindergarten	16%	21%	<.05
Mother-Child Home	13%	19%	—
High school dropouts			
Rome Head Start	50%	67%	<.05
Early Training	22%	43%	<.10
Perry Preschool	33%	51%	<.05
Additional Perry Preschool Findings			
Competence/Literacy (average or better score)	61%	38%	<.05
Postsecondary enrollments	38%	21%	<.05
Arrests	31%	51%	<.05
Teenage pregnancies per 100 girls	64	117	<.10
19-year-olds employed	50%	32%	<.05
19-year-olds on welfare	18%	32%	<.05

Source: Adapted from Berrueta-Clement, Schweinhart, Barnett, Epstein, & Weikart, 1984.

kindergarten Program (Irvine, 1982), Levenstein's Mother-Child Home Program in Long Island (Levenstein, O'Hara, & Madden, 1983), and Palmer's Harlem Program in New York City (Palmer, 1983)—indicate that good preschool child development programs for poor children help prevent school failure. First, they help improve children's intellectual performance as school begins; this improvement, on the average, reaches a maximum of 8 points on intelligence tests and lasts from the end of the preschool program to age eight. Second, they help reduce the need for poor children to be placed in special education programs or to repeat grade levels because they are unable to do the work expected of them. Third, participation in these programs leads to a lower high school drop-out rate.

Pursuing program effects beyond schooling, the High/Scope Foundation's Perry Preschool Program found impacts in many areas of early adult life (Berrueta-Clement et al., 1984). Nineteen-year-olds who had attended the program were better off in a variety of ways than a control group who did not participate in a preschool program. The program apparently *increased* the percentage of participants who were

- functionally literate, from 38 percent to 61 percent
- enrolled in postsecondary education, from 21 percent to 38 percent
- employed, from 32 percent to 50 percent.

The program apparently *reduced* the percentage of participants who were

- classified as mentally retarded during school years, from 35 percent to 15 percent
- school dropouts, from 51 percent to 33 percent
- pregnant teens, from 67 percent to 48 percent
- on welfare, from 32 percent to 18 percent
- arrested, from 51 percent to 31 percent.

The Perry study had an experimental group of fifty-eight participants in the preschool program and a control group of sixty-five persons who had no preschool program. These individuals were selected for the study at age three or four on the basis of parents' low educational and occupational status, family size, and children's low scores on the Stanford-Binet Intelligence test. Pairs of children matched on IQ, family socioeconomic status, and gender were split between the two groups. Both groups were virtually identical on a host of demographic characteristics such as race, welfare utilization, age of mother, father absent, and so on.

The Perry Preschool Program used the High/Scope Curriculum (Hohmann, Banet, & Weikart, 1979), an educational approach based on Jean Piaget's interactional theory of child development. Most children attended the program for two years at ages three and four. The classroom program was in session five mornings a week for seven months of the year, with a teacher visiting each parent at home once a week. Each class had about twenty-five children and four teachers, for a child-teacher ratio of between 1:5 and 1:6.

It is important to note that the studies mentioned here investigated many kinds of early childhood programs, but all of them were of *high quality*. They followed a specific curriculum methodology, had adequate supervision and in-service training, employed team teaching and daily program planning, featured extended parent involvement, employed some evaluation or monitoring strategy, and enjoyed competent administrative support.

The array of findings of preschool program effects from all programs may be divided into short-, mid-, and long-term results. The evidence indicates that good preschool programs for poor children

- *do* help improve children's intellectual and social performance as they begin school. These short-term effects have been found in many studies of Head Start and other programs.
- *probably* help children achieve greater school success. Half a dozen experimentally designed studies found the mid-term effect of lower percentages of poor children being placed in special education programs and repeating grade levels.
- *can* help young people achieve greater socioeconomic success and social responsibility. (This long-term evidence comes largely from the Perry Preschool study; few others have been able to

document long-term effects because of the difficulties of conducting the research.)

Cost-Benefit Analysis of High/Scope's Perry Preschool Program

Good preschool child development programs for poor children can be an excellent investment for taxpayers, according to the cost-benefit analysis of the Perry Preschool Program and its long-term effects. In the book *Investing in Our Children*, the research and policy arm of the Committee for Economic Development (1985), an organization of leading business executives and educators, summarized the analysis this way:

> If we examine the Perry Preschool Program for its investment return and convert all costs and benefits into current values based on a three percent real rate of interest, one year of the program is an extraordinary economic buy. It would be hard to imagine that a society could find a higher yield for a dollar of investment than that found in preschool programs for its at-risk children. (p. 44)

The total benefits to taxpayers for the program (in constant 1981 dollars discounted at 3 percent annually), depicted in table 10.2, averaged $28,000 per participant. For each program participant, taxpayers saved about $5,000 for special education programs, $3,000 in crime costs, and $16,000 for welfare assistance. Additional postsecondary education costs added about $1,000 per participant. Because of increased lifetime earnings (based on more years of school completed), the average participant was expected to pay $5,000 more in taxes.

One year of the Perry Preschool Program cost about the same as one year in a special education classroom. As an experiment rather than a test of cost-efficiency, the program was relatively expensive because of its teacher-child ratio of 1:6. The same kind of program has demonstrated equally good results with teacher-child ratios of 1:8 or even 1:10. With such ratios the program would cost about $3,000 per child.

For program outcomes to be as positive, however, there is a condition. The preschool programs that have demonstrated long-term effectiveness have been of *high quality*, and the key to

Table 10.2: Perry Preschool Program Per-Child Costs and Benefits to Taxpayers

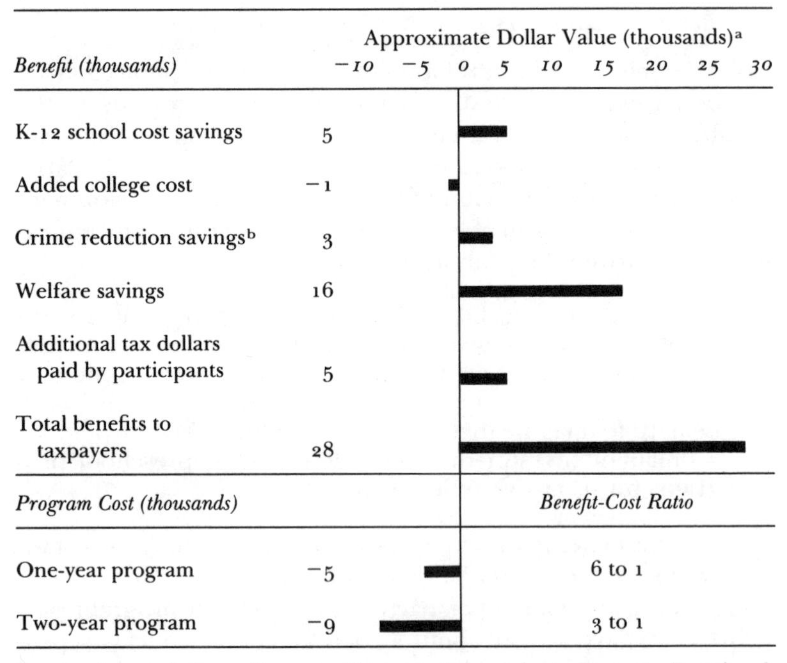

Benefit (thousands)		Approximate Dollar Value (thousands)[a] −10 −5 0 5 10 15 20 25 30
K-12 school cost savings	5	
Added college cost	−1	
Crime reduction savings[b]	3	
Welfare savings	16	
Additional tax dollars paid by participants	5	
Total benefits to taxpayers	28	
Program Cost (thousands)		*Benefit-Cost Ratio*
One-year program	−5	6 to 1
Two-year program	−9	3 to 1

Source: Adapted from Berrueta-Clement, Schweinhart, Barnett, Epstein, & Weikart, 1984.

a. Table entries are constant 1981 dollars, discounted at 3% annually.
b. Savings to citizens as taxpayers and as potential crime victims.

quality is a well-articulated curriculum. It was this issue of defining program quality that the High/Scope Preschool Curriculum Study addressed.

The High/Scope Preschool Curriculum Study

The High/Scope Preschool Curriculum Study (Schweinhart, Weikart, & Larner, 1986) operated in the public schools of Ypsilanti, Michigan, between 1967 and 1970. It served children three and four years old who lived in families of low socioeconomic status and who, according to test scores, were at risk of failing in school. The children were assigned to one of three curriculum models by a random-assignment procedure that was designed to ensure the comparability of the groups. The curriculum models all operated under similar administrative conditions and adhered to high standards of quality: a clearly articulated curriculum, ongoing training and supervision, highly trained teachers, low teacher-pupil ratios, extensive parent involvement, adequate resources, and so on.

The curriculum models used in the project represented three major theoretically distinct approaches to preschool programs. They differed with respect to the degree of initiative expected of the child and the teacher—whether the child's and the teacher's primary roles were to initiate or respond.

The *programmed-learning approach*, in which the teacher initiates activities and the child responds to them, was represented by the direct-instruction preschool program developed by Bereiter and Engelmann (1966) and later published as Distar. In this approach, classroom activities are prescribed by behavioral sequences of stimuli, responses, and positive reinforcements. Objectives are clearly defined academic skills.

Instructional goals consisted largely of drills in which teachers modeled correct language and children imitated them. Manipulation of concrete materials and self-initiated learning did not play a significant role. The program was intended to improve the children's self-confidence by providing opportunities for academic success in an atmosphere of friendly competition. It was also aimed at producing well-socialized students by bringing their behavior under the control of reinforcement contingencies common to elementary school. The day's schedule was as follows:

1. Unstructured time (twenty minutes): children played with materials of their own choice (puzzles, small blocks, table games, and so on).
2. Group singing (fifteen minutes): children learned songs and sang them under the direction of the teachers.
3. Structured time (sixty minutes, twenty minutes for each of three content areas): children were instructed in language, reading, and arithmetic, in small groups.
4. Semistructured time (twenty minutes): children were taught

such school-related skills as coloring, cutting, pasting, sharing of materials, group games.
5. Juice time (fifteen minutes): children had a snack and rested.
6. Story time (ten minutes): children listened to a story read by the teacher and answered questions about it that focused on current instructional goals.

The *open-framework approach*, in which teacher and child both plan and initiate activities and actively work together, was represented by the High/Scope Curriculum (Hohmann et al., 1979). Developed in the Perry Preschool Project, classroom activities revolve around key experiences intended to promote intellectual and social development. The underlying psychological theory is cognitive-developmental, as exemplified in the work of Jean Piaget.

The High/Scope Curriculum offered teachers a conceptual model of child development within which children's day-to-day behavior made sense, and a related set of goals and strategies that could be used to plan and evaluate a developmental program for three- and four-year-olds. It was assumed that children's development occurs not through rote learning but through their active exploration and manipulation of their environment and through transactions with their classmates as well as adults. Teaching strategies were designed to provide children with experiences that would help them achieve developmental goals. Children were encouraged to initiate activities and construct their own learning.

Specifically, the curriculum identified key experiences through which the child's mental abilities could be broadened and strengthened rather than accelerated or directly taught, and it offered strategies that would help teachers provide these experiences. The key experiences included *active learning* (such as direct exploration with all senses); *planning and evaluating* (such as verbally articulating a plan); *using language* (such as conversing about meaningful experiences with adults and peers); *representing* (such as recognizing objects by sound, touch, taste, and smell only); *classification* (such as investigating and labeling the attributes of things); *seriation* (such as comparing things and their attributes); *number concepts* (such as comparing numbers and amounts); *tem-*

poral relations (such as describing past events in words); and *spatial relations* (such as fitting things together and taking them apart).

The day's schedule was as follows:

1. Planning time (twenty minutes): children, assisted by adults, set daily activity goals for themselves.
2. Work time (forty minutes): children carried out plans in work areas.
3. Group time (ten minutes): this included self-evaluation and group discussion of work done, and teacher-initiated activities centering on cognitive goals.
4. Cleanup (fifteen minutes): as children cleaned work areas, teachers helped them classify and seriate the materials.
5. Juice time (twenty-five minutes): teachers worked informally on predetermined goals with small groups of children.
6. Activity time (fifteen minutes): teachers initiated group activities either indoors (music, games) or outdoors (games, use of playground equipment).
7. Circle time (fifteen minutes): teachers led a review of the day's work and sometimes read stories.
8. Dismissal (ten minutes): teachers introduced concepts experienced during the day into the process of preparing to go home.

The *child-centered approach*, in which the child initiates and the teacher responds, was represented by a nursery school program that incorporated the elements of what has historically constituted good nursery school practice. In this approach, classroom activities are the teacher's responses to the child's expressed needs and interests, and the teacher encourages children to actively engage in free play. The curriculum grew out of the traditional nursery school approach to early childhood education.

Units or themes (like holidays, farm animals, circus, seasons) were the focuses of activities and discussions over the course of the year. The teachers were guided in their day-to-day formulation of the educational program by their intuition and by several assumptions about child development: that children learn and develop by discovering for themselves through direct experience how the world works; that children are intrinsically motivated to learn about the world; that their motivation to learn may be stifled, however, by a restrictive environment or emotional insecurity; that different children have different needs, interests, and talents and that they develop in different ways at different rates; and that social, emotional, physical, and aesthetic development are just as important as intellectual development to the well-being of the whole child.

The day's schedule for this approach was as follows:

1. Circle time and music time (forty-five minutes): teachers worked with the entire group of children (usually seated), introducing unit-related materials, reading stories, singing songs, working with puppets, counting, learning body parts or one another's names.
2. Discovery time and cleanup (sixty minutes): children engaged in free play in one of four activity areas (housekeeping, large-motor activities, fine-motor activities, art).
3. Group time (fifteen minutes): teachers read stories or initiated relatively quiet activities (like coloring, pasting) and children had juice and cookies.
4. Outdoor time (fifteen minutes): children engaged in free play outdoors when weather permitted.
5. Dismissal (fifteen minutes): children prepared to go home.

All three programs in the study were part of the same research project, with the same director (Weikart), funding source, and personnel policies, and all operated within the Special Services Division of the public school system. All three programs had two components—classroom sessions and educational home visits. Classroom sessions lasting two and a half hours were held Monday through Friday. A teacher visited each mother and child at home in ninety-minute sessions every two weeks, during the part of the day when the class was not meeting. During the home visits, the teacher encouraged the mother to engage her child in learning activities that fit the curriculum approach used in that classroom.

Each year, the new three-year-old children were randomly assigned to three groups, with reassignments until the three groups were comparable in race, gender, and mean IQ at program entry. Children with IQs between 60 and 90, with no evidence of physical disability, were eligible for enrollment. Their mean IQ at program entry was 78.3. On this basis, before they attended the preschool programs, the children in the study could have been temporarily classified as slow learners at risk of school failure. The three groups were then randomly assigned to the three preschool curriculum models. Each school year, the preschool programs brought together two groups of children—one as four-year-olds and one as three-year-olds. Because of this feature, two additional groups of children participated in the preschool programs with the study participants—one group prior to the study sample, one after—but were not part of the study.

Some of the characteristics at program entry of the sixty-eight children in the program and their families were as follows: 65 percent were black; 54 percent were female; the families lived in poverty, with one out of three receiving welfare assistance; in the 75 percent of families for whom fathers were present, 98 percent of the fathers were employed in unskilled labor; 38 percent of the mothers were employed in unskilled labor; fathers averaged nine years of schooling, mothers, ten; the average household had 6.7 persons, or 1 person per room.

Curriculum groups were similar on the key characteristics of gender, family socioeconomic status, and child IQ at program entry. But the nursery school group did have some initial advantages over the other groups, particularly the High/Scope group: mothers had a higher level of schooling and fewer children in the group came from single-parent families. Also, fewer blacks and more whites were in the nursery school group.

Of the sixty-eight youngsters in the program, fifty-four were interviewed at age fifteen—a retention rate of 79 percent. Previous data collections from ages three to ten, which took place either in the preschool programs or in the schools, had retention rates of 90 percent or better. Comparison of these characteristics of the remaining sample at age fifteen to the original sample characteristics indicates that the age-fifteen sample was virtually equivalent to the original sample in every respect.

High/Scope Preschool Curriculum Effects

When the program-entry mean IQs (79, 80, and 81) of the three preschool curriculum groups are compared, the differences among the three groups are not significant. During the first year of the preschool program, mean IQs rose between 23 and 29 points, moving all three groups of children out of the at-risk category. During the second preschool year, mean IQs of the High/Scope and nursery school groups dropped 9 to 10 points, whereas that of the Distar group dropped only 3 points and thereby achieved the only statistically significant intellectual advantage among groups at any testing. From the end of kindergarten onward, however, curriculum groups did not differ in mean IQs and stabilized in the range of 90 to 100, significantly above their entry test scores. When all follow-up IQs (from ages four through ten) were averaged to give a mean IQ over time, the three preschool curriculum groups did not differ significantly from one another: the Distar group averaged 97, the High/Scope group 96, and the nursery school group 94. Each group differed significantly from their program-entry scores.

Achievement scores were gathered for all the children via the California Achievements Tests (CAT, lower primary form W) at the end of first and second grades. Each of the groups gained between 50 and 60 points between the two testings (using the same test form), and the groups were not significantly different from one another at either time. This is to be expected, since the early IQ differences that separated the groups diminished by kindergarten and disappeared by the second grade. The modest early advantage the Distar group had over the other two was not translated into superior achievement in elementary school.

At age fifteen the Adult Performance Level Survey (APL) was employed. This instrument measures a person's competence in solving real-world problems and coping with the cognitive demands of adult life. The APL total and subscale scores of the three preschool groups showed that the Distar group scored the lowest on nine of the eleven APL scales, to a statistically significant extent for occupational knowledge and approaching a statistically significant extent for writing.

On self-report ratings of social behaviors, there were clear-cut and significant differences between the Distar group on one hand and the High/Scope and nursery school groups on the other. The average member of the Distar group at age fifteen engaged in thirteen self-reported delinquent acts (girls, fourteen; boys, twelve), the average nursery school group member engaged in seven (girls, seven; boys, seven), and the average High/Scope member engaged in five (girls, four; boys, eight). On all but one item of the eighteen-item scale, the Distar group reported the highest frequency, or was tied for the highest frequency, of the three groups. On the delinquency scale, then, the Distar group reported a highly significant rate of juvenile delinquency when compared to the other two groups.

The eighteen-item delinquency scale is divided into five subscales—personal violence, property violence, stealing, drug abuse, and status offenses. The Distar group engaged in twice as many acts of personal violence as the other two groups. The Distar group engaged in five times as many acts of property violence as did the other two groups, reporting 1.7 acts per person as compared to only .3 acts per person in the other two groups. The Distar group had the highest frequencies of the three groups on each of the three items in that subscale; the difference in the arson category approached statistical significance. The Distar group also reported that they engaged in twice as many acts of drug abuse as did the other two groups, in use of marijuana and other illegal drugs. The Distar group reported that they engaged in twice as many activities that we have labeled "status offenses," exceeding the other two groups in fights with parents, trespassing, and, to a statistically significant extent, running away from home.

Curriculum groups at age fifteen did not yet manifest statistically significant differences in official contact with the police. Gold (1970) has reported similar findings—that group differences in self-reported delinquency do not yet show up in arrest rate differences for fifteen-year-olds. Regardless of curriculum group, half the members of the sample reported having been picked up or arrested by police by age fifteen; the average sample member reported contact with the police .5 times, while average self-reported delinquency acts for the total sample was 8. In the Perry Project police arrests "caught up" with self-reported delinquency by age nineteen, suggesting a bleak future for the Distar group.

Curriculum group members at age fifteen reported on family relations, activities, school behavior and attitudes, and mental health. Corroborating the juvenile delinquency reports of the Distar group, the few group differences found in these areas suggest greater problems experienced by the Distar group as compared to the other two curriculum groups. One out of three members of the Distar group said their families felt they were doing poorly, a response made by only one out of thirty-six members of the other two curriculum groups combined. And whereas one out of five members of the Distar group reported getting along poorly with their families, no one in the High/Scope group made this response. Finally, one out of three members of the High/Scope group reported contributing to household expenses, but fewer than one out of six members of the Distar group did so. Given the substantially higher rates of delinquent behavior reported by the Distar group, their greater frequency of poor family relations should come as no surprise.

In the area of activities, the biggest group difference was in sports participation: nearly all the High/Scope group participated in sports, whereas fewer than half of the Distar group did so. Compared to members of the Distar group, twice as many members of the High/Scope group had recently read a book.

No one in the Distar group had ever been appointed to an office or special job at school. The strongest contrast here was with the nursery school group, which reported one out of three members with some school appointment. Only half of the Distar group expected to pursue postsecondary education, whereas two-thirds of the nursery school group and three-quarters of the High/Scope group expected to do so.

Although the three curriculum groups reported about the same numbers of personal problems, the Distar group members were least likely to seek help for them. Only two out of eighteen did so, as contrasted with seven out of eighteen in the High/Scope group.

To summarize the group differences among the children at age fifteen, then, more of the Distar group members reported they were not socially well adjusted, compared to both the High/Scope and the nursery school groups. Clearly, these data suggest that there are social consequences to curriculum choice.

Summary and Policy Considerations

When the High/Scope Preschool Curriculum study was established in 1967, the most effective preschool programs were thought to be those that espoused a structured curriculum. Such a curriculum has been interpreted by many educators to mean a formal didactic program with instructional "cookbooks" to help teachers remediate the difficulties their students encounter. Other approaches, such as open classrooms and developmental models, were thought to be not structured enough to achieve success. The High/Scope study explored this issue of structure by examining three theoretically diverse curriculum approaches, none of them representative of chaotic nonsystematic models of education.

In a monograph that reported earlier data on participants through age ten (Weikart, Epstein, Schweinhart, & Bond, 1978), the startling conclusion was reached that, insofar as intellectual and scholastic performance could be measured, all three models appeared to achieve the same positive results. On the whole, the school-related results were better than those obtained with the experimental group of High/Scope's Perry Preschool study by the same age. These findings of equivalence in intellectual and academic outcomes were surprising at the time of the report because the central issue in early childhood education has long been the selection of curriculum. Early childhood educators have divergent views about how best to meet the needs of children and achieve instructional goals from their theoretical perspective. The curriculum study showed that diverse curriculum models can be *equally* effective in improving children's education and that this success does not appear to derive from the models themselves, but rather from the way the programs are administered and operated.

This unexpected finding of model equivalence has since been verified by the Consortium for Longitudinal Studies (1983). This careful analysis of fourteen early-intervention projects included several curriculum comparison projects as well as longitudinal-program versus no-program studies. The design permitted a search for differential curriculum outcomes. Royce, Darlington, and Murray (1983) summarized the findings as follows:

> We found no significant differences in later school outcomes related to curricula. All the curricula were successful in reducing school failure. . . . It may be that finer-grained outcome measures or *measures of social learning* would find dif-

> ferential effects, but the present indicators did not. It appears that a variety of curricula are equally effective in preparing children for school and that any of the tested curricula is better than no preschool program at all. (p. 442; emphasis added)

Now new data from the High/Scope Preschool Curriculum study suggests a more complex conclusion. The curriculum study through age fifteen has produced two major findings. First, it has replicated the central finding of the Perry Preschool study and others in the Consortium for Longitudinal Studies (1983), demonstrating once again that high-quality preschool programs for poor children can lead to improvements in their intellectual and scholastic performance.

Second, it has found significant differences at age fifteen in social behavior outcomes among the groups experiencing various curriculum approaches. In this study, the group that received a preschool program using the teacher-directed Distar model, when compared to groups receiving preschool programs that encouraged children to initiate their own activities, showed substantially higher rates of self-reported juvenile delinquency and associated problems. Given that the youngsters in this study were only fifteen years old, and building on the findings of the Perry Preschool study at this age, it is anticipated that the groups will continue to diverge in the coming years, making it likely that group differences in crime and delinquency will eventually be even larger.

The curriculum study's most recent data suggest, then, that there are important social consequences to preschool curriculum choices. In the earlier elementary school years, trends that were not statistically significant foreshadowed these later findings. According to the ratings of first- and second-grade teachers, the Distar group consistently was rated lower than the High/Scope group on sociability, cooperation, and academic orientation (Weikart et al., 1978, p. 89). These slight differences in social behavior were replaced by pronounced group differences in self-reported social behavior at age fifteen. In the report on the curriculum study through age ten, Weikart et al. (1978) said: "The ultimate outcome of any educational experience . . . is the kind of adult which each child becomes. Differential program impact upon adult development is an empirical issue, and one that must await further longitudinal research as individuals progress beyond the school years" (p. 136).

There is no evidence here that youngsters in the Distar group engaged in *more* delinquency than they would have if they had not attended the preschool program. Indeed, their self-reported juvenile delinquency pattern is no worse than that of the Perry Preschool study control-group youngsters. Therefore, we are inclined to believe that the preschool Distar experience did not actually harm the children's social development. After all, the program's major goals were academic. It is reasonable, therefore, to find few if any social behavior effects, positive or negative. The point is that the other two preschool curriculum approaches in this study did have social behavior goals and did appear to produce favorable long-term social effects indicated by lower rates of juvenile delinquency and other social behavior problems, as well as equivalent academic outcomes.

We can speculate about why social alienation occurred among such a substantial number of youths in the Distar group. Traditional early childhood educators recognizing the stress may be quick to say, "I told you so." Most cognitive-developmental theorists subscribe to the need for children to construct their own learning and build their own relationships with teachers and friends. Apparently a preschool curriculum that emphasizes direct transmission of knowledge is less successful in helping children adapt to the interpersonal realities of rules and conventions.

Social theorists such as Erikson (1950) state that the early childhood period of life is the time a child acquires a sense of initiative and overcomes a sense of guilt in exercising that capacity. Initiative promotes inquisitiveness and adventurousness. If the child is directed by adults and initiative is treated as misbehavior or failure to attend, then the child may develop a sense of guilt about the capacity to perform and not learn the skills of self-direction. The adolescent expresses this as alienation, which shows up in the home, school, and community. Poor relations with the family, failure to support the family, drug usage, delinquency offenses, and property violence all express this separation.

Young children appear to learn from both their relationship to their teachers and friends and the manner in which they gain knowledge. Although knowledge that young children gain for themselves in various curriculum approaches may appear to be the same as the knowledge that is dispensed to the child, the social consequences for the child may be very different.

For some years, we interpreted the early findings of the High/Scope Preschool Curriculum Study as implying that high-quality early childhood education could be built upon *any theoretically coherent model*. But the study with its age-fifteen data no longer permits that conclusion. Tenuous though the data are, it is now clear that a high-quality preschool curriculum is based on *child-initiated learning activities*.

This report requires major restraint in its use and interpretation. These are the data that traditional early childhood educators have been predicting since journalist Maya Pines introduced the Bereiter-Engelmann method to the world as a "pressure-cooker" approach in the mid-1960s. These are the findings that direct instruction specialists have considered unlikely, because academic skill improvement was seen to promote self-esteem and adjustment to the real world. Actually, what these data add to the debate is a plea for caution. The sample size for the study, while carefully drawn and randomly assigned over a three-year period, was small. The findings must be replicated in other projects with good enough data to explore this issue. We do plan to collect data on the curriculum study sample, as we did in the Perry study, in late adolescence after high school graduation, particularly data pertaining to delinquency and social behavior.

These findings cannot be generalized to types of children who were not included in our sample—we studied only poor children at risk of school failure. Both the Perry study and the curriculum study indicate the importance of the early childhood period, ages three and four, to the overall development of the child—look at the astonishing decade-plus period of commitment and positive outcomes on school and social performances found in both studies. But what these studies indicate is that intervention is helpful to children similar to those involved. Middle-class children who were not studied have not been either negatively or positively affected by early education experiences in other studies. Such children apparently are given their positive "intervention" from the traditional family-rearing methods. It is also important to note that even under the special conditions of these studies, not all disadvantaged children were "helped." Finally, and what the study set out to examine is that not all curricula work the same. The Distar participants did not improve their social behavior as the others did.

Although this single research study does not justify drawing policy recommendations, it does suggest some policy considerations. It confirms what child development experts over the years have said—that this age is an important period of time. Educators need to beware of treating the child too firmly, of being too domineering, and of not respecting the child's inherent growth patterns and rhythms. If they become too directive, the child will have problems. Therefore, there is good reason for the concern among child development professionals about the "superbaby" concept, the pressure cooker, and other *formal* academic approaches.

This study found consequences for later social growth based on early education experiences of children in the three-to-five age span, what Piaget calls the preoperational period. More broadly, it raised the issue of the role of formal schooling with any child in the preoperational age group from three to six and perhaps seven. Professionals and parents concerned with children's development at ages three and four need to involve elementary school principals in thinking about these issues, for they call into question the validity of the "push-down curriculum" of formal academic training from higher grades to kindergarten programs. Such an approach may be socially disruptive to disadvantaged children at this stage of development.

Certainly, these results must give pause to plans for formal academic schooling at age four. Although *good* early childhood programs are an effective way to improve the life chances of disadvantaged children, *formal academic* programs as represented by teacher-directed learning models may be inadequate to the task, because they fail to have the desired social behavior consequences.

Finally, current uses of teacher-directed learning methods in early childhood care and education should be subjected to careful scrutiny and rigorous evaluation. Although it would be inappropriate, on the strength of this curriculum study alone, to suggest across-the-board curtailment of teacher-directed models, the fact that direct-instruction approaches may be ineffective in reducing children's later social behavior problems should be carefully evaluated. We cannot continue to excuse an almost exclusive focus on the use of intellectual and academic measures for program evaluation because valid measures of social competence are difficult to develop. It is also time to initiate longitudinal studies on the long-term intellectual and social effects of teacher- and child-initiated curriculum approaches. As in the field of medicine, rigorous long-term evaluations under careful conditions must be conducted to uncover unintended consequences or undesirable side effects of programs based on any theory. This need is especially true when the programs differ from historically accepted approaches. Short-term research is not sufficient.

The High/Scope Preschool Curriculum study raises important questions for parents, professionals, and policymakers concerned with equity and the amelioration of social problems. It is not a definitive study by any means, but the critical issues it raises regarding the proper education of our children beg for further discussion.

REFERENCES

Bereiter, C., & Engelmann, S. (1966). *Teaching the disadvantaged child in the preschool*. Englewood Cliffs, NJ: Prentice-Hall.

Berrueta-Clement, J. R., Schweinhart, L. J., Barnett, W. S., Epstein, A. S., & Weikart, D. P. (1984). *Changed lives: The effects of the Perry Preschool Program on youths through age 19* (Monographs of the High/Scope Educational Research Foundation No. 8). Ypsilanti, MI: High/Scope Press.

Committee for Economic Development. (1985). *Investing in our children*. New York: Author.

Consortium for Longitudinal Studies. (1983). *As the twig is bent . . . Lasting effects of preschool programs*. Hillsdale, NJ: Lawrence Erlbaum Associates.

Erikson, Erik, H. (1950). *Childhood and society*. New York: W. W. Norton.

Gold, M. (1970). *Delinquent behavior in an American city*. Belmont, CA: Brooks/Cole.

Gray, S. W., Ramsey, B. K., & Klaus, R. A. (1982). *From 3 to 20—The Early Training Project*. Baltimore, MD: University Park Press.

Hohmann, M., Banet, B., & Weikart, D. P. (1979). *Young children in action: A manual for preschool educators*. Ypsilanti, MI: High/Scope Press.

Irvine, D. J. (1982). *Evaluation of the New York State Experimental Prekindergarten Program*. Paper presented at the annual meeting of the American Educational Research Association, New York City.

Jordan, T., Grallo, R., Deutsch, M., & Deutsch, C. (1985). Long-term effects of early enrichment: A 20-year perspective on persistence and change. *American Journal of Community Psychology*, *13*(4).

Levenstein, P., O'Hara, J., & Madden, J. (1983). The Mother-Child Home program of the verbal interaction project. In Consortium for Longitudinal Studies, *As the twig is bent . . . Lasting effects of preschool programs* (pp. 237–264). Hillsdale, NJ: Lawrence Erlbaum Associates.

Nebraska State Board of Education. (1986, Spring). What's best for 5-year-olds? Reprint in *High/Scope Resource*, pp. 3, 4, 8.

Palmer, F. H. (1983). The Harlem Study: Effects by type of training, age of training, and social class. In Consortium for Longitudinal Studies, *As the twig is bent . . . Lasting effects of preschool programs* (pp. 201–236). Hillsdale, NJ: Lawrence Erlbaum Associates.

Royce, J. M., Darlington, R. B., & Murray, H. W. (1983). Pooled analyses: Findings across studies. In Consortium for Longitudinal Studies, *As the twig is bent . . . Lasting effects of preschool programs* (pp. 411–460). Hillsdale, NJ: Lawrence Erlbaum Associates.

Schweinhart, L. J., Weikart, D. P., & Larner, M. B. (1986). Consequences of three preschool curriculum models through age 15. *Early Childhood Research Quarterly*, *1*, 15–45.

Weikart, D. P., Epstein, A. S., Schweinhart, L. J., & Bond, J. T. (1978). *The Ypsilanti Preschool Curriculum Demonstration Project: Preschool years and longitudinal results* (Monographs of the High/Scope Educational Research Foundation No. 4). Ypsilanti, MI: High/Scope Press.

CHAPTER 11

Comparing Preschool Curricula and Practices: The State of Research

DOUGLAS R. POWELL

The long-standing debate about the appropriateness and effectiveness of different approaches to early childhood education is returning to a central position in discussions about preschool education. The resurgence of interest in the methods and content of early education stems partly from questions about the education of four-year-olds in public schools. The debate also has been rekindled by recent reports of longitudinal research on the consequences of different curricula, and by efforts of national professional associations to determine appropriate educational practice with young children.

As a research issue, the question of "what works best" has not commanded center stage since the late 1960s and very early 1970s. The 1965 launching of Project Head Start and similar early intervention programs generated a flurry of curriculum development work, fueled by perceived inadequacies of the traditional middle-class nursery school model for children from low-income communities; excitement about the work of Jean Piaget, including applications of his theory of cognitive development to early education; and renewed interest in parent education. A host

Portions of this chapter appeared in an article entitled "Research in Review: Effects of Program Models and Teaching Practices," *Young Children*, September 1986.

of curriculum models were developed, implemented, reformulated, and sometimes abandoned. Supporters of the early intervention concept as well as advocates of different curriculum models wanted answers to an obvious research question: what approach is best? Several investigations were undertaken, including the ambitious Head Start Planned Variation experiment (Bissell, 1973).

But interest in curriculum comparison research waned in the early 1970s as the early education agenda shifted dramatically to other issues. The negative findings of the Westinghouse-Ohio study of Head Start (Cicirelli, 1969) significantly altered public debate about early intervention. Attention focused on whether early education was beneficial for disadvantaged children, not which curriculum to use. The lack of robust data on positive Head Start effects called into question the existence of the fledgling early intervention enterprise.

Moreover, serious questions were raised about the desirability and feasibility of curriculum comparison research. In the late 1960s and early 1970s, results of studies comparing alternative curricula indicated different preschool programs had roughly equivalent effects on children (Weikart, 1972; Smith, 1975). For instance, none of the twelve different preschool models examined in the Head Start Planned Variation study was more or less effective than the others on more than two of five child outcome measures. There were, "to put it bluntly, no overall winners or losers" (Smith, 1975, p. 108). These findings contributed to a prevailing notion in the 1970s and 1980s that any well-administered curriculum could achieve positive effects. The influential report of one study, which found no differential effects in a comparison of three preschool curricula, concluded that the key issue in early childhood education was "not *which* curriculum to use, but how to manage *any* curriculum to achieve positive results" (Weikart, Epstein, Schweinhart, & Bond, 1978, p. 136).

Large-scale studies of planned curriculum variation proved to be exceedingly difficult. The Head Start Planned Variation experiment encountered major implementation problems, including variations in the local adaptation of program models and a lack of precise goals and operational procedures for many program models (Lukas, 1975). A comparison study of Follow

Through program models experienced similar problems (McDaniels, 1975). Key leaders in curriculum comparison studies—members of the Brookings Panel on Social Experimentation—met in April 1973 to discuss what had been learned from large planned variation studies. The resulting publication was entitled "Planned Variation in Education: Should We Give Up or Try Harder?" (Rivlin & Timpane, 1975).

The phenomenal growth of all-day child care in the 1970s and 1980s also served to foreshadow interest in the debate about preschool curricula and teaching practices. Issues regarding the need for child care, and whether it is good or bad for children, dominated the field of early education. In addition to day-care effects, structural dimensions of child care directly related to cost (for example, staff-child ratios, group size, sponsorship, staff credentials) surfaced as key research questions.

The return of curriculum issues to the forefront of interest in early childhood education in the late 1980s is partly a function of the field's maturation. In an effort to improve its professional status and the quality of programs for young children, the field has moved in recent years to set forth standards of early education. Growing public school interest in the education of four-year-olds also has pushed early childhood professional associations to take positions on what early education should look like. The National Association for the Education of Young Children has issued guidelines for developmentally appropriate practice with young children (Bredekamp, 1986) and has established an accreditation system for preschool programs. The International Reading Association (1986) also has established parameters for the role of reading education in programs for preschoolers. These moves have forced the field to determine what is acceptable and unacceptable curricular practice. At the same time, recent long-term results of several curriculum comparison studies begun in the late 1960s suggest that, unlike the earlier reports, there do appear to be differences across preschool curricula in their consequences for children in later life. Perhaps there are some "winners" after all. The question of which curriculum to use in educating young children has regained its prominence in public and professional interest in early schooling.

As the field returns to a debate that has existed since the

development of formal educational programs for young children, it is important to consider the state of research on the consequences of different approaches to early education. This chapter critically explores the substantive yield and some methodological problems of research on the dimensions and effects of contrasting preschool curricula and teaching practices. The aim is to assess the extent to which existing research can answer the question of what practices should and should not be pursued in the education of four-year-olds.

Most of the studies examined in this chapter involved experimental preschool interventions with black children from low-income families. The programs were viewed as ameliorative in nature. The generalizability of findings from this research, however, is a major question. Program purposes and sample characteristics need to be considered. The closest fit of the existing work is to educational programs for four-year-olds that have ameliorative purposes and serve black children from low-income communities. To the degree educational programs for four-year-olds vary from these characteristics (for example, kindergarten readiness programs for children from middle-class homes), most of the existing research cannot be used as a firm basis for curriculum decisions. This is an important qualifier since the generalizability of findings from preschool studies has been problematic in the past—for example, using positive results of an idiosyncratic curriculum intervention with disadvantaged children to justify the existence of a custodial child-care program.

Two sets of questions have guided comparative research on curriculum and teaching practices. The main difference between these sets is the degree to which interactions between child characteristics and specific program practices are considered.

The first set of research questions has attempted to determine whether particular approaches to early education affect children differently. This set has two variants. One has sought to identify the superior curriculum or practice; it has assumed there is an ideal or best approach to early childhood education as measured by some outcome criterion, such as IQ. The other variant of this set has assumed different types of preschool practice influence children in different ways. The intent has been to investigate relationships between specific types of practice and child behavior or outcome (for example, practice A is associated with higher IQ but lower performance in interpersonal problem solving than practice B). These two variants differ primarily in the number or range of child outcomes considered. Both variants assume a given curriculum or teaching practice has similar effects on children. Operating here is a unidirectional model of influence, from program to child.

In contrast, the second set of questions guiding research on curriculum and teaching practices has assumed child attributes may influence the effects and/or the nature of the treatment. Variations in the effects of a particular curriculum or practice have been examined in relation to such child characteristics as gender (for example, do direct instruction techniques influence boys differently than girls?). Child gender also has been considered in relation to teacher behaviors (do teachers' instructional behaviors vary by child sex?). Rather than identify the superior early education model, this second set of research questions has sought to specify interactions between child characteristics and curriculum or teaching practice.

This chapter considers literature relevant to both sets of questions. As a preface to discussion of this work, methodological problems are examined.

Methodological Problems

Although most problems and issues found in field-based program evaluation work (such as subject attrition) are encountered in research on curriculum models and teaching practices, this section will consider only the methodological problems unique to this research. (A cogent discussion of these hurdles in research on early childhood programs is found in Clarke-Stewart & Fein, 1983.)

A major difficulty in research designed to determine relationships between classroom processes and child outcome is the confounding of content, activities, and materials with teaching techniques. Some teaching methods are inherently tied to program content. For example, because drill involves repetition, it cannot be used as a teaching technique for helping a child find alternative solutions (Miller, Bugbee, & Hybertson, 1985). This confusion of content and method makes it difficult to determine specific links between program components and child outcome. The relevant program dimension is not clear. What leads to what? This problem is found in two common research strategies employed to examine classroom practices and child outcome: comparison of intact curriculum models (like free-play nursery school versus direct instruction) and naturalistic observation of a variety of preschool classrooms (for example, Prescott, Jones, & Kritchevsky, 1967).

Some researchers have attempted to solve this problem of content-method confounding by experimentally varying teaching techniques while holding constant the program content. Teachers are trained to use different teaching methods with the same content. This approach, however, is not without its problems (for a detailed discussion, see Miller et al., 1985). First, it is not possible to manipulate teaching technique without modifying program content (for example, Wright & Nuthall, 1970). Second, discrete teaching practices may be effective when combined with other techniques to form a pattern but may not be important as a separate unit. Miller et al. (1985) offer a good example: the proper ratio of structuring a task to asking questions may be a necessary condition for adequate learning, but the absolute amount of either variable may not be important. The appropriate unit of instruction, then, remains elusive. Third, the generalizability of teaching behaviors—a positive feature of naturalistic observation of contrasting classrooms—is seriously limited when teacher roles and behaviors are rigidly prescribed and highly controlled.

The observation of classroom practices is essential to the naturalistic research strategy of comparing a variety of classrooms and should be (but has not always been) a part of the research strategy of comparing intact curriculum models or the procedure of manipulating teaching technique while holding content constant. Without precise observational data on classroom processes, curriculum comparison studies are unable to offer assurances that the models were implemented according to model specifications and, further, that the supposedly contrasting preschool programs were indeed different. An important lesson from the Head Start Planned Variation study is that substantial variation can exist across sites in implementing the same model (Lukas, 1975). Teacher acceptance and understanding of a model's approaches and practices can also be a major challenge in implementing some models (Weikart & Banet, 1975). While variations in the implementation of a model program pose an interesting set of research questions in their own right, curriculum comparison research concerned with child outcome is best carried out with a systematic check on the integrity of the model's implementation and existence of significant process differences between treatments.

This is easier said than done. When two or more pedagogical practices are being compared, measurement of program models entails some problems with no clear-cut solutions. A single comprehensive observational system is likely to be limited in generating descriptive data on classroom processes in theoretically diverse programs. Variables pertinent to one classroom might be of little significance to another (Shapiro, 1973). If separate observational systems are employed for each program, comparability across programs is compromised. Another problem surrounds the measurement of what is delivered versus what is experienced or consumed in a program. For example, to discover that teachers interact with boys differently than girls does not mean boys and/or girls experience the difference in the ways it has been observed. Persuasive arguments have been made for measuring program dimensions from the participant's perspective (see Zimiles, 1977), but how this idea can be operationalized in valid and reliable ways with young children is not clear.

Like the problem of measuring classroom processes across diverse educational approaches, the selection of outcome variables relevant to varying preschool programs can be difficult. Preschool models represent differing views about the goals of early education, and hence a study of program effects should include outcome measures appropriate to the aims of a particular model or cluster of models. For comparison, however, there needs to be a set of common measures to determine how models fare on the same criteria. A useful approach might include both types of measures, those appropriate to a specific model and a set of common outcome measures. This would allow models to be assessed both by their own objectives and in terms of the goals of other models (Rivlin & Timpane, 1975). The problem with this strategy is that reliable and valid measures have not been available. Academic or IQ performance has been used extensively as a child outcome variable in curriculum comparison studies, primarily because good assessment tools exist. Its relevance to the substance of program operations may be greater with some curricula (such as didactic instruction) than with others (nondidactic/experiential). Social competence is of great interest to researchers and practitioners alike, but again measurement is problematic (Zigler & Trickett, 1979).

Some recent research on the effects of preschool education has used social indicators like placement in special education, retention in grade, or crime record as outcome variables. These indicators are appealing to cost-conscious policymakers and to the general public, probably because they represent widely understood standards of child performance. Clarke-Stewart and Fein (1983) ask crucial questions, however, about the interpretation of positive findings: if there are no differences between comparison groups of children on school achievement, do positive findings on social indicators mean reasons other than academic criteria are operating? If so, what are these criteria?

Preschool Models and Dimensions

Ideological differences regarding the content and method of early childhood education are deep and long-standing. The differences are rooted in sharply contrasting conceptions of developmental processes and of the role of the environment in facilitating development. Major models of early education loosely parallel three theoretical perspectives on child development: maturationist, behaviorist, and cognitive-developmental (Kohlberg & Mayer, 1972). The philosophical and psychological underpinnings of educational approaches are manifest in such arguments as the amount of teacher versus child directiveness, group versus individual instruction, and the amount of teacher-giving versus teacher-asking information. To what degree should the teacher or child initiate activities in the classroom? Should teachers primarily give information or ask a child for information? If the latter, should the questions elicit a "right" answer or encourage divergent problem-solving processes? Should socioemotional needs be a central part of the teacher's concern? These are not esoteric questions, removed from the real lives of real children. There is evidence of a link between the experiences of children and the educational ideology operating in a classroom. For instance, children's play behavior has been found to differ in relation to the amount of teacher directiveness in both Head Start (Huston-Stein, Friedrich-Cofer, & Susman, 1977) and middle-class (Johnson, Ershler, & Bell, 1980) preschool classrooms.

Perhaps the sharpest debate regarding early education practices surrounds the use of such didactic methods as drill and practice to transmit information to children. This approach is at odds with both the maturationist perspective and the cognitive-developmental view of early education. The intensity of the didactic versus nondidactic difference is seen most clearly in the teacher roles assumed in respective models. For the nondidactic traditional nursery school approach, maturational growth is the boss in determining a child's interests and readiness to learn (Hymes, 1955). Adults should not "try to tamper with the process of a child's own development" (Jersild, 1946, p. 1). Yet for a developer of a didactic preschool model (Bereiter-Englemann, 1966), the "minimization of teaching" in the traditional nursery school model indicates the model is not "a distinctive approach to teaching, but a system of custodial child care" (Bereiter, 1972, p. 12).

Major curriculum comparison studies initiated in the 1960s included a program model representative of didactic and nondidactic approaches. The studies used a strategy of comparing intact curriculum models, typically involving a model's expert to train and monitor the teachers implementing the model. The remainder of this section provides an overview of the scope of major studies. Findings are reviewed in the next section.

The Louisville Experiment, initiated by Louise Miller and her colleagues in the Head Start program in Louisville, Kentucky, compared four preschool programs (Miller & Bizzell, 1983b). Two programs used didactic instructional methods with small groups of children. One of these programs was the direct instruction model developed by Bereiter and Englemann (B-E) (1966). In B-E direct instruction, teachers use a patterned drill procedure to elicit responses in unison from children. The pace is rapid and repetitive. The curriculum is organized into reading, language, and arithmetic.

The other didactic program in the Louisville Experiment was DARCEE, developed by Susan Gray (see Gray, Ramsey, & Klaus, 1982). It is designed to enhance perceptual/cognitive and language development, and to instill attitudes related to academic achievement (such as delayed gratification). Formal instruction in language is a major part of the program.

The two other programs in the Louisville Experiment did not entail group instruction. One was a Montessori (1964) program that emphasizes developing the senses, conceptual development, competence in daily activities, and character development. The child decides which activities to pursue. The other nondidactic program was a traditional nursery school that focuses on social and emotional development. Consistent with the child development point of view (Hymes, 1968), this program emphasizes development in all areas at each child's pace. The largest single portion of the school day is occupied by free play, a time when children engage in whatever activities they choose.

The Louisville Experiment included an initial sample of 214 four-year-olds in the four program models plus a control group of 34 children. Children were randomly assigned to programs by school. The study involved four each B-E, DARCEE, and traditional classrooms, and two Montessori classrooms (14 in all). The short-term effects (through second grade) are reported in Miller and Dyer (1975), and the long-term effects are reported in Miller and Bizzell (1983a, 1983b).

The High/Scope Curriculum Comparison Study (Schweinhart, Weikart, & Larner, 1986) was developed by David Weikart in Ypsilanti, Michigan, to compare three program models: B-E direct instruction, the High/Scope model, and a traditional child-centered nursery school. There was no comparison group. The High/Scope model uses an open-framework approach where teacher and child plan and initiate activities and actively work together. It is known as the High/Scope Cognitively Oriented Preschool Curriculum (Hohmann, Banet, & Weikart, 1979). Parents of each child in all program models received a home visit from the teacher every two weeks. Initially the study involved sixty-eight three- and four-year-old children from low-income families; 65 percent were black. Children were randomly assigned to program models. Study details and a follow-up of the children at ten years of age are reported in Weikart et al. (1978). A follow-up at fifteen years of age is reported in Schweinhart et al. (1986).

Discussion of the long-term effects found in the Louisville and High/Scope studies will be supplemented by findings from curriculum comparison studies by Karnes and her colleagues (Karnes, Shwedel, & Williams, 1983) involving preschool children, and by Stallings (1975) involving Follow Through classrooms in first and third grades. This chapter also draws on additional research reports of short-term studies of teaching practices and child outcome.

As noted earlier, a major limitation of curriculum comparison studies is that they confound content, activities, and materials with teaching techniques. To avoid this problem, Miller et al. (1985) conducted a study in which both content (language) and global teaching method (small group instruction) were controlled in order to determine whether specific teaching techniques (amount of reinforcement) were related to child outcome. This one-year study involved eight Head Start classrooms where teachers used the Peabody Language Development Program (Dunn, Horton, & Smith, 1968) in a standardized manner. The sample included 111 four-year-old children from low-income, predominantly black families. This research, which I will call the Preschool Dimensions Study, should not be confused with the Louisville Experiment; they were different investigations.

Preschool Pedagogy and Child Outcomes

Findings of the longitudinal curriculum comparison studies suggest that the kind of preschool attended by low-income children may affect them through their middle-school and early teenage years. The results raise questions about the effects of didactic approaches to early education, especially for boys, and also about reasons for variations in preschool effects by child gender. The differences in program effects by sex of child are particularly striking.

Follow-up data from the Louisville Experiment show that by eighth grade, boys who had been enrolled in a nondidactic preschool program (Montessori or traditional) were superior in school achievement to boys who had been enrolled in a didactic preschool program (B-E or DARCEE). Nondidactic boys had a twelve-month advantage in reading and a ten-month advantage in math compared to didactic boys, and in the sixth and seventh grades, their reading and math scores were also superior. By eighth grade, didactic girls performed better in reading than nondidactic girls but not in earlier years and not in math at any year beyond second grade.

There were also differences in IQ scores. Over the period from prekindergarten to eighth grade, the boys who had been in a didactic preschool program lost 9.2 points while the boys formerly in a nondidactic preschool program lost 3.1 points. Both didactic and nondidactic girls lost 11.8 points from the end of prekindergarten to the end of eighth grade (Miller & Bizzell, 1983a). There was a greater IQ decrease for B-E children than for the other program groups. Boys formerly enrolled in the Montessori preschool program performed significantly higher than all other groups in math and reading in the sixth, seventh, and eighth grades. This was not the case for girls. The DARCEE boys performed significantly lower in reading in the sixth, seventh, and eighth grades than boys in the other three programs combined. They also scored lower in sixth-grade math (Miller & Bizzell, 1983a). By tenth grade, the superior performance of Montessori boys in achievement tests had continued. They performed above national norms academically and were in the normal IQ range. In preschool, Montessori boys started at the same IQ level as DARCEE boys, but by tenth grade the Montessori boys were 15.3 points above the DARCEE boys (Miller & Bizzell, cited in Stallings & Stipek, 1986). The IQ scores of Montessori girls increased at the end of preschool and then dropped dramatically.

It is important to note the Louisville Experiment was well designed and executed. The original sample was large, and 60 to 65 percent were secured for the follow-up. Also, longitudinal research by Karnes et al. (1983) indicates there were a higher percentage of high school graduates, higher school success ratings, and a lower grade-retention rate among former Montessori preschool children compared to children who were enrolled in four model preschool programs.

Results of the High/Scope Curriculum Comparison Study indicate that at age fifteen (ninth grade), children who had attended the direct instruction program reported twice as many delinquent acts as the children who had been in the High/Scope and traditional preschool programs. The self-reported delinquent behavior included five times as many acts of property violence. This juvenile delinquency pattern, however, was no worse than that of the control group in the Perry Preschool study. The B-E direct instruction children participated less often in sports and held fewer appointments to a school office or job. Also, in response to the question, "How does your family feel you're doing?" a greater percentage of direct instruction children (33 percent) expressed a negative impression ("poorly") than children enrolled in the High/Scope (0 percent) and traditional (6 percent) preschool programs. These social behavior outcomes are based on self-report data. School achievement scores and IQ performance were not reported for the sample at fifteen years of age. Follow-up data at earlier points (four through ten years) indicated no significant differences by curriculum model in IQ and achievement scores (Weikart et al., 1978). Schweinhart et al. (1986) caution that the High/Scope study is not definitive. Although an impressive 79 percent of the original children were included at fifteen years of age in the follow-up, the sample is relatively small.

Proponents of the direct instruction model have raised serious questions about the methodology of the High/Scope study (Bereiter, 1986; Gersten, 1986). Criticisms include the reliability and validity of the self-report measures, differences across the preschool groups regarding family background characteristics, whether the preschool treatments actually differed from one another, and the interpretation of findings. Interested readers are referred to the fall 1986 issue of the *Early Childhood Research Quarterly* (*1*, no. 3) for reports of these critiques and a rejoinder by Schweinhart et al.

One of the lessons of the early Head Start work was that early intervention cannot serve as an inoculation against subsequent difficulties in life; supportive programs may be needed at each stage of life. A variation of this theme appears in the finding that didactic preschool programs may not sustain higher IQs and achievement scores unless they are followed by a similar program in kindergarten and elementary school. Children who entered a nondidactic program after attending a direct instruction B-E preschool program did not perform well on achievement tests in the Louisville Experiment (Miller & Dyer, 1975). Similarly, Becker and Gersten (1982) found that without continued involvement in the direct instruction Follow Through program, most children demonstrated losses when compared to a standardized sample. Perhaps *continuity in type* of educational curriculum is important in sustaining positive child outcomes.

Short-term studies provide additional data on the effects of different program approaches and teaching practices. In the Preschool Dimensions Study, where content and global methods were held constant across eight classrooms, Miller et al. (1985) found that didactic teaching (drill) was negatively related to boys' auditory and visual receptive skills but positively associated with verbal expression. The researchers questioned the use of didactic methods to improve boys' expressive abilities, noting there are likely to be alternative methods that may not have a negative impact on important receptive skills.

Stallings's (1975) study of first- and third-grade Follow Through classrooms found higher scores in reading and mathematics among children in highly controlled classrooms where teachers used systematic instruction and a high rate of positive reinforcement. In flexible classrooms where there was more exploratory material and children had more choice, they scored higher on a test of nonverbal perceptual problem solving, showed greater willingness to work independently, and had lower absence rates (perhaps an indicator of attitude toward school). Also, children from more flexible classrooms took responsibility for their own successes but not for their failures. Children in the highly structured classrooms took responsibility for their failures but attributed their successes to the teachers or some other outside force. Similarly, a two-year study of elementary schoolchildren by Fry and Addington (1984) found that children in open classrooms had higher scores in social problem solving and self-esteem than children in more closed, traditional classrooms.

The types of questions asked and the information provided by teachers also relate to child behavior. In a preschool program that used teacher questioning to enhance children's representational thinking, children showed significantly greater competence in tasks that required prediction than children in a traditional nursery school program. Also, parents of children in the inquiry program reported their children had more hobbies and interests, and were more curious compared to parent reports of children in a traditional nursery group (Sigel, 1979).

Smothergill, Olson, and Moore (1971) compared two teaching practices with nursery school children. In one group, teachers used an elaborative style by giving detailed task information and encouraging child comment and involvement. In the other group, teachers used a nonelaborative style, giving only necessary task information and not encouraging child involvement. Children in the elaboratively taught group performed better from pre- to posttests on a verbal similarities task and on a storytelling task.

In addition to the sex differences in program outcome noted previously, it appears that boys and girls may have different day-to-day experiences in the same classroom. In three classroom observation studies, Fagot (1973) found that teachers appeared to instruct girls more than boys. They answered girls' questions more often and gave girls more favorable comments. Similarly, in all four of the preschool models examined in the Louisville Experiment, girls received more instructional contact than boys (Biber, Miller, & Dyer, 1972).

A number of differences in teacher behavior was related to sex of the child in the Preschool Dimensions Study (Miller et al., 1985). Girls received twice as much drill from teachers as boys. Moreover, it appeared that when boys were uninterested in group work they received individual instruction; girls in the same situations were reprimanded. Positive reinforcement from the teacher was associated with boys' volunteering and offering opinions, but with girls' peer interactions. Also, girls who volunteered more and asked more questions received relatively more negative than positive reinforcement. The data suggest that this child behavior pattern probably was viewed by teachers as disruptive even though it was task-related.

One of the most striking findings of the Preschool Dimensions Study was that relationship between child behavior and child outcome varied by sex of the child. The effect of participation in group work was especially notable. For boys, group participation was related to higher scores in divergent thinking and logic, but for girls group participation was related to lower scores in logic and curiosity.

What We Know and Do Not Know

The amount of data available for making decisions about preschool practices has advanced significantly since the 1960s when curriculum comparison studies were launched. The research findings, although subject to the generalizability limitations noted earlier, point to two major themes:

1. *Preschool curriculum does matter.* The type of curriculum and teaching practices employed with young children is associated with later child outcomes. The assumption that any well-administered curriculum can achieve long-term positive results—a popular idea in the late 1970s and early 1980s—is wrong.
2. *Preschool effects appear to be a function of interaction between child characteristics and preschool practices.* The unidirectional model of preschool influence, from program to child, is incomplete. We need a bidirectional view of preschool effects that recognizes interactions between child characteristics (especially gender) and program practices.

The existing research is not of sufficient breadth and depth to permit an elaboration of these two themes in definitive terms. We cannot advocate one educational approach over others, and we cannot specify with confidence what contrasting preschool practices should be used with boys and with girls. But we do have enough program research findings to help frame the questions and guide the search for answers. Curriculum decisions need not be dominated by philosophical ideologies and intuitions alone. Some of the major questions inspired by the data are discussed below.

Why would the nondidactic Montessori program prove to be

beneficial for low-income boys but not girls? Why would there be a tendency for girls but not boys to benefit from the didactic B-E direct instruction and DARCEE programs? Miller and Bizzell (1983a) have speculated that because girls mature faster than boys, girls may be more ready to process information gained through observation and verbal instruction in a didactic preschool group setting. Boys may need more hands-on manipulation of materials like that provided by the Montessori approach. The individually paced, self-correcting, cognitive materials of the Montessori program may be a good match for four-year-old boys' cognitive receptivity (see Stallings & Stipek, 1986).

The High/Scope study raises questions about the long-term value of direct instruction especially regarding social behavior. The popular press and other periodicals have given the findings of this work considerable attention (for example, Hechinger, 1986). But the methodological limitations of this research prevent its use as an indictment of direct instruction as an educational strategy in general. With elementary schoolchildren, direct instruction has been shown to have positive effects on school performance. For example, it has been found that fifth graders who had been in a direct instruction program for four years had significantly higher achievement scores than comparison children (Meyer, Gersten, & Gutkin, 1984). Also, Meyer (1984) examined three direct instruction Follow Through classrooms for three to four years, and found superior reading and math performance in the ninth grade when contrasted to a comparison group.

It appears that the direct instruction program in the High/Scope study did not actually harm the children's social development, because there is no evidence that the direct instruction program children engaged in more delinquency than they would have if they had not attended the preschool program. Yet children enrolled in two nondidactic preschool programs (traditional nursery and High/Scope models) reported lower rates of juvenile delinquency and other social behavior problems. Why might this be the case? Schweinhart et al. (1986) speculate that the presence of social behavior goals and child-initiated learning activities in the nondidactic programs may account for the differences. This is speculation, however, not evidence. The High/Scope data cannot be used as a definitive research argument for child-initiated activities.

Caution must be used in our assumptions about why various preschool curricula might yield different results. The dimensions of a preschool classroom that relate most strongly to child outcomes are not always the ones that discriminate between programs. For instance, Soar and Soar (1972) found the amount of teacher (versus child) talk in a classroom was related to complex-abstract cognitive growth (for example, word meanings) in children, yet the dimension of teacher versus child talk did not differentiate programs. We need more research such as the Preschool Dimensions Study (Miller et al., 1985) to identify the specific aspects of programs that relate to child behavior and outcomes.

Researchers and designers of programs in early childhood education have struggled for many years with the role of individual differences in child functioning and learning. Interactions between personal attributes and program environments are difficult to study, partly because of uncertainty in identifying the appropriate child characteristics and treatment properties. The sex of the child is a relatively straightforward way to consider the role of individual differences in preschool programs. No doubt other personal attributes are important as well. For instance, findings of one study suggest high-arousal children may be ill-suited for an open classroom environment (Koester & Farley, 1982). Finding the best match between child and preschool approach is a tempting pursuit for the early education field, yet the program design and research method hurdles pose crucial challenges.

Some investigations have failed to uncover differential effectiveness in early education when certain subgroups of children are compared across outcome measures. The Consortium for Longitudinal Studies, for instance, found no significant interaction between early education and such child background characteristics as gender, family structure (one-parent versus two-parent homes), mother's education, and number of siblings (Lazar & Darlington, 1982). Fallible measures may be partly responsible for the absence of significant findings in this study. For instance, there was a restricted range of mother's education level, and dichotomous rather than continuous measures of school competence variables. The consistent findings of gender differences in long-term preschool effects in the Louisville Experiment (Miller & Bizzell, 1983a), and gender differences in the nature and consequences of the child's preschool participation in the Preschool Dimensions Study (Miller et al., 1985) suggest that preschool effects are mediated by child gender and perhaps other characteristics.

In discussing the results of the Preschool Dimensions Study, Miller et al. (1985) stop short of calling for different instructional practices with boys and with girls. It is an interesting idea, but the existing data do not support such a move. The excellent work of Louise Miller and her colleagues does point to potentially fruitful areas of further research on relations between instructional strategies and child outcome. The determinants of contrasting teacher behaviors with boys versus girls also need careful examination.

With regard to the education of four-year-olds, then, the bottom line of research on preschool practices is this: a key issue in early childhood education is finding an effective match between curriculum and child characteristics. Our program development and research efforts should be focused toward this end.

REFERENCES

Becker, W. C., & Gersten, R. (1982). A follow up of Follow Through: The later effects of the direct instructional model on children in fifth and sixth grades. *American Educational Research Journal*, *19*, 75–92.

Bereiter, C. (1986). Does direct instruction cause delinquency? *Early Childhood Research Quarterly*, *1*, 289–292.

———. (1972). An academic preschool for disadvantaged children: Conclusions from evaluation studies. In J. C. Stanley (Ed.), *Preschool programs for the disadvantaged* (pp. 1–21). Baltimore: Johns Hopkins University Press.

Bereiter, C., & Englemann, S. (1966). *Teaching the disadvantaged child in preschool*. Englewood Cliffs, NJ: Prentice-Hall.

Biber, H., Miller, L. B., & Dyer, J. L. (1972). Feminization in preschool. *Developmental Psychology*, *1*, 86.

Bissell, J. S. (1973). Planned variation in Head Start and Follow Through. In J. C. Stanley (Ed.), *Compensatory education for children ages two to eight: Recent studies of educational intervention*. Baltimore, MD: Johns Hopkins University Press.

Bredekamp, S. (Ed.). (1986). *Developmentally appropriate practice*. Washington, DC: National Association for the Education of Young Children.

Cicirelli, V. G. (1969). The impact of Head Start: An evaluation of the effects of Head Start on children's cognitive and affective development (Vols. 1 and 2). Washington, DC: National Bureau of Standards, Institute for Applied Technology.

Clarke-Stewart, K. A., & Fein, G. (1983). Early childhood programs. In P. Mussen (Ed.), *Manual of child psychology* (pp. 917–999). New York: Wiley.

Dunn, L. M., Horton, K. B., & Smith, J. O. (1968). *Peabody Language Development Kits for Level P*. Circle Pines, MN: American Guidance Service.

Fagot, B. (1973). Influence of teacher behavior in the preschool. *Developmental Psychology*, *9*, 198–206.

Fry, P. S., & Addington, J. (1984). Comparison of social problem solving of children from open and traditional classrooms: A two-year longitudinal study. *Journal of Educational Psychology*, *76*, 318–329.

Gersten, R. (1986). Response to "Consequences of three preschool curriculum models through age 15." *Early Childhood Research Quarterly*, *1*, 293–302.

Gray, S. W., Ramsey, B. K., & Klaus, R. A. (1982). *From 3 to 20: The Early Training Project*. Baltimore: University Park Press.

Hart, B., & Risley, T. B. (1975). Incidental teaching of language in the preschool. *Journal of Applied Behavioral Analysis*, *4*, 411–420.

Hechinger, F. M. (1986, April 22). Preschool programs. *New York Times*, p. 17.

Hohmann, M., Banet, B., & Weikart, D. P. (1979). *Young children in action: A manual for preschool educators*. Ypsilanti, MI: High/Scope Press.

Huston-Stein, A., Friedrich-Cofer, L., & Susman, E. (1977). The relation of classroom structure to social behavior, imaginative play, and self-regulation of economically disadvantaged children. *Child Development*, *48*, 908–916.

Hymes, J. L. (1968). *Teaching the child under six*. Columbus, OH: Merrill.

———. (1955). *A child development point of view*. Englewood Cliffs, NJ: Prentice-Hall.

International Reading Association. (1986). IRA position statement on reading and writing in early childhood. *Reading Teacher*, *39*, 822–824.

Jersild, A. T. (1946). *Child development and the curriculum*. New York: Bureau of Publications, Teachers College Press, Columbia University.

Johnson, J. E., Ershler, J., & Bell, C. (1980). Play behavior in a discovery-based and a formal-education preschool program. *Child Development*, *51*, 271–274.

Karnes, M. B., Shwedel, A. M., & Williams, M. B. (1983). A comparison of five approaches for educating young children from low-income homes. In Consortium for Longitudinal Studies. *As the twig is bent . . . Lasting effects of preschool programs* (pp. 133–170). Hillsdale, NJ: Lawrence Erlbaum Associates.

Katz, L. (1985). Dispositions in early childhood education. *ERIC/EECE Bulletin, 18*, 1–3.

Koester, L. S., & Farley, F. H. (1982). Psychophysiological characteristics and school performance of children in open and traditional classrooms. *Journal of Educational Psychology*, 2, 254–263.

Kohlberg, L., & Mayer, R. (1972). Development as an aim of education. *Harvard Educational Review, 42*, 449–496.

Lazar, I., & Darlington, R. (1982). Lasting effects of early education: A report from the Consortium for Longitudinal Studies. *Monographs of the Society for Research in Child Development, 47*(2–3, Serial No. 195).

Lukas, C. V. (1975). Problems in implementing Head Start Planned Variation models. In A. M. Rivlin & P. M. Timpane (Eds.), *Planned variation in education: Should we give up or try harder?* (pp. 113–125). Washington, DC: Brookings Institution.

McDaniels, G. L. (1975). Evaluation problems in Follow Through. In A. M. Rivlin & P. M. Timpane (Eds.), *Planned variation in education: Should we give up or try harder?* (pp. 47–60). Washington, DC: Brookings Institution.

Meyer, L. (1984). Long-term academic effects of direct instruction Follow Through. *Elementary School Journal, 4*, 380–394.

Meyer, L., Gersten, R., & Gutkin, J. (1984). Direct instruction: A Project Follow Through success story. *Elementary School Journal*, 2, 241–252.

Miller, L. B., & Bizzell, R. P. (1983a). Long-term effects of four preschool programs: 6th, 7th, and 8th grades. *Child Development, 54*, 725–741.

———. (1983b). The Louisville Experiment: A comparison of four programs. In Consortium for Longitudinal Studies. *As the twig is bent . . . Lasting effects of preschool programs* (pp. 25–90). Norwood, NJ: Ablex.

Miller, L. B., Bugbee, M. R., & Hybertson, D. W. (1985). Dimensions of preschool: The effects of individual experience. In I. E. Sigel (Ed.), *Advances in applied developmental psychology* (Vol. 1, pp. 25–90). Norwood, NJ: Ablex.

Miller, L. B., & Dyer, J. L. (1975). Four preschool programs: Their dimensions and effects. *Monographs of the Society for Research in Child Development, 40*(5–6, Serial No. 162).

Montessori, M. (1964). *The Montessori method*. New York: Schocken.

Prescott, E., Jones, E., & Kritchevsky, S. (1967). *Group day care as a child-rearing environment*. Pasadena, CA: Pacific Oaks College. (ED 024 453).

Rivlin, A. M., & Timpane, P. M. (1975). Planned variation in education: An assessment. In A. M. Rivlin & P. M. Timpane (Eds.), *Planned variation in education: Should we give up or try harder?* (pp. 1–21). Washington, DC: Brookings Institution.

Schweinhart, L. J., Weikart, D. P., & Larner, M. B. (1986). Consequences

of three preschool curriculum models through age 15. *Early Childhood Research Quarterly, 1*, 15–45.
Shapiro, E. (1973). Educational evaluation: Rethinking the criteria of competence. *School Review, 8*, 523–549.
Sigel, I. E. (1979). On becoming a thinker: A psychoeducation model. *Educational Psychologist, 14*, 70–79.
Smith, M. S. (1975). Evaluation findings in Head Start Planned Variation. In A. M. Rivlin & P. M. Timpane (Eds.), *Planned variation in education: Should we give up or try harder?* (pp. 101–111). Washington, DC: Brookings Institution.
Smothergill, N. L., Olson, F., & Moore, S. G. (1971). The effects of manipulation of teacher communication style in the preschool. *Child Development, 42*, 1229–1239.
Soar, R. S., & Soar, R. M. (1972). An empirical analysis of selected Follow Through programs: An example of a process approach to evaluation in early childhood education. In I. Gordon (Ed.), *71st yearbook of the National Society for the Study of Education Part 2*. Chicago: University of Chicago Press.
Stallings, J. (1975). Implementation and child effects of teaching practices in Follow Through classrooms. *Monographs of the Society for Research in Child Development, 40*(7–8, Serial No. 163).
Stallings, J. A., & Stipek, D. (1986). Research on early childhood and elementary school teaching programs. In M. C. Wittrock (Ed.), *Handbook of research on teaching* (3rd ed., pp. 727–753). New York: Macmillan.
Weikart, D. P. (1972). Relationship of curriculum, teaching, and learning in preschool education. In J. C. Stanley (Ed.), *Preschool programs for the disadvantaged* (pp. 22–66). Baltimore: Johns Hopkins University Press.
Weikart, D. P., & Banet, B. A. (1975). Model design problems in Follow Through. In A. M. Rivlin & P. M. Timpane (Eds.), *Planned variation in education: Should we give up or try harder?* (pp. 61–77). Washington, DC: Brookings Institution.
Weikart, D. P., Epstein, A. S., Schweinhart, L. J., & Bond, J. T. (1978). *The Ypsilanti Preschool Curriculum Demonstration Project: Preschool years and longitudinal results*. Ypsilanti, MI: High/Scope Press.
Willert, M. K., & Kamii, C. (1985). Reading in kindergarten: Direct versus indirect teaching. *Young Children, 40*, 3–9.
Wright, C., & Nuthall, G. (1970). Relationship between teacher behavior and pupil achievement in three experimental elementary science lessons. *American Educational Research Journal, 1*, 477–491.
Zigler, E., & Trickett, P. K. (1978). IQ, social competence, and evaluation of early childhood intervention programs. *American Psychologist, 33*, 789–799.
Zimiles, H. (1977). A radical and regressive solution to the problem of evaluation. In L. Katz (Ed.), *Current topics in early childhood education* (Vol. 1, pp. 63–70). Norwood, NJ: Ablex.

PART IV

The Policy Challenge

CHAPTER 12

Early Schooling: A National Opportunity?

SHARON L. KAGAN
AND EDWARD F. ZIGLER

Throughout this volume, well-known scholars and practitioners have shared their experience and research findings regarding early schooling. Nearly all agree that concern for young children and their families has risen to a new level of importance, drawing national attention beyond that accorded early childhood education in the 1960s. All recognize that much of the impetus for increased concern over early schooling comes from America's rapidly changing social fabric that propels mothers of young children into the work force. Many point out that the increased attention also has its origins in the popularization of research findings that support the benefit of high-quality early intervention programs for some children. Most important, contributors agree about the elements that constitute high-quality early childhood programs and the need for such programs to be age-appropriate.

Given the extent of this agreement, one might logically ask, is there really a national debate, or are we dealing with a pseudo-issue? Our contention, based on a review of the chapters in this volume, coupled with our experience, is that, although agreement may exist on the need for expanded services for young children and on variables associated with quality in preschool, there is still strong disagreement on such questions as who shall be served? For how long? By whom? And at whose expense? In addition to confusion regarding these critical programmatic and policy issues, our reading of the current situation suggests that elements of current demographics and recent research findings are being grossly misinterpreted and these misinterpretations are obfuscating the early schooling debate. Our purpose in this concluding chapter is, first, to delineate areas where controversy exists and to shed light on the misinterpretations we see; second, to codify points of agreement into guiding principles; and third, to champion a specific role for schools, both in the immediate future and in the long run.

Unresolved Issues: Misinterpreted Data

The recent push for early schooling has been both intense and widespread. Legislators and parents alike are bringing pressure to bear for quick solutions to address the lack of available services. These solutions tend to focus on where to locate services and at what costs. Certainly, it is most appropriate for legislators to be responsive to broad social needs and for parents to attempt to meet their personal child-care needs. Yet this pressure for additional high-quality early childhood services, coupled with the frenetic activity of establishing and procuring services, obscures a critical concern of many child developmentalists: whether or not young children should be in *any* program at all. Whether young children should be separated from the intimacy of family and home is widely debated not only in this volume but in the field in general. Zimiles states this issue clearly when he asks what it means for a young child to be in an environment that is not his home for much of the day (Zimiles, 1985). He questions the readiness of young children to attend programs, particularly those that meet for a full day. Early childhood professionals express concern about overtaxing young children, even if they are in low-keyed and child-oriented programs. Scholars not only worry about the impact of out-of-home services on children and families but also raise questions about the values we are transmitting to young children by placing them in out-of-home care at early ages (Bettleheim, 1987). In chapter 8 of this book, Sigel pointedly asks, "Are we revealing to the children that their value is only in terms of achievement?" Although unresolved, the issue of whether children should be away from family and home is receiving little attention. It is the hidden issue of the early schooling debate.

This concern about whether or not children should be in *any* program is complicated by the reality of the situation: very young children already *are* in programs in record numbers (Chorvinsky, 1982). Not only are more children attending programs than in our recent past, but the programs tend to have longer days and some place much more emphasis on academic preparation. Thus, the focus of the debate has moved from whether children should be in out-of-home situations to what kinds of programs should be made available to them. Hence, there is currently a tremendous focus on questions of pedagogy and of appropriate delivery systems (Miller & Bizzell, 1983). Culling research findings of the past twenty years, early childhood professionals generally agree that certain elements are associated with high-quality programs—elements such as parental involvement, training and experience of personnel, and appropriate staff-child ratios (Ruopp, Travers, Coelen, & Glantz, 1979). Yet confusion persists on specific curricular considerations and on how comprehensive the programs can and should be. To what degree should the curriculum be teacher directed versus child initiated? How much freedom should children be accorded? Are health services, such as dental care, absolutely necessary to a quality program, as Campbell and others suggest, or are they prohibitive in cost? Essentially, then, the second issue focuses not on *who* shall be served but on *how* services shall be rendered: what kind of program will be best for children who need to be somewhere other than the home for whatever reason?

As a logical consequence of the above issues, a third unresolved issue arises regarding *where* children should be served: is the existing mélange of programs the best way to provide the range of services needed? Are existing programs of sufficient quality? Should schools expand their services in this area? Do schools have the ability to accommodate young children and their families? As the varied opinions of the contributors reveal (particularly Elkind and Sarason), not all are willing to champion a role for the schools in early childhood education. Yet the importance of these questions is intensified as a growing number of states consider funding expanded services for preschool-aged children.

Taken together, these three unresolved questions—*should* children be served in out-of-home care, *how* should they be served, and *where* should they be served—embrace many of the fundamental issues inherent in the early schooling debate. Yet, even when taken together, they do not present the dilemma in its entirety. We believe that the issue of early schooling is being exacerbated because data on changing demographics and data from research are being misinterpreted, thereby skewing the very context of the debate.

Data clearly indicate that divorce rates remain at a high level, as does the number of single-parent families and the number of women with children under the age of six who are in the work force. Although the demographics are quite clear, as are the pleas from working parents for more child care, the nation seems to equate the need for more child care with a call for more schooling, thereby confounding the debate. Child care and early schooling are not the same. What working parents need is different from the programs schools provide. Shorter than the eight to ten hours of operation needed by working parents, conventional school-based preschool programs are different from full-day programs in pace and orientation. Typically, school-based programs serve low-income children, are half day, and have a heavy cognitive orientation (Bereiter & Englemann, 1966; Huston-Stein, Friedrich-Cofer, & Susman, 1977; Karnes, Shwedel, & Williams, 1983). To assume that expanding these half-day categorical programs into full-day child care is feasible or even desirable is premature. We need to better discern whether the schools *can* offer full-day care and *if* they are the best vehicle for doing so. In the meantime, though, we must disaggregate the need for child care from the need for half-day programs. They serve different purposes and different populations.

Given the disagreement that arises when we attempt to meet child-care needs with educational programs, it is instructive to examine why this confusion exists. One reason that may account for the difficulty is related to the popularization and potential misinterpretation of research findings. Until fairly recently, reports of research studies were confined to scholarly journals. Although the desire to make research "useful" is not new, popularization of research by the media has intensified considerably. As a consequence, many of the findings from longitudinal studies have been given front-page attention by the media who, often faced with limited print space or broadcast time, consolidate the findings, focusing on those that are most dramatic. No one can doubt the impressive results obtained by low-income children in the Perry Preschool Program (Berrueta-Clement, Schweinhart, Barnett, Epstein, & Weikart, 1984) and in the Consortium for Longitudinal Studies (Lazar & Darlington, 1982). When these findings are translated to the American public, however, important, sometimes more technical, dimensions of the studies have been overshadowed by the more impressive findings. The fact that these programs have been of very high quality and that gains have been achieved with very low-income children seems to have been lost on the American public. Many middle-class parents who are trying to deal with unmet child-care needs personalize the findings and interpret them to mean that early education will make important differences for their children. Further, parents tend to associate education with schools. They feel that facilities that promise to "educate" their children will be the ones to provide the best opportunity for development. Assured of the benefits of early learning, parents are turning more and more to the system they associate with children's education, the school system.

Schools have additional advantages that help account for their appeal to parents in search of the best for their young children. Schools are convenient for parents; they are close to home and often they may already be serving the young child's older siblings. Further, schools do not charge direct fees for services, as do day-care or nursery facilities. Given the convenience, lack of fees, and perceived benefits of an "educational" orientation, it is not surprising that many parents would like to see programs in schools that address both child care and child development needs. To that end, any proposed solution to the early schooling debate must clearly take the needs of working and nonworking parents into consideration and must offer a range of services to meet their diverse situations.

The Resolved Issues: Guidelines for Policy Development

Authors in this volume have indicated that schooling and child care emanate from different traditions and are the end products of different funding sources. Historically, day care was equated with custodial care, a service that connoted little more than meeting basic physical needs—in short, baby-sitting. Preschool education, by contrast, emphasized a developmental and/or cognitive orientation. Although programmatic differences are narrowing, distinctions that separated child care and early education continue to exist not only in the rhetoric but in reality. As pressure mounts for children to become achievers at ever younger ages, early education is shifting to a more didactic emphasis, thus evoking images of academic pressure and expectation, rigid classrooms, and formalized learning methods. In spite of the fact that in many child-care settings, early education is being provided, child care may still conjure images of children playing with little guidance or, worse, with youngsters lodged in front of a television set.

And unfortunate as these images are, replacing them may be no small task. First, *child care* and *education* are handy terms, which have become set over time. Second, they are terms familiar to all parents, for whom more technical but complex terms, such as *developmental program*, may signify little. Moreover, *child care* and *education* have meaning because they identify the administrative auspices through which services are delivered, even though they say little about what is actually transpiring in the program.

Fully recognizing these difficulties in rhetoric and in practice, in 1986, the National Association for the Education of Young Children (NAEYC) published the guidebook *Developmentally Appropriate Practices* for programs serving young children (Bredekamp, 1986). This landmark work delineates practices that are appropriate regardless of sponsorship or setting. The NAEYC publication is critically important on two counts. First, it clearly suggests that emphasis needs to be placed on a common understanding of quality in all programs, not on distinctions between auspices such as child care or schools. Second, NAEYC has helped popularize the term and the concept of "developmental appropriateness" through this volume. Although the phrase *developmentally appropriate services* is more cumbersome than *child care*, *preschool*, or *education*, it aptly conveys the orientation we seek and the orientation that has been advocated throughout this volume. No word is more appropriate than *developmental* to convey the mission and philosophic orientation that should characterize services for young children.

Contributors have agreed that young children need "rich, carefully designed developmental experiences" (Shanker, chapter 3). The composite portrait of a quality program for young children includes the freedom for children to explore at their own rate, and on their own; the opportunity to learn to interact with others and acquire socialization skills; and individualized attention to social, emotional, physical, and cognitive growth, provided by an appropriate adult:child ratio. There is more agreement of what this rich experience is not—it is not an accelerated program of academics at too young an age—than there is identification of any single program type that will provide such an experience. Nevertheless, there is agreement that programs, whatever their auspices, should adhere to developmentally appropriate practices. Further, in advocating a developmentally appropriate orientation for programs, we believe the emphasis on youngsters as "students"—as only "cognitive systems"—should be converted to an emphasis on "children" as developing human beings, with as much attention given to the development of humane values (caring, consideration, concern, and thoughtfulness) as to the development of dispositions for learning (motivation, persistence, and thoroughness) or cognitive processes.

Inherent in a commitment to developmentally appropriate services is the existence of curricula that will be sensitive to each child. Variations in children's needs, with special attention to handicapped and non-English-speaking youngsters, must be addressed. Parent participation and parent education need to be integral features of the programs; staffs need to be appropriately trained with opportunity for participation among AA, CDA, BA, MA, and PhD level individuals. Developmentally appropriate services will include screening children and, if necessary, referring them to existing community services.

Although we advocate implementing developmentally appropriate services, we also strongly support program diversity, particularly in the length of time services are offered. It is critical to disentangle part-day, educational-day, and full-day service needs for the preschool child. Part day means a two-and-a-half- to three-hour program; educational day means programs that run four and a half hours, typically from early morning to mid-afternoon; full day means programs that operate from 6:30 A.M. to 6:30 P.M. Naturally, as the length of the program varies, so will program pacing, emphases, activities, and priorities. Within the context of developmentally appropriate services, there is ample room for variation in program length. Such variation includes the array of services offered and provides sufficient diversity to meet varying family needs.

Variation in program length and type arises more out of the needs of families than of children, many of whom will be fatigued by a long day away from home. Yet the child-care needs of America's children and families are dictating the future growth of early childhood programs: both the early childhood field and society at large are struggling to create a system that provides for both the developmental needs of children and the child-care needs of working parents. As our nation attempts to create a well-organized and highly defined system of developmental services, concerns arise about how to make such care accessible to families on a widespread, even nationwide scale. To that end, we turn to a discussion of the schools' role, specifically considering their capacity to provide both developmentally appropriate services and a range of programmatic alternatives.

The Role of Schools

Throughout this volume, authors have presented their views on the schools' capacity to mount and maintain developmentally appropriate programs for young children and their families. Some authors have expressed legitimate concern regarding the content orientation of school pedagogy, the curriculum versus the child orientation of school practice. Schools have been criticized on the ground that they are too product-oriented and not sufficiently process-oriented, and on the ground that they have systemic difficulty in providing comprehensive developmental services that stress parental involvement and health, nutritional, psychological, and social services. Further, as Moore has pointed out, there is healthy skepticism about the schools' capacity to meet the needs of minority children and families.

Nevertheless, there are definite arguments in favor of the schools. The salience of schools as a delivery system for some programs is as much philosophical as it is practical. Philosophically, schools' very existence bespeaks an American commitment to services for all. A fundamental principle of our democracy is that education is a right of all Americans, and therefore it is a collective, societal responsibility to ensure the availability of education to all. By conceptually aligning the administrative structure of early childhood programs with this philosophical orientation and with education, developmental services are advanced as a mainstream need. The earlier vision of early childhood services as those established primarily to ameliorate the deficits of the poor is put to rest, and the stigma associated with social services and with conventional child-care delivery mechanisms is eliminated.

Beyond philosophy, there are practical reasons the schools are attractive sites for preschool services: schools are more ubiquitous than any other delivery system, they are universally available, and not only have they had experience administering programs for children, but some districts already have mounted services for children and their families. New York State's experimental prekindergarten is one example. The efforts of the Missouri and Minnesota departments of education to involve parents in the education of their young children is also noteworthy. Newer efforts (for example, New York City's Giant Step), acknowledging the difficulty many schools face in providing family-oriented services, have incorporated family service workers who foster links between the program and the families as a routine part of the team that serves a specific group of children. Other efforts launched in public schools have sought union waivers from duty-free lunch periods so teachers and staff can eat with the children. The point, made well in the chapters by Sarason and Moore, is that although schools may not be the ideal structural or bureaucratic repositories for developmental programs as they now stand, with attention to institutional regularities, curriculum, parents' roles, and special services, schools potentially can serve the needs of youngsters and their families quite well.

Before schools can provide developmentally appropriate and varied services to young children, however, three key problems need to be addressed. The first is the academic orientation of the classroom. As numerous contributors to this volume have pointed out, early childhood professionals fear that classrooms for preschoolers may simply result in a downward extension of kindergarten. Although schools embrace early childhood education, frequently their emphasis remains educative rather than developmental by virtue of existing academic goals and orientations. Under the rubric of early childhood education, we have observed public school kindergartens where five different workbooks are the norm and preschools where children are expected to write their names. This is happening in so-called early childhood classes. So even the term *early childhood*, although implying something quite different from elementary education, may not be sufficiently developmental in orientation.

In addition to a developmental orientation, schools need to become flexible in their schedules, ideally offering part-day, educational-day, and full-day services for children as well as a range of services for parents. Therefore, expanding the scope and content of direct services is the second problem that must be addressed. We would like to see schools open to all families in the neighborhood. Families would register with the school at the time of a child's birth, much as they do now when children are five. During the postnatal to preschool years, an array of services would be offered to children and families. These services would be voluntary and available to parents at their option. Parents could attend parenting education classes and other programs designed to meet their needs. They could receive help in determining what services they want for their children and in locating them. Early screening for handicapping conditions would be available. The extent of resource and referral, and direct, services could be quite limited, or it could be quite extensive, expanding to provide, for example, parenting education, home-visitor programs, or toy and book lending libraries.

Models for these types of services exist, some within the public education sector and some as privately funded services. Sometimes they function as part of schools or other institutions; often they called by other names, such as family support programs. In communities where such programs exist, schools should not replicate the services, but should link with the already available programs.

When children are three and four, they should be able to come to school, should parents so desire. Full-day services would be offered, but children would be able to attend for only a half day, should parents so decide. Ideally, services for young children would be housed in the school building, but located in a wing away from older children. Here, furniture and facilities would be more intimate in scale, close to outdoor facilities, and more appropriate to the needs and activities of preschoolers.

Program staff would be made up of both certified teachers and CDAS who would work in concert with one another, planning a sound program for the children. Programmatically, the morning program, attended by all enrolled children, would be slightly more focused, whereas the afternoon program (for children whose families selected the full-day option) would be devoted to more restful and relaxed activities.

This structure seems ideal in that it would meet the needs of working and nonworking families alike, providing options for parents. Furthermore, by serving families whose children are not yet five and enrolled in formal classes, the school would have the opportunity to expand its constituency to include more parents and to expand the quality of its services. For example, by providing services to younger children, schools could identify handicapped and special needs youngsters earlier and guide them to appropriate services earlier than they are now being referred.

The third problem that needs to be addressed relates to the role of the school with regard to other services in the community. Our vision of the role of public schools in the delivery of services for young children and their families differs starkly from the isolationist orientation that has characterized public education. We see the schools as being proactive and highly interactive with other providers of services for young children. In our vision, schools would lend their educative authority and use their central position in the community to facilitate coordination among existing child-care services for young children.

Because public schools will receive the bulk of five-year-olds and because schools exist in every community, it seems appropriate that they take the initial leadership in facilitating communication and collaboration with other providers of services to preschoolers. Establishing a citywide Early Childhood Council composed of providers of services to preschoolers in day care, Head Start, public schools, and the public and private sectors is one vehicle for linking services. Such councils could be used to coordinate the placement of new programs in the short run and to establish community-wide planning efforts for young children in the long run. Such linkages not only would bring service providers into contact with one another but should lead to the establishment of systems that would promote continuity for the children, as they moved from one year to the next. In communities where interprogram continuity has been made a priority, not only are children's records transferred from programs serving four-year-olds to programs serving five-year-olds, but professionals have engaged in joint training, regardless of program auspices; visits have been made from one site to another; and children and families have been guided as they make the transition from one program to another.

In our vision, the schools have three specific roles: (1) to provide high-quality developmentally appropriate programs; (2) to provide a range of services to parents that will accommodate their need for support, information, and direct services, including programs that will be part day, educational day, or full day in length for three- and four-year-old children; and (3) to facilitate the coordination of other deliverers of developmental programs, ensuring that continuity and collaboration exists among providers of services to preschool children. We regard the latter two components as essential to any school's effort to offer developmental services. Providing part-day programs to children addresses an important but small part of what we consider to be an ideal early childhood role for schools. Offering educational and full-day services where necessary, facilitating interagency continuity, coordinating existing services, and providing resource and referral services to parents are also critical if developmental services for young children and their families are to emerge in the nation.

In the Short Run: In the Long Run

The above services, although ideal, are at least twenty years away. Given the existing needs of families in the 1980s and their projected needs into the 1990s, what is an effective interim strategy that will build toward the provision of these diversified developmentally appropriate services?

We suggest two concurrent strategies. First, school districts, rather than adding and subtracting programs at will with no well-thought-out strategy, should develop comprehensive long-range plans that forecast the needs of young children and their families. Within the context of the long-range plan, a strategic short-term plan should assess available programs and delineate strategies to compensate for a lack of specific services. We propose that when schools expand current services, they consider not only adding more half-day classrooms of children but establishing the rudiments of a community-based, early childhood system that will build in continuity, as well as mechanisms of resource and referral for parents. By providing such services, schools will lay the foundation for public support from a broad range of families and garner support from other preschool service providers in the community. This strategy demands considerable commitment on the part of school personnel and the community. To that end, we ask that states where early childhood–child development initiatives are taking place allow districts to use funds for long-range planning. Legislators are usually anxious to boast of increased numbers of children in direct service. Although we support expansion of direct services to youngsters, we also see great benefit in facilitating district planning processes, particularly when services that offer parents options, that meet their child-care needs, and that promote continuity are envisioned.

Beyond what efforts are already underway, we support the development of models that would shed light on implementation costs and strategies. Although the societal importance of attending to children's development is acknowledged, we as a nation are a long way from recognizing it as a national priority and from garnering adequate financial support. Clearly, any expansion will need not only finely tuned financial information but also a range of programmatic models and studies to ascertain the effects of such programs. Put simply, we need to ascertain what works and what doesn't work from fiscal and programmatic perspectives before we call for broadly based public support. To that end, we suggest that model programs as outlined in the previous section be established on a pilot basis in a limited number of schools in the nation. We would hope that the number would be sufficiently large so as to enable the development and implementation of different types of services with different funding mechanisms. Such efforts should be closely evaluated to ascertain effects on children, families, staff, and institutions, and to ascertain ease of replicability.

At the present time, there is not sufficient support at the national level to create an entirely new system to deliver developmentally appropriate services to young children. Yet there is growing momentum at the state level and in foundations to support early childhood services generally. Given the present state of interest and funding, we have a responsibility to encourage states, municipalities, and foundations to support the advance planning that is necessary if America's schools are to capitalize on the current opportunity afforded them. We have a responsibility to do more than simply support business as usual or continue to provide limited services without options for parents. The anticipated growth in services to young children represents an opportunity for America to utilize its schools better and for America's schools to serve their constituents more effectively.

Early schooling: a national debate? Yes, definitely. Early schooling: a national opportunity? Yes—potentially.

REFERENCES

Bereiter, C., & Englemann, S. (1966). *Teaching the disadvantaged child in the preschool*. Englewood Cliffs, NJ: Prentice-Hall.

Berrueta-Clement, J., Schweinhart, L., Barnett, W., Epstein, A., & Weikart, D. (1984). *Changed lives*. Ypsilanti, MI: High/Scope Press.

Bettleheim, B. (1987, March). The importance of play. *Atlantic Monthly*, pp. 35–46.

Bredekamp, S. E. (1986). *Developmentally appropriate practices*. Washington, DC: National Association for the Education of Young Children.

Chorvinsky, M. (1982). *Preprimary enrollment 1980*. Washington, DC: National Center for Education Statistics.

Huston-Stein, A., Friedrich-Cofer, L., & Susman, E. (1977). The relation of classroom structure to social behavior, imaginative play, and self-regulation of economically disadvantaged children. *Child Development*, *48*, 908–916.

Karnes, M. B., Shwedel, A. M., & Williams, M. B. (1983). A comparison of five approaches for educating young children from low-income homes. In Consortium for Longitudinal Studies (Ed.), *As the twig is bent . . . Lasting effects of preschool programs* (pp. 133–170). Norwood, NJ: Ablex.

Lazar, I., & Darlington, R. (1982). Lasting effects of early education: A report from the Consortium for Longitudinal Studies. *Monographs of the Society for Research in Child Development*, *195*(4).

Miller, L. B., & Bizzell, R. P. (1983). The Louisville Experiment: A comparison of four programs. In Consortium for Longitudinal Studies (Ed.), *As the twig is bent . . . Lasting effects of preschool programs* (pp. 25–90). Norwood, NJ: Ablex.

Ruopp, R., Travers, J., Coelen, C., & Glantz, F. (1979). *Children at the center. Final report of the National Day Care Study* (Vol. 1). Cambridge, MA: Abt Books.

Zimiles, H. (1985, April). *The role of research in an era of expanding preschool education*. Revised version of a paper presented at the meeting of the American Educational Association, Chicago, IL.

INDEX